A
HISTORY
OF
ENGLISH
IN ITS
OWN WORDS

A HISTORY OF ENGLISH IN ITS OWN WORDS

CRAIG M. CARVER

BARNES & NOBLE BOOKS
NEW YORK

❧ CONTENTS ❧

Introduction

Our words are windows into our past. Scenes from political history, for example, are often glimpsed in word origins, as in *coach* (from the name of a Hungarian town where carriages were manufactured, made famous in Europe when the Hungarian king's son married the duchess of Milan and drove off in one); *cravat* (the Serbo-Croatian word for "a Croat," with reference to the linen scarf worn by Croatian mercenaries in the French military); *despot* (the Greek word for "master of the household" and the title of the Christian ruler of a province in the Turkish Empire); and *chancellor* (Latin for "court secretary," originally the officer stationed at the *cancelli,* the latticework or grating that separated the judges from the public in a court of law).

The histories of some words are vignettes from the history of western science. The old model of the universe from astrology, the precursor of modern astronomy, for example, is revealed in *disaster* (from Latin *dis-,* "without," and *astro,* "star," because an unfavorable configuration of stars and planets could result in calamity) and *jovial* (meaning literally "under the influence of the planet Jupiter," because those born under the sign of this planet were thought to be of a good-humored, cheerful disposition).

The development of western European physiology, psychology, and medicine is hinted at in words like *frenetic* (from Greek meaning "inflammation of the brain," from *phren,* "mind," ultimately from an Indo-European root meaning "diaphragm," because the diaphragm was thought to be the seat of intelligence); *irascible* (originally referring in the medieval anatomy of the soul to the part responsible for the irrational nature of humans, from Latin *ira,* "anger"); *influenza* (a contagious disease originally thought to be due to the "influence" of the stars); and *creosote* (from Greek *kreas,* "flesh," and *soter,* "savior," literally "flesh saving" because this oily liquid was formerly used as an antiseptic).

Tantalizing ancient views of the western religious heritage are seen in such words as *Easter* (from the name of the Germanic goddess of dawn, *Eastre* [whose high holiday was celebrated at the spring equinox], from *east,* because dawn or sunrise is in the east); *soul* (from a Proto-Germanic root meaning "coming from or belonging to the sea," because to the ancient Germanic peoples the sea was the sacred abode of the soul before birth and after death); and *rosary* (from the figurative sense of "rose garden," implying a "garden" of prayers).

Our vocabulary is also peppered with the myths of the ancient world. *Lethal,* for example, is from the name of the river Lethe in Hades, whose waters caused forgetfulness of the past. *Panic* is from the Greek god Pan, who caused contagious fear in herds of animals and crowds of people. And *tantalize* is from the mythic Tantalus, who was punished for betraying the gods' secrets by being made to stand in a river under branches of fruit, the water and food always receding out of reach whenever he tried to drink or eat.

English through its word histories is particularly suited to telling the story of the culture it arose from, because it is arguably the richest of the European languages. Most languages develop from a single parent language, but English received its wealth of words from two major sources: the Germanic family of languages, including the Scandinavian, and the Romance or Latin family, primarily from French after the Norman French invasion of England in 1066, but also from Italian and Spanish and directly from Latin.

English is first and foremost a Germanic language, stemming directly from the speech of the Angle, Saxon, and Jute tribes of northern Germany who settled England in the fifth century, the beginning of the Old English period. But long before those settlers left Germany, their ancestors spoke Proto-Germanic, a language that linguists have inferred or "reconstructed" from the rules of phonological and semantic change, like a prehistoric skeleton inferred from fragments of a jawbone.

Proto-Germanic was the mother tongue of all the modern Germanic languages, including German, English, Dutch, Swedish, Danish, and Norwegian. It in turn was a main branch off the trunk of a prehistoric language called Indo-European. Because Proto-Germanic and Indo-European words were only spoken and never written, linguists mark them with an asterisk to indicate that they are reconstructed or hypothetical forms.

The following chapters outline the broad historical periods in the development of English. And within the chapters themselves, the word histories are presented in chronological order. That is, the histories are ordered according to the first-known written or printed appearance in English of the word itself or of a specific sense or usage of the word. The only exception to this is in Chapter I, on Old English, where the words are instead ordered thematically. This is because relatively few Anglo-Saxon manuscripts survive, making it very difficult to date accurately the first appearance of a word in the Old English period. The individual histories themselves, however, often reach back to prehistoric times.

BOOK,* for example, first appears in Old English in the eighth century and is accordingly treated in the first chapter, though its history can be traced to Indo-European roots. BEAR and BULL also date from the Old English period, and written examples exist from the ninth and tenth centuries respectively. But the financial-market senses of *bear* (a falling mar-

---

*A word whose history is treated in this book is indicated by small capital letters.

ket) and *bull* (a rising market) do not appear until about 1700, and accordingly these two words are treated in the third chapter, dealing with Early Modern English.

The earliest-known printed or written use of a word, of course, only very roughly approximates when the word or a new sense first entered the language. This approximation gets fuzzier and more inaccurate the further back in time one goes, and can be as much as a century or two off in the Old English period. In modern English after the advent of the printing press, the increasing mass of printed material raises the odds that the first printed appearance of a word closely matched its actual first use. But because language is foremost a spoken medium, the appearance of the uttered word will almost always precede the written word (except perhaps in highly technical or scientific language).

Occasionally odd-appearing or non-English alphabet letters are used in this book. English before about 1100 had three additional letters. The Modern English combination *th* was represented with either "thorn" (þ) or "eth" (ð). And the vowel in Modern English *bat* and *hat* was usually represented by the symbol "ash" (æ). The pronunciation symbol "schwa" (ə), which is not an alphabet symbol, is used to represent the sound of the vowel in *but* or *the*.

Something that might strike the reader as odd is that for a given word there are frequently two or more plausible alternative histories. Though etymologists and philologists might not like to admit it, word histories are not based on exact science, in part because the record is never complete. The ideal etymologist is a student of history and a polyglot linguist, one who knows several, preferably defunct, languages, and who not only has a knowledge of the workings of language and how it changes but has an intuitive feel for it, a "sprachgefühl." But even where the etymology is in dispute, it is entertaining and informative to see what the scholars have come up with.

❖ I ❖

THE ANGLO-SAXON TONGUE

The Old English Period
(450—1150)

BACKGROUND

A thousand or so years ago after English had evolved into a distinct language separate from the speech of the original Angles and Saxons, it looked and sounded from our vantage point like a foreign language. Reminiscent of modern German, it had a highly inflected grammar (*dol cyning,* "foolish king"; *doles cyninges,* "of the foolish king"), and the word order in its sentences was often, from our point of view, a bit turned around (*Tha sealde se cyning him sweord,* "Then gave the king him a sword"; *God geseah tha thaet hit god waes,* "God saw then that it good was").

Old English lacked the tens of thousands of words of Latin and French origin that have since been added. And yet, of the one thousand words that we use most frequently today, about 83 percent are of Old English origin. After this first thousand, roughly 30 percent of our vocabulary consists of Anglo-Saxon survivals.

Many Old English words have come down to us practically unchanged in form and meaning, such as many of the words whose histories are presented in Chapter I. Many other Old

English words are still recognizable, though they have changed in meaning or form, such as:

> *folc* (people) now *folk*
> *mynd* (memory) now *mind*
> *feond* (enemy) now *fiend*
> *gast* (spirit) now *ghost*
> *burg* (walled town) now *borough*
> *wieldan* (control) now *wield*
> *cwethan* (to say) now *quoth*
> *scieppan* (to create) now *shape*
> *with* (against, opposite) now *with.*

Then there are Old English words that have not survived at all, such as:

> *dryhten* (lord)
> *hyge* (mind, thought)
> *rice* (dominion, German *Reich*)
> *theod* (people, nation)
> *wuldor* (glory)
> *aetheling* (nobleman, prince)
> *scop* (poet, singer)
> *lic* (body, corpse)
> *feorh* (life)
> *wer* (man)
>
> *hatan* (to be called)
> *weorthan* (to become)
> *beorgan* (to protect)
> *munan* (to remember)
> *ece* (eternal)
> *swith* (strong)
> *eft* (later)
> *swithe* (very, extremely)
> *mid* (with, accompanying)

Old English was more than just the language of simple everyday life. It was very flexible and capable of adapting old words to new uses. For example, *mod* (mind, spirit, heart)—our word *mood* (a mental state)—could also mean "boldness," "courage" and even "pride" or "haughtiness," depending on the context. By the addition of certain endings or suffixes, many new terms could be created whose meanings were extensions of the root idea:

> **mod**ig (spirited, bold, arrogant)
> **mod**iglic (magnanimous)

*mod*iglice (boldly, proudly)
*mod*ignes (magnanimity, pride)
*mod*igian (to bear oneself proudly, to be indignant)
ge*mod*od (minded, temperamentally disposed)
*mod*full (haughty)
*mod*leas (spiritless)

Another strategy for expanding the vocabulary, also characteristic of German, was to combine a base word with other words. *Mod*, for example, was compounded with *cræft* (strength, power, skill, cunning) to give *mod*cræft (intelligence) and *mod*cræftig (intelligent). Combined with other words, *mod* could express various mental states:

glaed*mod*nes (kindness) combined with *glaed* (cheerful)
*mod*lufu (affection), with *lufu* (love)
un*mod* (despondency, depression)
*mod*caru (sorrow), with *caru* (care)
*mod*leas (lack of courage), with *leas* (without, deprived of)
mad*mod* (folly)
ofer*mod* (pride), with *ofer* (over)
ofer*mod*ig (proud)
heah*mod* (noble), with *heah* (high)
micel*mod* (magnanimous), with *micel* (much)
stith*mod* (resolute, obstinate), with *stith* (stiff, strong)
torht*mod* (glorious), with *torht* (bright).

This is only a handful of the some one hundred words formed with *mod* as the base.

When a new concept or object needed a name in the original English tongue, self-explanatory compounds were frequently used, the same method used by German (as in *Fernsprecher,* literally "far speaker" for telephone, and *Staubsauger,* "dust sucker" for vacuum cleaner). In Old English:

"lamp" was *leohtfaet:* from *leoht* (light) and *faet* (vessel)
"dawn" was *daegred* (day red)
"minstrel" was *ealoscop:* *ealo* (ale) and *scop* (poet, singer)

"geometry" was *eorthcraeft* (earth craft)
"purple" was *fiscdeag* (fish dye)
"gout" was *fotadl: fot* (foot) and *adl* (disease)
"jeweler" was *gimmwyrhta* (gem worker)
"epilepsy" was *fielleseocnes* (falling sickness).

Although Old English is overwhelmingly the Germanic speech of the Anglo-Saxons, it also borrowed from church Latin, estimated at about 450 words, and from Old Norse. Most of the Latin words adopted with the introduction of Christianity to the island in 597 naturally have to do with religion and its trappings and have survived into Modern English with very little change. For example, *alms,* ANGEL, *Antichrist, candle, cell, chalice, cloister, creed, deacon, demon, dirge, disciple, idol, martyr, noon, offer, organ, prime, prophet, relic,* and *temple* were all borrowed before 1050. The Church also influenced other aspects of the life of the people, and in the process gave English such domestic words as *cap, lentil, pear, radish, oyster, sock, silk, chest,* and *sack,* and words dealing with education, such as *school, grammatical, verse,* and *gloss.* Other Latin borrowings of this period include *anchor, fever, sponge, elephant,* and *phoenix.*

Beginning in the eighth century the Vikings, the warlike inhabitants of Scandinavia, began plundering the lands adjacent to the Baltic and the North Sea, eventually conquering and settling them. This period of invasion culminated in the early eleventh century when Cnut, king of Denmark, conquered Norway and England, usurping the English throne, and from there ruling most of the Scandinavian world.

Throughout the Old English period large numbers of Scandinavians settled in England, leaving their mark on the land with more than 1,400 Scandinavian place names. Names ending with *-by* (from Danish *by,* "farm, town"), as in *Rugby, Grimsby, Derby,* and *Thoresby;* or *thorp* (village), as in *Althorp* and *Linthorpe;* or *toft* (piece of ground) as in *Brimtoft* and *Nortoft;* or *thwaite* (an isolated piece of land) as in *Applethwaite* and *Langthwaite,* are all of Scandinavian origin.

More important, the Scandinavians enhanced English by giving it several thousand common words. The culture of the invaders was very similar to that of the English themselves.

Consequently most of the loan words are from everyday life. Some examples are *awkward, band, bank, birth, bull, crook, dirt, dregs, flat, freckle, gait, gap, ill, loan, loose, mire, muggy, odd, root, rotten, scab, sly, tattered,* and *weak,* as well as a surprising number of verbs, such as *to bait, bask, call, cast, crave, crawl, die, droop, gape, gasp, give, glitter, lift, raise, rake, scare, scowl, screech, snub, sprint, take, thrive,* and *thrust.*

Despite our dark image of the Dark Ages, the Anglo-Saxon period had its lightness. It was a time of great learning, especially during the enlightened reign of King Alfred the Great (849–899), and of literature, such as the great folk-epic poem *Beowulf.* It was also a time when a LORD and his LADY LOVED the GLEE craft of poets and minstrels, and ALE and BEER flowed freely in their hall, and CHURLs plowed the manor's ACRES in LENTEN and reaped the fruits in HARVEST; a time when PERIWINKLE and PEONIES flowered and forests were populated with many an ELF and WARLOCK, and magical MISTLETOE grew on oaks. It was also a fearful time of IRON and LAW and LEECH, when an EARL's WEIRD (fate) was to wage WAR for his king and if successful be SCOT-FREE; a time when one told his BEADS with fierce fervor lest GOD on DOOMSDAY send him, like a fallen ANGEL, to HELL with the other DEAD and unsaved HEATHEN, instead of to HEAVEN and FREEDOM.

ANGLO-SAXON (c. 885). Today about the only time we hear *Anglo-Saxon* is in reference to WASPs (*White Anglo-Saxon Protestants*), who are as often as not Americans or Australians. But in the eighth and ninth centuries, the *Angel-Seaxans* were "English Saxons" or "the Saxons of England" as distinguished from the *Ald-Seaxans* or "Old Saxons" of the continent. Borrowed from Late Latin *Anglo-Saxones,* the term is a compound of *Anglus,* the people of *Angul,* a district of Holstein, Germany, and *Saxonem,* the inhabitants of Saxony, Germany. *Angul* means literally "angle" and refers to the hook or angled shape of the German district, ultimately from Indo-European **ank-* (to bend).† The Angles, along with the Saxons and Jutes, settled in Britain during the fifth century,

---

†An asterisk indicates that a root word is reconstructed or hypothetical.

and formed the kingdoms of Northumbria, Mercia, and East Anglia. But by the time Old English speakers used *Angles* or *Engles,* the original sense (of or belonging to the Angul German tribe) had already been lost. Instead, *Engle* referred collectively to all of the Germanic peoples who had settled Britain. Soon it was broadened even further to include the Celtic and Scandinavian elements of the population. By the eleventh century, *Englisc,* the adjective of *Engle,* applied to all native inhabitants of *Engle-land* or England. The *Saxons* probably got their name from an Old Germanic word, **sahsom* (knife), appearing in Old English as *seax* (a short sword or knife) and in Old High German as *sahs* (knife, sword). The Saxons, then, were literally "men of the knife or sword." In recent times English speakers have reinterpreted *Anglo-Saxon* as being "Anglo and Saxon," instead of the original "English Saxon." This has made *Anglo-* (English) into a free form that can be used in combinations where "English and ——" is meant, as in *Anglo-Irish, Anglo-American, Anglo-Jewish,* and *Anglo-French.*

ALE (c. 940), **BEER** (c. 725). These are among the oldest alcoholic beverages, going back at least to the ancient Egyptians. During the Old English period, *ealu* or *alu* (ale) and *beor* (beer) were synonymous. A characteristically bitter drink, *ealu* or *ale* is from a root meaning "bitter," a meaning only preserved through the non-Germanic languages, such as Latin *alumen* (alum) and Greek *alydimos* (bitter). In England, an *ale* is also a traditional festive gathering at which much ale is drunk, especially at a wedding feast, which was called a *bridealu* or *bridal* or later *bridals* ("And clothed her for her *bridals* like the sun," 1859, Alfred Tennyson, *The Marriage of Geraint*). In Old English, *ealu* or *alu* was the more common term, *beor* being reserved primarily for poetic language, or as the Old Icelandic saga *Alvismal* puts it: "It is called 'ale' among men, and among the gods 'beer' " (*Ol* heitir meth monnum, en meth Asum *bjorr*). But after hops was introduced as a flavoring agent in the early 1400s, *beer* referred specifically to the hopped beverage. Some etymologists try to link *beer* and its numerous Germanic cognates with Latin *bibere* (to drink). Others claim it is cognate with Old Norse *bygg* (barley), ultimately from the Indo-European root *bheu-* (to grow), since beer is usually made from malted barley. Yet another version tries to associate it with the Germanic root for "brew," *breuro-*. All of these proposed histories, however, are so problematic that most dictionaries label the ultimate history of *beer* as "uncertain" or "unknown."

BED (c. 700). *Bed* has some odd linguistic bedfellows, including the siblings Latin *fodere* (to dig), Greek *bothros* (pit), and Welsh *bedd* (grave). All of these are the offspring of the Indo-European parent *bhedh-* (to dig). The connection between "bed" and "digging" is that a place dug out of the earth is a den or lair for an animal or person to lie in. Though this primitive connection disappeared even before the Proto-Germanic word *badja-* (bed) came into use, faint echoes of it remain in the two surviving primary senses, "a sleeping place" and "a garden bed."

BOOK (c. 725). An Anglo-Saxon version of the New Testament translated around the year 1000 uses *boc* (writing, book) in two of the senses common in Old English. In John 21:25, where the Old English plural *bec* is used, it means simply, "book or bound manuscript" ("Ealle tha *bec*" [All of the books]). This sense derives from the older meaning, "a writing or a written document," which appears in Matthew 5:31 ("Swa hwylc swa his wif forlaet, he sylle hyre hyra hiwgedales *boc*" [King James version: "Whosoever shall put away his wife, let him give her a writing of divorcement"]). It derives from Germanic *bok-s* (writing tablet, leaf, sheet), which originally referred to an inscription made on a beechwood tablet or cut into the bark of a beech tree. Its earlier form was *boko,* which referred more specifically to a beech staff that had runes carved on it. And before that, *boko* was the word for "beech," which is why Old English *boc* means both "book" and "beech." Toward the end of the Old English period, *boc* meaning "beech" became *bece,* but its oldest form survives virtually unchanged in *buck-mast* (beechnuts used as animal fodder) and *buckwheat,* literally "beech wheat," the seeds of which resemble beechnuts. The same development of senses, from "tree bark" to "book," occurred with BIBLE.

CHURL (a. 800). To be called *churlish* during the Old English period was not necessarily an insult. A *churl* or *ceorl* was merely a man or husband, and *to churl* was to take a husband, a usage that, unlike *to wive* (to take a wife), did not survive past the eleventh century. In the Anglo-Saxon laws, a churl was a man without rank, or technically, a member of the lowest rank of freemen ("Ærst he sloh thae eorles and thrallede thae *chaerles*" [First he slew the earls and enslaved the *churls*], c. 1205, Layamon, *Brut, or Chronicle of Britain*). It was not until after the Norman Conquest that the churls were reduced to serfdom and bondage ("For may no *cherle* chartre make ne his catel selle With-outen leaue of his lorde" [For a churl may not make a contract nor sell his cattle without permission of his lord], 1377, William Langland, *Piers Plowman*). From that time on, the reputation of the churl made a rapid decline, from "peasant" or "rustic" to "boor and villain" to "miser," and finally to "rude," "uncouth," "stingy," "ill-natured" in the adjective *churlish*. Old English *ceorl* is kin to Old Norse *karl* (a man, freeman), Old High German *karal* (man, husband, lover, hence the proper name Karl or Carl), Sanskrit *jarant* (old), and Greek *geron* (old man), all deriving from the Indo-European root **ger-* (to grow old, ripen).

EARL (a. 616). *Earl* fared better after the Norman invasion than did CHURL. After 1066 it was used to designate a man of rank equivalent to a count. Originally in Old English, an *earl* was a man of noble rank as distinguished from freemen or churls. And later, during the Danish occupation, *earl* was essentially synonymous with *alderman*, the native word for "viceroy or governor of a county," from *aldor*, "patriarch," from *ald*, "old." *Earl* is of Germanic origin and has kin in Old High German (*erl*, "man," "nobleman"), Old Icelandic (*jarl*, "chieftain") and Old Norse (*erilaR* "a magic-religious function"), but cannot be traced back any further. At least one etymologist speculates that it was coined as a counterpart to *churl.* If so, then we may ask, why did *churl* develop into *churlish,* whereas *earl* did not become *earlish?*

CRANK (c. 1000). To fall wounded or dying in battle is in Old English to *crincan* or *cringan,* literally to draw or contract oneself together into a "bent" or "crooked" posture of pain, the same underlying meaning as the modern descendant *cringe.* The root sense, which also gave *crinkle, crumple,* and *cripple,* is to "bend together," "crook," "curl up" and is expressed literally by *crank* (a bent axle or shaft used to impart circular motion), in Old English *cranc,* found only in the compound *cranc-staef* (a device used in weaving). The figurative extension of the root sense is to "shrink," "give way," "become weak or ill," found in German and Dutch *krank* (sick) and in English dialect *crank* and *cranky* (sickly). The modern *crank* (an eccentric) is a distant offshoot from the Old English word ("I moved amidst *cranks,* Bohemians, unbelievers . . . and riffraff of all sorts," 1889, George Bernard Shaw, *London Music in 1888–89*). Its development is from "crooked" to "a crooked or eccentric notion" or "a mental twist" to "one who has eccentric ideas." The *crank* that means "grouch" is probably a back formation of *cranky,* literally "having a crooked temper," hence "ill-tempered" ("We view our maids as *cranky* self-willed machines for getting our work done," 1876, Charlotte Yonge, *Womankind*).

DEAD (c. 725). In England before about 1200, when Uncle Hrothgar died, his nephew could not say simply "he *died,*" because there was no verb *to die.* Although it was probably used very early in the Old English period, *die* died out, as it did in Gothic and later in German and Dutch, and was then reborrowed around 1200 from Norse *deyja.* During the interim, there was no dearth of ways to express dying and death. The nephew could say of his departed uncle, *he waes dead* (he was dead), or more likely he would use *swelten* or *steorfan.* We know *swelten* today in *sweltering* (oppressive with heat), but its original sense was "to die," which survived in general use into the seventeenth century ("With swappis of hor swordes *swelt* mony knights" [With violent blows of their swords (they) killed many knights], c. 1400, *The Gest Hystoriale of the Destruction of Troy*). *Swelten* · derives ultimately from the Indo-European root *swel-* (to shine, burn), the "burning" or consuming power of fire, especially in cremation, being associated with death. A similar association is made between "rigidity" and "dying" in Old English *steorfan,* from the Indo-European root *ster-* (to be stiff or rigid). This sense was still current in Chaucer's time, though it had acquired the nuance of a slow, lingering death ("[Christ] Upon a cros . . . / First *starf,* and ros [rose], and sit yn heaven above," c. 1374, Chaucer, *Troilus and Criseyde*), which became modern English *starve* (to die from hunger). *Dead, death, die,* and *dwindle* all have the same ancient root, *dheu-* (to become exhausted, to die).

EIGHT (c. 725), **NINE** (c. 840). *Eight*—in Old English *eahta* or *aehta*—along with its cognates in German *(acht),* Latin *(octo),* and Sanskrit *(astau),* ultimately derives from the Indo-European root *okto.* The form of the root may be the dual *oktou,* "dual" being a grammatical category, as in Greek and Sanskrit, that indicates two persons or things, just as "singular" indicates one and "plural" many. *Oktou,* as dual, may refer to "two" fours, hence, "eight." The origin of *nine*—in Old English *nigen*—supports this notion. *Nine* is from the root *newn,* which in turn may be related to the root *newo-* (new). In a number system based on four ("eight" being "two fours"), *nine* would be "new" because it would be the beginning of the third group of fours.

ELEVEN (a. 900), **TWELVE** (a. 900). *Endleofan,* the ninth-century English precursor of *eleven,* is from Proto-Germanic *ain-lif-,* a compound of *ain-* (one) and *-lif-* (leave), literally, "one left over" after ten. Similarly, Old English *twelf* is from the Germanic compound *twa-lif-,* "two left over" after ten. In English for numbers larger than twelve, the names refer to the numbers added to ten, instead of "left over" after ten. *Fiftene* or *fifteen,* for example, is from the Germanic compound *fimf-tehun,* the sum of *fimf* (five) and *-tehun* (ten). For multiples of ten (twenty, thirty, etc.), the Germanic suffix *-tig* (tens) is used. Old English *fiftig* (fifty), for example, is a compound meaning "five tens" and is ultimately from Indo-European **penkwe-dkonta* (five tens).

ELF (c. 725). In Germanic mythology, an *elf* is a supernatural creature, small and mischievous ("Fram thanon untydras ealle onwocon, eotenas and *ylfe*" [From him sprang every misbegotten thing, monsters and elves], c. 725, *Beowulf*). Old English *ælf* or *ylf* is related to Old High German *alp* (evil spirit, goblin, nightmare) and Old Norse *alfr* (elf). In ancient times, the elves must have appeared to the Indo-Europeans as ghostlike apparitions, because *elf,* through Proto-Germanic *albiz,* is from the root **albho-* (white) with reference to the whiteness of an apparition. In Old English, if one was crazy or touched one would be *ylfig* or "elf-possessed" (compare *giddy* at GOD). And to have *elf-shot* was to have a disease caused by evil spirits or elves that supposedly shot people and cattle with *elf-arrows.*

FREEDOM (a. 1200). *Freedom* is so ordinary that we rarely notice it as a word, but it is everywhere in our free press and in the mouths of our politicians (Ronald Reagan lobbying for *perestroika* to a group of Russian dissidents: "The *freedom* to keep the fruits of one's own labor, for example, is a *freedom* that the present reforms seem to be enlarging. We hope one *freedom* will lead to another," 1988, *Time*). Being especially fond of it, Americans combine it with other words; some recent examples: *freedom fighters,* which—the Nicaraguan Contras notwithstanding—first referred to members of resistance organizations during World War II; *freedom march* and *freedom rider* from the civil rights movement of the 1960s; and in a similar vein, *freedom cut,* an Afro haircut, and *freedom war,* what many blacks used to call the Civil War. *Free,* from Old English *freo,* is ultimately from the prehistoric Indo-European root **pri* or **prai* (to love). In Sanskrit, this root became *priya* (dear, precious, friend, husband). A parallel development occurred in English, but through different sound changes, becoming Old English *freon* (to love) and *freond* (friend). Because of the pervasiveness of slavery in the ancient world—wealthier families commonly owned slaves—the Germanic root **frijaz* (dear) was naturally applied to one's family or clan as distinct from slaves. In time the word referred to any person who was not in bondage or servitude and then to the concept itself of nonservitude or freedom. Already by the ninth century in England, its abstract meaning "free will" was well established ("Forthaem he yesceop twa yesceadwisan yesceafta *freo,* englas & men" [Therefore he created two kinds of *free* creatures, angels and men], c. 888, King Alfred, trans. of Boethius, *Consolation of Philosophy*). The *dom* of *freedom* was a separate word in Old English, meaning "statute" or "jurisdiction" (see DOOMSDAY), and was occasionally combined with other words as in *cyningdom* (kingdom), *haligdom* (holiness), *freodom* (freedom), and *theowdom* (slavery), the condition of being a *theow* or slave (see SLAVE). In modern English *dom* is not a free word, but exists only as a suffix meaning "condition," "state," "domain," "realm" as in *boredom, Christendom,* and *martyrdom.* It was not until the Age of Enlightenment, however, that *freedom* moved into the political realm ("In this then consists *Freedom,* in our being able to act, or not to act, according as we shall choose, or will," 1690, John Locke).

GLEE (c. 700). With writing confined to priests and the jurisdiction of the Church, an already old tradition of spoken literature, usually in the form of easily memorized alliterative verse, flourished in Anglo-Saxon culture. The keepers of this tradition were the *gleomen* or *gleemen* (minstrels) and *scops* (poets). The kings and aristocracy maintained *scops* at their court, while the *gleomen* practiced their *glee-craft* (minstrelsy) on the road, wandering from place to place with their *glee-beams* (harps, literally "music or song wood"). *Gleo* or *glee* is cognate with Old Icelandic *gly* (joy) and is from a Germanic root cognate with Greek *chleue* (joke) and Old Lithuanian *glaudas* (amusement, pastime). In Old English, it first meant "entertainment and merriment," and then more specifically "musical entertainment" and "music" itself. From the twelfth century, it also had the more general sense "mirth," "joy," but after some three centuries of primarily poetic use, it was so little used that by 1755 Samuel Johnson could give it this heady usage note in his famous dictionary: "It is not now used, except in ludicrous writing, or with some mixture of irony and contempt." Then, within fifty years of Johnson's pronouncement, it was mysteriously revived and is still widely used today in its twelfth-century sense. In Shakespeare's time, the diminutive of *glee* was the odd-sounding *gleek* ("a jest," hence "to jest or gibe at someone"), which is now obsolete ("I have seene you *gleeking* and galling [scoffing] at this Gentleman twice or thrice," 1599, Shakespeare, *Henry V*). As for *scop,* it is kin to Old High German *scopf* (poetry, jest, derision) and Old Norse *skop* (mockery), which also gave English *scoff* (to make fun of).

BEAD (c. 725). Long before a *bead* was a small ball of glass it was a prayer, in Old English *bed* or *gebed,* literally an "asking" of God. It ultimately derives from the Indo-European root **bhedh-* (to bend), referring to "bending the knees" as in prayer or supplication, the same root that gives English *bid* (command, offer), in Old English *biddan* (to entreat, command, ask for, pray). Often the two related words, *bid* and *bead,* were used together in the phrase *bid one's beads* (to pray), an expression that remained current well into the eighteenth century ("The *Beades* that we will *bid,* shall be sweet Kisses," 1598, Michael Drayton, *England's Heroicall Epistles*). In the 1300s, small glass balls perforated so they could be threaded on a string (later called a *rosary*) were used to count prayers. Once the practice of telling beads (counting prayers) using rosaries became a common practice, *bead* (prayer) was transferred to the glass balls themselves. After the Middle English period, whenever *bead* (prayer) was used by itself it usually alluded to rosary beads ("Be briefe in praying,/ Few *beads* are best, when once we goe a maying," 1648, Robert Herrick, *Hesperides*). By the modern English period, the original sense was lost completely.

GOD (c. 725). This single syllable is exclusively Germanic, appearing in slightly different forms in Scandinavian, German, and Dutch. The Proto-Germanic source word, **gudam* or **gutham,* like Old Norse and Gothic *guth,* was neuter in declension. After the Christian conversion of the Germanic tribes, their word for "god" became masculine in declension. *Gudam* probably derives from the Indo-European root **gheu-,* meaning "to invoke" and "to pour." This primeval version of English *god* meant "that which is invoked" or "that which is worshiped by pouring libations." Some etymologists suggest that the root sense "to pour" might refer to the making of a molten image. In Anglo-Saxon times, if one was insane as though "possessed by a god," one would be *gidig,* from *gudam* (god) and the suffix *-ig,* which became modern English *giddy* (dizzy). Similarly, *enthusiasm,* borrowed from sixteenth-century French, also means "god-possessed," originating from Greek *entheos* (inspired), literally "in god."

DOOMSDAY (c. 975). To an Englishman in the Middle Ages, *domes daey* or *doomsday* (Day of Judgment) was not a day of doom and gloom, because *doom* had not yet acquired its meaning "final fate," "ruin," "death" (not until about 1600). Originally a *doom* was a "statute" or "decree" ("Thys synd tha *domas* the thu him taecan scealt" [These are the laws which thou shalt take to them], c. 1000, Ælfric, trans. of Exodus 21:1), and the *doombook* or *Domboc* was a book of dooms or Old Teutonic laws compiled by the great King Alfred (c. 925). It is also the suffix *-dom* in words like *kingdom, wisdom,* and FREE-DOM. *Doom,* which has many cognates in the Germanic languages, derives from the Indo-European root **dhe-* (to set or put), the root sense being "that which is set or put down." When a written law or doom was applied in litigation, the result was a judgment. In the popular mind, law and judgment were so closely associated that Old English *doom* or *dom* came to mean "a judgment or sentence formally pronounced," which did not survive much past the eighteenth century ("O! Partial Judge, Thy *Doom* has me undone," 1709, *Tatler*). Because *doom* is a judgment, a *doomsday* is a judgment day, a *doom house* is a judgment hall, a *doom settle* is a judgment seat ("He saet tha pilatus on his *dome-setle*" [Pilate sat on his judgment seat], c. 1000 trans. of Matthew 27:19), and a *doomsman* is a judge. In Scotland, a doomsman was known as a *doomster* or *dempster*, whose voice surely struck a feeling of doom in a courtroom defendant, for he was appointed to read out the sentence delivered by the court (" 'And this,' said the *Doomster*, aggravating his harsh voice, 'I pronounce for *doom,*' " 1818, Sir Walter Scott, *Heart of Midlothian*). The doomster was also the executioner of the sentence.

HELL (c. 725). In Anglo-Saxon times *hell* (the netherworld where the dead continue to exist) had two senses. The older sense was a remnant of the ancient Germanic myth of *Hel*, which is the origin of the English word. *Hel* was the underworld of the dead, later personified as the ugly goddess that ruled there. Originally, it was not a place of torment, though it was decidedly gloomy, resembling Sheol of the ancient Hebrews or Hades of the Greeks, where dead souls wandered about unhappily ("Cyme death ofer hie and astigen hie in *helle* lifgende." [Death came over them and they descended into living hell], c. 825, *Vesper Psalter*). *Hel* in the Old Norse version was a dreary, frosty place situated downward and northward and was reserved for the dead who had not been killed in war. Warriors who fell in battle went to Valhalla. With the advent of Christianity, *hell* became a place of punishment, where the wicked burned in an eternal fire ("Swa byrnende saw thæt fyr on thære *helle*, seo is on thæm munte the Ætne hatte" [Just as the fire burns in this hell, so it does on that mountain called Etna], c. 888, King Alfred, trans. of Boethius, *Consolation of Philosophy*). The Indo-European root of *hell* is **kel-* (to cover or conceal), because hell is "concealed" or hidden in the dark regions near the earth's center. Through the Germanic branch, the root also gave English *hall* (a covered place), *hull* (that which covers), *hole,* and *hollow.*

HEAVEN (c. 725). Oddly enough, like *hell, heofon* or *heaven* also derives from an Indo-European root meaning "to cover" (**kem-*), which also gave Old English *hama* (covering) and *ham* (undergarment). Instead of concealing, however, this cover forms the overarching, stony vault of the sky, since **kem-* itself is from **ak-men* (stone, sharp stone used as a tool). *Heaven's* earliest meaning in English is "sky" or "firmament" as a vast vault in which are embedded the stars and across the face of which float the moon, sun, and clouds ("He aerist scop aelda barnum *heben* til hrofe" [He first shaped for the sons of men heaven as a roof], c. 685, Caedmon, "Hymn"). But toward the later Old English period, *heaven* took on its common Christian interpretation as the abode of God and angels beyond the sky, in opposition to the infernal precinct of hell beneath the earth.

ANGEL (c. 950). Traced far enough back, an *angel* (a divine messenger and attendant of God) is a "hireling." In the course of trade with the Orient, the Greeks often borrowed words from the strange languages they met, such as Old Persian, which is the source of Greek *angaros* (mounted royal courier) and *angelos* (messenger), both akin to Sanskrit *angiras* (a divine being). The Old Persian word in turn probably derives from *agru* (hireling) and *agaru* (to hire), words from Akkadian, the semitic language of ancient Mesopotamia. When the Old Testament was translated into Greek, *angelos* was used for Hebrew *mal'ak*, in full *mal'ak Yehowah* (messenger of Jehovah). All of the doctrinal trappings surrounding angels then began to adhere to *angelos*, which was borrowed in Latin as *angelus*, and adopted by Old English as *engel* ("Sint suelce *englas* godes in heofnum" [Are as the angels of God in heaven], c. 950 trans. of Matthew 22:30).

HEATHEN (c. 725). In translating the Bible into Gothic in the fourth century, when Ulfilas (Gothic for "little wolf"), Bishop of the Goths, came to Mark 7:26 ("The woman was a Gentile, a Phoenician of Syria by nationality") he used Gothic *haithno* (Gentile or heathen woman). Ulfilas's choice is probably derived directly from the Gothic word for "heath," *haithi*, and means literally "dweller on the heath." Early Christianity was primarily an urban religion, not having penetrated the remoter areas of the countryside, where traveling was dangerous. This created a clear distinction between the Christians associated with the cities and the rural pagans associated with the heaths. The Gothic word would have been a loose translation for *pagan*, which also has its roots in the countryside, deriving from Latin *paganus* (villager, rustic), from *pagus* (rural district). Bishop Ulfilas may have been influenced by Armenian *het'anos* (heathen), borrowed from Greek *ethnos* (nation), which, when used in the plural, means "nations," "heathens." When Mark 7:26 was translated into Old English independent of the Gothic Bible, *haethen* or *heathen* was again the word of choice ("Thaet Wif waes *haethen* sirofenisces cynnes," c. 1000, *Anglo-Saxon Gospels*).

IRON (c. 700). Man's discovery of iron in meteorites made it seem as if it were a substance of divine origin. Egyptians as early as 4000 B.C. wore iron beads made from meteoritic iron. It took another two millennia before smelting iron from ore became common enough to make ceremonial weapons and ornaments. The Hittites developed the techniques of tempering iron and kept them secret until the fall of their empire in 1200 B.C. Iron technology then spread throughout southern Europe and the Middle East, and with it the association of the metal with the divine. The Venetic-Illyrian term used by the ancient Italian tribes was *eisarnon,* which is related to Etruscan *aisar* (god) and Umbrian *esono-* (divine). Beginning in the fifth century B.C., the Celtic tribes borrowed the Italic term and carried it and the technology to western Europe and the British isles. This Celto-Germanic term, *isarno-,* meant "holy metal" and was also related to Greek *hieros* (filled with the divine, holy) and Latin *ira* (anger). In Old English, it became *isern,* then *iren* ("Thurh thaet *isern* is getacnod thaet maegen thara threatunga" [Through iron is betokened the strength which threatens], 897, King Alfred, trans. of Gregory the Great, *Pastoral Care*).

LAW (a. 1000). The native English word for "law" was *ae* and was used, for example, in translating John 15:25: "In *ae* hiora awriten is" [(It) is written in their law] (c. 1000). A later version has "On heora *laga* ys awritan" (c. 1150). The difference between the two translations, *ae* and *laga* (law), shows the influence of Scandinavian on English, which reached its height at the beginning of the eleventh century when Cnut, king of Denmark, obtained the throne of England. *Lagu* (law), which usurped the native *ae,* was borrowed from Old Norse *log* (law), the collective plural of *lag* (something laid or fixed, a layer or stratum). The root sense is to "lie" or "lay," and is also the source of English *lie* and *lay.* Although *lagu* was often used to translate Latin *lex* (law) and was thought to be cognate with it, there is no historical connection between the two, *lex* deriving from the root *leg-* (to gather, read). In many languages the word for "law" derives from roots meaning "that which is laid or set down," such as English *doom* (see DOOMSDAY), Latin *statutum,* and German *gesetz. Outlaw* was also a direct Scandinavian borrowing (Old Norse *utlagi*) and meant "one who is put outside the law" ("Gif he man to deathe gefylle, beo he thonne *utlah*" [If he kills a man, he is an outlaw], *Laws of Edward and Guthrum,* c. 924).

LEECH (c. 900). The Old English translation of Luke 4:23 is "La *lece lecna* thec seoline," or in modern form, *"Leech, leech thyself"* (the King James version: "Physician, heal thyself"). In Anglo-Saxon England a physician was a *lece* or *laece* or *leech,* not because he tried to suck his patients' pocketbooks dry, but because that was the way the word came down from the Proto-Germanic source, **lekjaz* (counselor, enchanter, speaker of magic words). The lekjaz spoke healing words—both words of magic and of medical advice. The Indo-European root **leg-* (to collect or gather) was extended very early to "speak," that is, to "gather" one's words together and speak them. This gave English not only *leech* through Proto-Germanic **lekjaz;* but also, through Latin *legere,* it gave *lectern, lecture, legend,* and *elect,* and through Greek *legein* gave *lexicon, dialect,* and *dyslexia.* The *leech's* art was called *leechcraft,* his medicines or remedies *leechdoms* ("Micel wund behofath micles *laecedomes"* [Many wounds behoove or require many remedies], c. 900, trans. of *Bede's History*), and to cure or heal was to *leech.* A *leech* was held in such high esteem that God and Christ were often likened to a *leech* well into the Middle English period ("God that is our lyves [life's] *leche,"* c. 1386, Chaucer, *Canterbury Tales*). The *leech-finger* is the ring finger (next to the little finger), and was also called the *medicinal finger, physic finger,* or *physician's finger,* a translation of Latin *digitus medicus.* It was so called because in ancient medicine there was supposed to be a small artery in this finger that came directly from the heart and was used in diagnosis. During Anglo-Saxon times another word, *laece* or *leech* (blood-sucking worm)—same pronunciation and spelling—was current. It has cognates in Middle Dutch and Flemish, but its origin is unknown. By the Middle Ages, leeches (the worms) were widely used by leeches (the doctors) to "bleed" patients, a remedy prescribed for almost any ailment, and a practice that led to a strong association between the two words. In time, the association became a confusion, especially when calling a "physician" sounded increasingly like calling him a "blood sucker," which eventually forced the "physician" *leech* to become obsolete.

WOMAN (a. 766). *Woman* has a venerable Anglo-Saxon history, often misunderstood down through the centuries. One popular etymology claimed *woman* was a blend of *womb* and *man*. A more widely circulated false etymology said that it was a compound of *woe* and *man* (Richard Flecknoe wrote punningly: "Woe has end, when 'tis alone: But in *woman* never none," 1653). But, in fact, *woman* derives from Old English *wifman*, a compound of *wif* (woman, wife), perhaps from *wifan* to weave, a standard occupation for women in olden days, and *man* (human being, person). In all the Germanic languages, *man* meant both "human being" and "adult male person." In Old English, it was usually, but not always, used in the sense of "human being," since the language already had perfectly good words referring to persons on the basis of their sex: *wer* and *wif*, *wæpman* and *wifman* (see MAN). King Alfred translated Deuteronomy 22:5 using both woman words: "Ne scride nan *wif* hiy mid wæpmannes reafe, ne wæpman mid *wifmannes* reafe" (Let no woman clothe herself with man's clothing, let no man [clothe himself] with woman's clothing). But even the Indo-European root **man* meant "a man," as well as "mankind." Maleness and humankind, then, appear to be confused, if not outright equated, in the history of our language. *Female*, however, has no connection with *male*, but derives from Latin *femella*, the diminutive of *femina* (woman, female).

MAN (a. 725). *Wer* or *were* meant in Old English both "a male person" and "a husband." It derives ultimately from Indo-European **wiros*, which, through Latin *vir* (man), also became English *virile* and *virtue*. *Wer*, however, did not survive past the Old English period except in *werewolf* (man-wolf) and *world*, from *wer* and *ild* (age), literally "the age of man." *Wæpman* or *wapman* is an Anglo-Saxon compound of *wæpn* (weapon) and *man*, literally, a human equipped with a "weapon," that is, with a penis. With *man* increasingly favored as the word for an individual male as opposed to humankind in general (see WOMAN), *wapman* became more nearly redundant than it already was and by the fourteenth century had died out of use completely.

LORD (c. 725). When times are lean—as was often the case in the Middle Ages—the person who holds the keys to the larder holds authority and power. In Germany, this person was a *brotherr* (an employer of labor), literally "a bread-master or lord." Similarly in Scandinavia, the mistress of the servants was a "meat-mother" (Swedish *matmoder,* Danish *madmoder*). In Anglo-Saxon England, this person was a *hlafweard* or *hlaford,* literally "a bread keeper," from *hlaf* (loaf, bread) and *weard* (ward, keeper), the precursor of *lord* (one having power and authority over others). It is not clear which sense of *hlaf,* "bread" or "loaf," is the earlier, but the word is certainly Germanic in origin, possibly related to Old English *hlifian* (to rise), alluding to the "rising" of leavened bread. Originally, the *hlaford* was the head of the household and the master of the dependents and servants who "ate his bread." The servants themselves were likewise called *hlaf-æ tan* (loaf eaters), which, after the Norman Conquest, was replaced by Old French *servants*. *Hlaford,* however, survived, the *f* (pronounced *v*) gradually being dropped, so that by the sixteenth century the single syllable, *lord,* was fully established. Most of the primary senses of *lord* were already established well before the 1100s, including "prince or sovereign" and "husband," and the ecclesiastical *The Lord* (God), which was originally a translation (c. 1000) of Vulgate *Dominus* (Lord, Master) with its own domestic origins in Latin *domus* (house).

LADY (c. 750). If the LORD is the warden of the loaves of bread, then the *lady* is the maker of the bread. Like *lord, lady* is not found outside of English. Its earliest Old English form was *hlaefdige,* literally "bread kneader," a compound of *hlaf* (loaf, bread) and *dige* (to knead). *Dige* is from Old English *dag* (dough), ultimately from the Indo-European **deigh* (to form or shape, to build). Like the earliest sense of *lord, lady* meant "mistress of the household and servants" ("Swe swe eyan menenes hondum *hlafdian* hire" [As the eyes of a maiden (look) unto the hand of her lady (mistress)], c. 825, trans. of Psalms 123:2), though this sense died out by about the fourteenth century. And as counterpart to *lord,* in the late Old English period and after, a *lady* was a woman who ruled over subjects, a title often used instead of *cwen* (queen) when she was the consort of a king. And just as *Lord* figuratively referred to Christ and God, *Lady* referred to the Virgin Mary. Unlike *lord,* however, whose connotations remained as "ruler" and "person of high social degree," the meaning of *lady* as "ruler of subjects" was gradually supplanted, first by the broader reference to any "woman of superior social position," and then by its use as a courteous synonym for "woman," without reference to social status, the analogue of *gentleman.*

LOVE (c. 725). In the Germanic languages the Indo-European root **pri* (to love) was not used in its original sense.

Instead, the root gave English, for example, FREE and *friend*. Having coopted the root for "love," the Germanic languages used **leubh* (desire) instead. In English, it became *love,.* from Old English *lufu* ("Naefth nan man maran *lufe* thonne theos ys thaet hwa sylle his lif for his freondum" [Greater *love* hath no man than this, that a man lay down his life for his friends], c. 1000, trans. of John 15:13), as well as *leave* (permission) and *believe*. In Latin, the word deriving from Indo-European **leubh* stayed closer to the root sense, becoming *libido* (pleasure, desire). The Romance languages used neither of the Indo-European roots for "love" or "desire." Instead, they adopted the early Latin nursery word for "mother," *amma*. Its reduced form, *am-*, became in Latin *amare* (to love) and *amicus* (friend), ultimately enriching English with *amour, amateur, enamor,* and *paramour,* and *amicable, amigo,* and *enemy*.

MISTLETOE (c. 1000). The Druids and other ancient Europeans revered this parasitic plant as sacred, especially when it was found growing on an oak. When taken as a tea, it was believed to be a cure for sterility and an antidote for poisons. The superstitions surrounding the plant still live in vestigial form at Christmastime ("The *mistletoe* is still hung up in farmhouses and kitchens at Christmas; and the young men have the privilege of kissing the girls under it, plucking each time a berry from the bush. When the berries are all plucked the privilege ceases," 1820, Washington Irving, *Sketch Book*). *Mistletoe,* or in Old English *mistiltan,* is a compound of the older word for the plant, *mistil* (mistletoe), and the Old English word for "twig," *tan*. *Mistil* derives from a Proto-Germanic root that appears in Gothic as *maihstus* and Old High German as *mist,* both words meaning "dung." *Misteltoe,* then, is literally a "dung twig," because the plant grows out of the droppings of birds that have eaten the berries with the seeds. In time, the meaning of *tan* (twig) in *mistiltan* was lost and was mistakenly interpreted as the plural of *ta* (toe), just as *oxen* and *children* are plurals with the ending *-n*. This gave the singular form **mistilta,* and when *ta* itself was eventually altered to *toe,* **mistilta* also became *mistletoe*.

NORTH (c. 725). For the ancients, the sun's movement naturally defined and named the cardinal directions. Although all of the Germanic words for north (Dutch *noord*, German, Norwegian, and Swedish *nord*), including the Germanic root *nurthra*, simply mean the direction "north," the non-Germanic cognates, Oscan *nertrak* (on the left), Umbrian *nertru* (from the left) and Greek *nerteros* (nether, infernal), preserve the original meaning of the Indo-European root *ner-teros* (under, on the left). When worshipers prayed toward the sun rising in the east, the direction on the left was north.

SOUTH (c. 725). To the Europeans who lived in the northern hemisphere, the lands of the sun, or the direction leading toward sunnier regions, were *sunth* (south). This Germanic root derives from Indo-European **sawel* (the sun) and became Old English *suth* (south), the *n* being dropped, as in *tooth* from *tanth*. Not surprisingly, then, *suth* or *south* is akin to *sunne* or *sun*.

EAST (c. 725). Old English *east* is from the root *aus* (to shine). This root also gives Latin *aurora*, Lithuanian *auszra*, and Sanskrit *ushas*, all meaning "dawn." The sense progression is from the root "shine" to "the shining of the rising sun," and then, as in Germanic *aust*, to "the direction of sunrise."

WEST (c. 725). Since *east* was associated with sunrise and morning, *west* was logically from a root meaning "sunset or evening," which was then extended to "the direction of sunset." This root was **wespero* (evening, night), which appears in *Visigoths* (western Goths), as distinguished from *Ostrogoths* (eastern Goths), and gave Greek *hesperos* and Latin *vespera* (evening star, evening), hence, English *vespers*.

PEONY (c. 1000). This beautiful flower has been known since ancient times, when its roots, flowers, and seeds were used in medicine ("About an Infant's neck hang *Peonie*. It cures Alcydes cruell maladie," 1591, Josuah Sylvester, *Du Bartas*). The seeds were also used as a spice ("I haue peper and *piane* and a pound of garlek," 1362, William Langland, *Piers Plowman*). Old English *peonie* is, via Latin, from Greek *paionia* (peony), which derives from *Paion,* the name of the physician of the gods in Homer's *Iliad,* his name being related to Greek *paionios* (healing, medicinal). The flower is named in honor of the physician for its supposed medicinal qualities. *Paion* or *Paean,* "The Healer," was also an epithet applied to Apollo, and, because certain songs of thanksgiving to Apollo began *ie paieon,* "Io! the healer," *paean* came to mean "song of tribute or praise."

PERIWINKLE (c. 1000). This trailing evergreen herb with solitary blue or white flowers was known in Old English as *perwince,* a borrowing of the Latin name *pervinca.* Latin *pervinca* may be a compound of *per* (through) and *vincere* (to bind, tie), with reference to the tielike vines of the plant, or it may derive from *pervincere* (to conquer completely). This latter sense is found in the figurative use of "flower" as the finest example of something, a sense in which *periwinkle* (one who surpasses, the fairest) was formerly used ("Corteys lady and wyse . . . thou arte *pervenke* of pryse [prize]," a. 1440, *The Romance of Sir Degrevant*). *Pink* (a flower species of *Dianthus*) is also used in this way ("Nay, I am the very *pinck* of curtesie," 1592, Shakespeare, *Romeo and Juliet*). In Italy, the periwinkle is known as *fiore di morto*, "the flower of death," because it was a custom to wreathe dead infants with the plant. In the Middle English period, a similar custom placed a garland of periwinkle on the heads of prisoners on their way to execution ("Y-fetere . . . were ys legges under hys horse wombe: . . . A gerland of *peruenke* set on ys heved" [Fettered were his legs under his horse's belly. . . . A garland of periwinkle sat on his head], c. 1306, a political song, "The Execution of Sir S. Fraser").

SCOT-FREE (a. 1066). To be *scot-free* (in Old English *scotfre*) had nothing to do with the Scots, but with *scot* (contribution or tax). If an Anglo-Saxon churl was *scotfre,* he was exempt from paying royal tax. *Scot* is a Scandinavian borrowing, perhaps Old Norse *skot* (contribution), from the Proto-Germanic **skutaz* (shooting, shot), ultimately from the Indo-European **skeud* (to shoot, throw). The root sense is "to *throw* down money," or in the modern vernacular, "to *shoot* one's wad." By the Middle English period, *scot* also meant the tab or charge incurred at a tavern or for entertainment *("Scot-free* the Poets drank and ate; They paid no taxes to the State!," 1792, John Wolcot, *Odes of Condolence). Church scot* or *ciric-sceat* was literally "church tribute or tax," also known as *food-rent.* It was paid in food on St. Martin's Day (November 11), usually as corn and sometimes poultry, and was supposed to go to the support of the parish priests ("Hi agefen elce yere threo mittan hwaetes to *ciric-sceatte"* [He gave each year three mits (a measure) of wheat as church-scot], c. 890, King Alfred, trans. of *Bede's History). A sceat* was also a small, thick Anglo-Saxon coin of silver.

WINTER (c. 725). In Old English as now there were four seasons, or as *Byrhtferth's Handboc* (c. 1050) puts it: "Tha feower timan . . . lengten, sumor, haerfest, & winter." The prehistoric division of seasons was probably "winter" and "nonwinter," in many places interpreted as "wet season" and

"nonwet season." This latter dual season is probably the origin of English *winter*. Often used figuratively for "year," especially when talking about old age ("He geheold tela fiftig *wintra*" [He ruled for fifty winters], c. 725, *Beowulf*), *winter* is ultimately, through Germanic **wentruz*, from the Indo-European root **wend* or *wed* (wet), the same root that gave Old English *waeter* (water), *waet* (wet), and *otor* (otter).

LENTEN (c. 700, spring). In Old and Middle English there was no *spring*, only *lencten* or *lenten* or *lent*. *Lencten* comes from West Germanic **langi-tinaz*, which originally referred to the lengthening of the days in spring, compounded of *langa-* (long) and *tinaz* (days) ("Thar after com *leinten* and dayes gonne longy" [Thereafter comes spring and the days get longer], c. 1275, Layamon, *Brut, or Chronicle of Britain*). In England, *lenten* (spring) and its abbreviated form *lent* were transferred to the forty days of penitence and fasting that precede Easter, which of course occurs in the spring. By the early 1400s, the ecclesiastical sense had pushed out the "spring" meaning altogether, which did not happen in the other Germanic languages, where "spring" is the only sense. This created a hole in the English vocabulary that was immediately filled by *springtime* and *spring*, probably short for *spring of the leaf* (c. 1530), the time when the leaves "spring" forth.

SUMMER (a. 830). Old English *sumor* or *sumur* comes in a direct line from the ancient Indo-European root **sema*, meaning simply "summer." This root is the source for all of the

Germanic words for "summer" (except Gothic). But other European languages chose different roots, some being cognate with words for "hot" or "burn," for example, Greek *theros* (summer) is akin to *thermos* "warm," and Latin *aestas* (summer) is from *aestus* (fire, heat), giving Italian *estate* and French *été*. Others, such as Rumanian *vara* and Lithuanian *vasara* (summer), are akin to words for "spring."

HARVEST (c. 750, autumn). In English, autumn has had the greatest number of names. In Old English, it was called *haerfest,* which survived well into the eighteenth century, only gradually being supplanted by *autumn.* Cognates of *haerfest* or *harvest* (autumn) are common in all of the Germanic languages (Swedish *höst,* German *herbst,* Dutch *herfst*) and derive from the root **kerp* (to pluck, pick, gather), possibly in the form **korpistos* referring to the time "most fit for picking." *Autumn* does not appear in English until the 1300s, when it was borrowed from Old French, in turn taken from Latin *autumnus,* whose ultimate origin is unknown. Although *fall* originated in England in the mid-1600s, it is not much used there, but is the common name in the United States. Like *spring*'s reference to the growing season of leaves, *fall* refers to the dying time, when leaves fall from the trees, it being a shortening of the expression *fall of the leaf* (c. 1545).

ACRE (c. 975). In Old English an *aecer* or *acer* was simply "a field," a sense that survives today only in *God's acre* (churchyard, cemetery) and certain proper names. The root is **ag-*

meaning "to drive," as in Greek *agros* and Sanskrit *ajras* (field), because cattle were "driven" to the "field" or pasture. From **ag* comes Indo-European **agro,* the source not only of *acre* but also of *agriculture, agrarian,* and *peregrine. Acre* evolved from "an untenanted field" ("Fortham is se *aecer* gehaten . . . blodes *aecyr"* ["Wherefore that field (i.e., the potter's field) was called . . . field of blood"], c. 1000, trans. of Matthew 27:8) to "a cultivated field" and then to "a definite measure of tilled land." In the Old English period, an *acre* was the amount of land that a team of oxen could plow in a day. Later, under Kings Edward I and III and Henry VIII, laws defined it more precisely.

THING (c. 685). *Things* have changed since the days of Old England. Back then a *thing* was "an assembly, council, court." Although this sense died out early in Middle English, it survives in the Scandinavian languages (Norwegian, Danish, Swedish *ting*). In Iceland, the parliament is still called the *Althing.* The cognate in Gothic is *theihs* (a time scheduled for something), which strongly suggests that the original Germanic word meant "the time or day of assembly." Ultimately, it is from the Indo-European **tenk-* (to stretch, draw out), extended to "a stretch of time." Old English *thing* (court, assembly) was transferred to "the matters or suits brought before a court or assembly," then to any "saying" or "utterance" and finally to any "entity" or "object." A parallel development occurred in the Romance languages when Latin *causa* (judicial process, legal case) evolved into French *chose* and Spanish and Italian *cosa,* all meaning "a thing."

HUSTING (1012). In contrast to a public THING, also called a *folkmoot,* literally a "folk meeting," was a *husthing,* literally a *"hus* or house assembly,"* which was a council convened by a king or nobleman attended only by members of his immediate court or "house." With the weak stress on the second syllable, *th* was very early pronounced *t* giving *husting.* (The same process occurred in *nostril* from *nosthril,* literally "nose hole.") From "court council," *husting* became the name for "the supreme court of London." Used primarily in the plural form *hustings,* it was then transferred to "the upper end of the hall where the court convened," then to "the platform on which the mayor and aldermen sat in the hall." By the eighteenth century it referred to another platform, the one raised above the crowd from which candidates for parliament spoke to the voters and from which they were nominated. Finally, it was extended to political stumping and electioneering itself.

2

WAR (c. 1050). The early Germanic tribes, despite their warrior cultures, had no native word for "war." The speakers of the Romance languages had perfectly good "war" words from Latin *bellum,* but they avoided using them because they sounded too much like *bello* (beautiful). To fill this gap in the language, Old North French speakers borrowed a Germanic word for "confusion," "discord," such as Frankish or Old High German *werra* (confusion, strife), ultimately from **wers* (to confuse, mix up), also the root of English *worse* and German *wurst* (sausage). The Old North French *werre* became French *guerre,* Spanish, Italian, and Portuguese *guerra,* and derivatives such as Spanish *guerrilla* (little war), borrowed into English as "one who fights in a guerrilla band." Latin *bellum* is usually translated in Old English with *gewinn* (struggle, strife, battle, warfare). ("Thaer bith swythe mycel *gewinn* betweonan him" [There was a very great war between them], c. 900, King Alfred, trans. of Orosius's *Historiae adversum Paganos*). *Gewinn,* from Old English *winnan* (to strive, labor, contend), however, did not survive, except indirectly in *win* (to gain victory, defeat, prevail), nor did Old English *orlege* (hostility, war). Instead of using its own native words, English borrowed the North French *werre* in the late Anglo-Saxon period (c. 1050); this usage was reinforced by William the Conqueror's great Norman *werre* (1066) a few years later. The other Germanic languages went their own ways and developed words for "war" independently. The Germans had *Krieg,* borrowed by the Swedes and Danes as *krig.* The Dutch had *oorlog,* and the Icelanders had *ofrithur,* literally "unpeace."

WARLOCK (a. 900). *Warlocks* may be warlike, but the history of the word is not. The *war* in *warlock* is from Old English *wær* or *wer* and means "covenant," "faith." It is from an earlier sense of *wær,* meaning "true," and is related to Latin *verax* (truthful), the root of *very, verify, verity,* and *verdict.* The *lock* of *warlock* is from Old English *loga* from *leogan* (to lie). A *waerloga* or *werloga,* then, was literally a "covenant liar," that is, an "oath breaker," and by extension "a traitor." Similarly, a *treow-loga,* from *treow* (faithful, loyal) and *wed-loga,* from *wedd* (pledge), the same *wedd* as in *wedlock* (marriage vow), are "oath breakers." *Wed-loga,* however, is not the origin of *wedlock,* whose ending, *-lock,* is from the noun-forming suffix *-lac,* not from *-loga,* its Old English form being *wedlac.* *Waerloga* usually referred to "The Devil," since Satan was a traitor and deceiver. In Middle English, *waerloga* became *warlowe* and developed its only surviving sense (a sorcerer, wizard, male witch) from the notion that one who is in league with the Devil has occult powers. The origin of the *-ck* ending of modern *warlock* is a mystery, though it clearly originated with Scotch and northern English writers in the sixteenth century. It may come from the influence of a lost or unknown word, perhaps a Scottish dialect term.

WEIRD (c. 725). *Weird,* from Old English *wyrd,* is not always strange or uncanny unless fate dictates it so. *Wyrd* originally meant "fate" or "destiny" ("Ac thaet thaet we *Wyrd* hatath, thaet bith Godes weorc thaet he aelce daeg wyrceth" [That which we call *Wyrd* is (really) the work of God about which He is busy every day], c. 888, King Alfred, trans. of Boethius, *Consolation of Philosophy*). When used in the plural, *wyrdes* was personified as three goddesses, the Fates, who were supposed to determine the course of human life. These fair fays in time turned into witches and sometimes wizards ("Puir auld [poor old] wives . . . / Were seized in Superstition's clutches, / An' brunt [burnt] to death for *wierds* [sic] an' witches," 1834, Alexander Smart, *Rambling Rhymes*). In this aspect, Shakespeare immortalized them in *Macbeth* as the three *weird sisters,* which was the fuller Middle English name for the Fates. It was this *weird* that the Romantic poet Shelley first used to mean "supernatural, of unearthly or uncanny character" ("In lone and silent hours, / When night makes a *weird* sound of its own stillness," 1815, Percy Bysshe Shelley, *Alastor*) and then extended to its most common modern sense "strange," "unusual," "fantastic" ("Mutable As shapes in the *weird* clouds," Shelley, *Alastor*). *Weird* or *wyrd* is ultimately from Proto-Germanic **wurth,* which developed the sense of "to turn into" or "to become" from the Indo-European root **wert* (to turn). From the same root comes Old English *weorthan,* or later *worth* (to come to be, happen, befall), *wyrd* being "that which befalls one" ("Unc sceal *weorthan* . . . swa unc *wyrd* geteoth" [It shall happen as fate decides], *Beowulf*).

✳ II ✳

THE
LANGUAGE
OF CHAUCER

The Middle English Period
(1150—1500)

BACKGROUND

When William the Conqueror landed in England in 1066 with his invading Norman army, he established French domination of the island kingdom for the next two hundred or so years. This had a greater influence on English than any other event in its history. The Normans were originally Danes or "Northmen," who in the eighth and ninth centuries settled the northern coast of France known as Normandy, directly across the channel from England. Like the Scandinavian settlers in England, the Normans quickly adopted the customs, culture, and language of their new homeland in France. At the time of the Norman Conquest of England, Normandy was essentially French.

In the course of subduing the English, William, who was crowned king of England, in a series of ruthless campaigns virtually wiped out the Old English nobility. In 1072 only one of the twelve earls in England was an Englishman, and four years later he was executed. Soon all of the important positions and great estates were held by Normans, and French became the language of the aristocracy and government. The speech of the masses, however, remained English.

England until about 1200 was essentially bilingual, English being the language of the uncultivated and socially inferior classes. Even so, Norman nobles identified with their new country, married Englishwomen, founded monasteries on their estates, and were buried along with their families in their adopted land. It was advantageous for both nobles and common people to know a bit of each other's language. Soon French words filtered into the everyday English of the commoners and became part of the English vocabulary itself.

In addition to those presented in this chapter, a sampling of new words that entered English during the French domination of England might include *lecher* and *lackey* (from Old French *lechier,* "to lick"); *pavilion* (ultimately from Latin *papilionem,* "butterfly," because a tent resembles a butterfly's outstretched wings); *butler* (from *butiller,* "cupbearer," from *bouteille,* "wine vessel," "bottle"); *nape* (from *hanap,* "goblet," from the resemblance of the concavity at the base of the skull); *tennis* (from *tenez!* "receive!," "take!"); *umpire* (from *nonper,* "odd," "not even"); *trance* (*transir,* "pass on," "die," "numb with fear"); *nasty* (from *villenastre,* "infamous," "bad," "villainous"); *bribe* (from *briber,* "to go begging"); and *truant,* ("beggar," "rogue").

French words were very quickly assimilated and combined with native English words and affixes. For example, *gentle* was adopted early in the 1200s and almost as soon was compounded with English elements to give *gentlewoman, gentleman, gentleness,* and *gently.* Many English words died out, especially when there was a French synonym. French *envy,* for example, replaced Old English *anda; uncle* replaced *eam; people* replaced *leod.* Other examples of Old English words that were lost to French were *firen* (crime), *cempa* (warrior), *sibb* (peace), *adl* (disease), *ieldu* (age), and *earm* (poor).

Often, however, when an English and a French word meant the same thing at the time of the borrowing, the English word or sometimes its French counterpart was kept by gradually altering or shading its meaning. This process greatly broadened and enriched the English vocabulary, enhancing its ability to express nuances of meaning. This happened with the originally synonymous English DOOM and French *judgment* (hence *to deem* and *to judge*), English *hearty* and French *cordial,* *smell* and *aroma* (or *odor*), *house* and *mansion, ask* and *demand, shun* and *avoid, seethe* and *boil,* and *wish* and *desire.* It is also seen in the group of words that distinguish between the animal and its meat: English *ox, sheep, swine,* and *calf,* and French *beef, mutton, pork,* and *veal.*

Some of the many French loan words in English come in closely related pairs that have the same ultimate Latin source, though they have quite different meanings. For example, English *ransom* is from Old French *rançon* and English *redemption* is from Old French *redemption,* but both French words are ultimately from Latin *redemptionem* (a redeeming, especially by ransom); *chance* is from *cheance* (accident, dice game) and *cadence* is from *cadence* (rhythm), while both are from Latin *cadere* (to fall). Other examples: *abridge* and *abbreviate, chieftain* and *captain, constraint* and *constriction, costive* and *constipation, fashion* and *faction, frail* and *fragile, loyal* and *legal, naïve* and *native, poor* and *pauper* (borrowed directly from Latin), *prove* and *probe* (directly from Latin), *pursue* and *persecute, ration* and *reason, restraint* and *restriction, royal* and *regal, sample* and *example, sever* and *separate,* and *surface* and *superficies.*

By the mid-1300s English had reasserted its place as the proper language for Englishmen. In 1362 parliament enacted a statute requiring all lawsuits to be conducted in English. Several historical events conspired to give English the ascendancy. The first was the severing of England's ties to the continent when in 1204 King John lost Normandy to the king of France. The English king and aristocracy were now forced to see England as their first concern, having its own political and economic ends that were not the same as those of France. French soon became a cultivated rather than a native language for the upper classes, so that by about 1300 the mother tongue of the children of the nobility was English.

With the outbreak of the Hundred Years' War (1337–1453), it became clear to soldier and citizen alike that French was the language of the enemy country. At the same time, the improvement in the lot of the laborers and the rise of the middle class gave English new prestige. And the effect in 1349–50 of the Black Death, which killed off some 30 percent of the entire population of England, was to increase the economic importance of the laboring classes, and with it the importance of their language.

It was during the fourteenth century that Geoffrey Chaucer, writing in his native English tongue, became court poet, receiving pay and patronage from the royal family. In one of the illuminated manuscripts of his *Troilus and Criseyde,* he is shown reading aloud that masterpiece of vernacular English narrative to King Richard II and his court. By the next century very little spoken French could be heard in England. Chaucer's English—the variety or dialect spoken in London—had established itself as the standard language of England.

Oddly enough, while English was reclaiming its rightful place in the years 1250 to 1400, it adopted the greatest number of French words. At least 40 percent of all French words in English came in during that time. Of the nearly 10,000 French words borrowed during the Middle English period, about 75 percent are still in current use.

English changed during the Middle English period in more extensive and fundamental ways than at any time before or since. Some of these changes were the result of the Norman Conquest, but many others were a continuation of changes begun in Old English, especially the radical changes that occurred in pronunciation and grammar. Not only did a large part of the Old English word stock disappear with the addition of thousands of French and Latin borrowings, but the changes in grammar shifted English from a highly inflected language to a very analytic one. It was now sounding less like the original Germanic tongue and more like the unique hybrid that Shakespeare inherited.

PARADISE (a. 1175). In medieval art, Adam and Eve before the fall are usually depicted in a park or garden that is walled in, with a gate through which they are later cast out. This portrayal of Eden is close to the etymological origin of *paradise* from Old Persian *pairidaeza,* which referred to the extensive walled parks or pleasure grounds of the Persian kings. *Pairidaeza,* literally "walled around," is a combination of *pairi-* (around), close relative to the prefix *peri-* (around) as in *perimeter* and *peristalsis,* and *daeza,* ultimately from Indo-European

*dhoigho (mud wall) from **dheigh-* (to form, mold, build), also the root of English *dough* and *figure*. After the ancient Greeks borrowed the Old Persian word, the Greek Jews who in the 3rd century B.C. translated the Old Testament, the so-called Septuagint, used *paradeisos* for the Garden of Eden. Later, the New Testament writers extended *paradeisos* to mean "the abode of the blessed in heaven." This is the oldest sense in English, borrowed shortly after the invasion of the French. Before the French, the native English expression for "paradise" was *neorxna wong* (plain of delights) or *se haliga wong* (the holy plain), though the Old English translations of the New Testament often used the Latin word ("To-daey thu bist mid me on *paradiso*" [Today you will be with me in paradise], Luke 23:43). To distinguish it from the *heavenly paradise,* Eden was also called the *earthly paradise.* A *fool's paradise* (happiness based on ignorance or false hopes) was first used about three centuries after the appearance of *paradise* in English.

CORONER (1194). An early seventeenth-century survey of Devon notes that "If any man die . . . in the forest, the *coroner* of Lidford shall *crown* him," and a similar survey of Cornwall enumerates the coroner's "sundry large privileges," among which is the *"crowning* of dead persons." These officials were not empowered to conduct posthumous royal coronations, but were acting as *crowners* (coroners), who *crown* (hold inquests). *Crowner* ("The *Crowner* hath sat [held an inquest] on her, and finds it Christian buriall," 1602, *Hamlet*) is a later popularized version of *coroner* that is incidentally close to the etymological meaning. *Coroner* was borrowed from French *coruner* or *corouner* and is from *corune* (crown) in the coroner's original title *custos placitorum coronae* (custodian of the pleas of the crown). In England he was originally an officer of the royal household, and later, of a county or district, charged with the interests of the private property of the crown. Under Edward I (1239–1307), the coroner's duties were codified and included the investigation of crimes "where any be slain, or suddenly dead or wounded, or where houses are broken, or where treasure is said to be found." By the nineteenth century, the coroner's authority had diminished to simply holding inquests on the bodies of those supposed to have died by violence.

DRAGON (c. 1200). The *dragon* was one of the most popular and fearsome creatures in the medieval bestiary, and could be found everywhere, from the royal war standard or banner to illuminated manuscripts and paintings depicting St. Michael or St. George or St. Margaret or St. Romain or St. Clement or St. Martha or St. Florent, among other saints, slaying a dragon. The Middle English *dragun* was first and foremost a huge serpent or snake, and as such was closely identified with Satan and evil ("And he caugte the *dragoun,* the olde serpent, that is the devel and Sathanas," 1382, Wyclif, trans. of Revelation 20:2). The Greek origin of the word, through the French learned borrowing of Latin *draconem* (serpent, dragon), incidentally complemented this association of snake and Satan. Greek *drakon* (serpent, sea-fish) meant literally "monster with the deadly glance or evil eye." It is based on a lost noun, **drak* (glance), akin to Greek *derkesthai* (to flash, gleam, look at), from Indo-European **derk-* (to see). The root sense of "seeing or watching" also appears in the classical legends of the dragon that watches or guards a treasure, as in the story of the golden apples of Hesperides, or in the medieval romance variation of the dragon guarding a captive lady. *Draconian* (c. 1700, harsh, cruel) is also from Greek *drakon* (dragon), but as the personal name of a seventh century B.C. lawgiver. *Drakon* codified laws that had never been written down, but in the process he made them extremely severe. As Plutarch explained, these laws demanded the same penalty "for nearly all crimes . . . death. The man who was convicted of idleness, or who stole a cabbage or an apple, was liable to death no less than a robber of temples or the murderer" (*Life of Solon*).

FELLOW (c. 1200). In Middle English, a *fellow* (associate, comrade) was as often as not a woman ("She wente with confessours [to] hir *felowes*, that were wymen," c. 1450, *Prose Legends*). Sometimes one's wife or mate was a *fellow* ("He wroght a *felau* of his ban Till adam" [He made a fellow (i.e., Eve) out of his (rib) bone for Adam, a. 1300, *Cursor Mundi*), who, long before feminism, was considered (more or less) a *fellow* or "equal" ("Thy wyfe . . . thof sche be servant in degre, / In som degre sche *felaw* ys" [Your wife . . . though she is a servant in degree, / In some degree she is a fellow or equal], 1869, in William Hazlitt *English Proverbs*). *Fellow* is from late Old English *feolaga* (partner) borrowed from a Scandinavian source, probably Old Norse *felage*. It is a compound of *fe,* or in Old English *feoh* (property, money), and *lag* (to lay). A *feolaga* or *fellow,* then, was literally a "money layer," that is, one who "lays down money" in a joint venture with others, in short, a business partner. Old English *feoh* originally meant "cattle" or "livestock," which from ancient times has been a measure of one's wealth, extending the meaning of *feoh* or *fee* to "property," "money." It is from the Proto-Germanic **fehu,* ultimately from Indo-European **peku-* (movable property, wealth), the source of Latin *pecus* (cattle) and *pecunia* (money). *Fee* meaning "payment due a lawyer or other professional" is a different word, though ultimately it is probably from the same Germanic root, **fehu.* Earlier in Middle English *fee* or *fe* meant "land held from a lord in return for homage or service," and was taken from Old French *fieu* or *fief,* also the source of English *fief* (a feudal estate) and *feudal.* Middle English rarely used *fellow* in combinations, the way we do today, as in *fellow countrymen* and *fellow worker.* Instead, *even* (level, equal), from a Germanic root of unknown origin, was used, as in *even-disciple, even-servant,* and *even-worker.*

CONSTABLE (c. 1200). As with MARSHAL, which has a closely parallel equine history, *constable* was borrowed from Old French, *conestable,* which in turn is from Late Latin *comes stabuli* (count or officer of the stable), earlier known as the *tribunus stabuli* (tribune of the stable). The importance in the Middle Ages of horses and a mastery of them, especially in the military, is apparent in the titles "Constable of France" and "Lord High Constable of England," who were the chief officers of the royal household. Eventually these posts were elevated to chief of the army. Along with the Earl Marshal, the Lord High Constable was also the judge of the Court of Chivalry, deciding on matters relating to tilts, tournaments, and trial by combat. By the fourteenth century, a *petty* or *parish constable* was an officer of the peace, a sense that survives in England but, unlike MARSHAL, was never adopted in America.

CALENDAR (c. 1205). In ancient Roman "banking," because monthly interest payments were usually due on *calendae* (calends), the first day of the month, the moneylender's account book was called a *calendarium.* The Roman method of reckoning the days of the month was, so to say, byzantine and extremely inconvenient. And, in fact, it was backward. Instead of counting the days in ascending numerical order, the Romans counted backward from three different points: the *ca-*

lends, the *nones,* and the *ides.* The calends were invariably the first day of the month, ides were the thirteenth or fifteenth day, and nones were the ninth day before ides. By this retrograde way of reckoning, January 14, for example, was the "nineteenth day before the calends of February," counting inclusively (31 days of January minus 14 plus the 14th and the 1st equals 19). *Calendae* or *calends* itself is from Latin *calare* (call out, proclaim) from Indo-European **kel-* (to shout), because on the first day of the month the priests "called" the people together to announce the days during the month on which the festivals would fall, to ensure they would be properly observed and kept sacred. After Latin *calendarium* (a list of accounts) became Old French *calendier,* it was used for any list or register of items. Around the twelfth century, when Middle English borrowed the French word, its meaning had changed to refer to the system of dividing up the year in the Julian calendar. Then, in the next century, it more specifically referred to a register or table listing the days and months of the year.

COWARD (a. 1225). Although a *cow* is a timid creature, it has nothing to do with the history of *coward,* nor does *cowherd* (a herder of cows, a low bumpkin). And *coward* is not related to *cower* (to crouch in fear or shame) or *cow* (to intimidate, frighten), which were borrowed from Scandinavian sources. Instead, it is probably from Old French *coart,* a compound of *coe* or *cow* (tail) from Latin *cauda* (tail), and the derogatory suffix *-art* or *-ard.* The tail is that of a frightened animal "turning tail" and running, or else one cowering with its tail clapped between its legs. In heraldry, a lion with its tail tucked under is called a *lion coward.* However, there may be another tale of a tail to tell here. In France, an old hunting term for "hare" was *couard,* or in the language of an old glossary, "le *coward,* ou le court cow" (the coward or short tail), a reference to its bobtail. In an Old French version of the fable "Reynard the Fox," the hare is named *Coart.* Because rabbits are considered to be flighty, fearful creatures, *couard* or *coart* may have come to mean "coward" in reference to their apparently cowardly traits.

OSTRICH (a. 1225). An ostrich and a sparrow may seem at opposite ends of the spectrum of bird life, but they are next to each other etymologically. The original Greek for ostrich was *strouthos megale* and meant literally "great sparrow." To confound avian categories further, Greek *strouthos* is ultimately not a sparrow at all, but a thrush, from the Indo-European root **trozdo-* (thrush), which is also the root of English *thrush*. The Greek phrase was then shortened to *strouthion* (ostrich), and eventually adopted into Vulgar Latin as *avis struthio*, literally "ostrich bird." The Latin phrase was then condensed in Old French to *ostrusce* and borrowed by Middle English, which spelled it in numerous odd ways *(hostryche, astridge, estryge, estritch)*. Most of the folk myths about the ostrich ("The *hostryche* by his nature eteth [eats] well yron [iron]," 1481, William Caxton, trans. of *The Mirrour of the World*) originated during the Middle Ages ("Like the *Austridge*, who hiding her little head, supposeth her great body obscured," 1623, cited in the *Oxford English Dictionary*).

HARLOT (a. 1225). One old theory of the derivation of *harlot* (an immoral or debauched woman), no longer given much credence, says that it is from Arlotta or Harlotha, the concubine of the Duke of Normandy and the mother of William the Conqueror, also called William the Bastard. But in the thirteenth and fourteenth centuries, and earlier in France, a harlot was not even a female. When Chaucer called the Summoner "a gentil harlot," he was not referring to the man's sexual proclivities, but was simply calling him a "gentle fellow." Its first meaning, closest to the original Old French *herlot* or *arlot,* was a "vagabond," "rascal," or "knave." It also referred to an itinerant who worked from time to time as a jester or buffoon, sometimes with other traveling showmen ("Mynstrel and jogelour, tumbler and *harlot,* wole not take of the puple bifore that thei han shewid ther craft" [Minstrel and juggler, tumbler and harlot, will not take (money) from the people before they have shown their craft (i.e., performed)], c. 1380, Wyclif, *Selected Works*). A male servant was a harlot, such as the one that follows the friar in Chaucer's *Summoner's Tale* ("A sturdy *harlot* wente ay hem bihynde . . . and bar a sak" [A sturdy harlot went ever behind him . . . and bore a sack]). It was not until well into the fifteenth century that it referred to a woman, specifically a prostitute or strumpet, though *harlotry* (unchastity, sexual profligacy) appeared fifty years earlier. It is not known why *harlot* shifted its reference from men to disreputable women, but a similar shift occurred in the histories of BROTHEL, *bawd,* and BIMBO, and is undoubtedly rooted in sexist cultural attitudes. *Strumpet* (a. 1327) was another favorite Middle English term for a debauched woman. Like *harlot,* its ultimate origins are unknown. One theory says it derives through French *strupe* or *stupre* (debauchery, concubinage) from Latin *stuprare* (debauch). In Irish Gaelic it is *striopach* (strumpet) and in English dialect it is often abbreviated to *strum.* Wyclif often used both *hoore* (whore) and *strumpet* in his translation of the Bible ("There shal be no *strumpet* [in the 1388 edition: *hoore*] of the doughters of Yrael," 1382, Deuteronomy 23:17). Sixteenth-century translations uniformly preferred the more euphemistic *harlot.*

CUCKOLD (a. 1250). In European folklore cuckoos are considered love oracles, their distinctive song being a good omen for marriage. But *cuckoo* is a resoundingly bad omen

,after marriage. Dr. Johnson notes in his famous dictionary that "it was usual to alarm a husband at the approach of an adulterer by calling out 'Cuckoo,' which by mistake was applied in time to the person warned." The Elizabethans loved to pun on *cuckoo* and *cuckold* ("The cuckoo, then, on every tree, / Mocks married men, for thus sings he— / Cuckoo . . . O word of fear Unpleasing to a married ear!," 1588, Shakespeare, *Love's Labour's Lost*). The cuckoo's habit of laying its egg in another bird's nest is the underlying metaphor. A *cuckold* (the husband of an adulterous wife) is like a bird, secure in its nest, hatching another bird's egg, witless of the deception. The Romans called an adulterer a "cuckoo" *(cuculus)*. And in Germany and France both the adulterer and the husband of the adulteress are cuckoos, in German *gauch* or *kuckuk* and in French *cocu*. In English, however, only the duped husband is a *cuckold* ("Brother Osewold . . . hath no wyf, he is no *Cokewold,*" 1386, Chaucer, *Miller's Prologue*). When Middle English borrowed *cukeweld* or *cokewold,* pronounced with three syllables, from the Old French *cucuault,* from *cucu* (cuckoo) plus the perjorative suffix *-ault,* the reference to the adulterer was lost. The cuckoo gets more bad publicity beginning in the sixteenth century, when a foolish or silly person was called a *cuckoo,* probably in reference to the bird's maddening, monotonous song. This may be the source of the American slang sense (c. 1918) "crazy," perhaps reinforced by the crazy monotony of a cuckoo clock, which typically seemed to run down and sound the hours at the wrong times.

MARSHAL (1258). When the "marshal of the army of God and Holy Church," Baron Robert Fitzwalter, led his fellow barons and their forces against King John in 1215 for redress of grievances that resulted in the Magna Carta, he was not acting as a mere "horse servant," the original and literal meaning of *marshal*. A marshal originally tended horses, treating their diseases (in modern French, the *maréchal vétérinaire*) and shoeing them (the *maréchal ferrant*). In the Middle Ages, this was an occupation of no small importance, especially for a marshal attached to the royal household, who in time became a chief functionary of the royal court. The English borrowed *marshal* from Old French *maresc(h)al* (farrier, marshal), and the French had taken it from the title of the *marescalci* or "masters of the horse" of the early Frankish kings. Ultimately it is a Germanic word, **marhoskalkoz,* compounded of **marho* (horse), the feminine form (**marjha*) giving English *mare,* and **skalko* (servant). *Skalko* also appears in Old English as *scealc* (servant) and is cognate with Middle High German *schel* (jumping), the original sense perhaps being a "jumper" or "errand boy," ultimately from Indo-European **skel-* (to jump). The importance of the cavalry in medieval warfare raised the marshal to the rank of a military commander. In the armed forces of England, *marshal* is still used in titles of rank, such as *Field-Marshal* and *Marshal of the Royal Air Force.* As early as the thirteenth century a marshal was also an officer of a court of law, who took charge and custody of prisoners. This sense is probably at the root of the American usage of *marshal,* a civil officer of a judicial district similar to the sheriff of a county. CONSTABLE has a very similar history.

CURFEW (1285). In medieval Europe, cities were built of wood, and a home had a hearth that was little more than a hole in the middle of the floor under an opening in the roof for the smoke to escape. To prevent a conflagration of these tinderboxes, ordinances required a *curfew* or bell to signal that fires be extinguished or "covered" after dark. In France it was called *cuevre-fu,* literally "cover fire," from *couvrir* (to cover) and *feu* (fire). It is commonly thought that William the Conqueror instituted the *corfu* or *curfewe* in England to control the populace; however, in the reign of Alfred the Great (849–900) a curfew bell was rung each night at Carfax, Oxford. The existing lights-out regulations that William strictly enforced were abolished by Henry I in 1100. But the practice of tolling an evening bell, usually at eight or nine o'clock, survives to this day in some parts of England, a relic of the old curfew.

GARGOYLE (1286). One of the common popular images of the medieval period is the grotesque water spouts or *gargoyles* projecting from the gutters of building roofs. The imaginations of the Gothic architects went wild with these sculptures of deformed humans, fabulous beasts, and demonic spirits ("And euery hous keuered [covered] was with lede [lead]. And many *gargoyl,* and many hidous hede [hideous head]," 1412–20, John Lydgate, *Troy Book*). Because these sculptures spewed rain water from their throats, the French called them *gargouille* (gargoyle, throat) from Latin *gurges* (throat, whirlpool) and *gula* (throat). *Gurges* is ultimately from Indo-European **gwerə-* (to swallow), probably an imitation of the sound of swallowing, and is the source of English *gargle, gurgle, gorge, gurgitation,* and *regurgitate*. *Gula* is from another Indo-European root meaning "to swallow," **gwel-*, which gave English *gullet, glut,* and *glutton*. With the introduction of lead downspouts and gutters in the sixteenth century, gargoyles rapidly began to disappear.

GOUT (c. 1290). This inherited metabolic disease that affects the joints is one of the oldest to be described in medical literature. The ancient Greek physician Galen attributed it to overindulgence and luxury, and Seneca noted the prevalence of gout among Roman ladies as a result of debauchery and gluttony. Middle English *goute* ("The *goute* lette hire nothyng for to daunce" [The gout did not prevent her from dancing], c. 1386, Chaucer, *Nun's Priest's Tale*) is a French borrowing from Latin *gutta* (a drop), in allusion to the belief that morbid or diseased humors from the blood were "dropped" into the joints. (In Old French *goute* also gave *goutiere* (gutter, spout), literally a "receptacle for drops of water," which is the source of English *gutter*.) In addition to gout, Medieval Latin *gutta* referred to other diseases that were attributed to a "defluxion" of HUMORS, including dropsy and catarrh. By the beginning of the sixteenth century, *gout* (a large splash or clot) was also used in its etymological sense of "a drop" ("I see thee still, / And on thy blade and dudgeon [handle], *gouts* of blood," 1605, Shakespeare, *Macbeth*).

TESTAMENT (c. 1290); **TESTIMONY** (1382). When a witness gives *testimony,* he is literally "standing as a third party" to the defendant and the plaintiff. The Latin root of *testament* and *testimony* is *testis* (witness), from **tristis,* a compound of *tres* (three) and *stare* (to stand). *Testimony* originally referred to the tablets containing the Ten Commandments in the Ark of the Covenant ("Moyses . . . berynge in hoond two tablis of *testymonye* wrytun on eithir side" [Moses . . . bearing in hand two tablets of testimony written on either side], 1382, Wyclif, trans. of Exodus 32:15). This is taken as a literal translation from the Vulgate Latin *testimonium,* which is a translation of the Septuagint Greek *tò martýrion,* which in turn translates the original Hebrew *eduth* (attestation) from *ed* (witness), Moses' tablets bearing witness of God's law. *Testimony* (evidence given under oath), borrowed from Old French *testimonie,* appears in English about fifty years later. The earliest meaning of *testament* (covenant) is also taken from Biblical Latin, but from the New Testament. The Latin *testamentum* is a translation of Greek *diatheke* in the account of the Last Supper ("This cuppe is the newe *testament* of my blood," 1382, Wyclif, trans. of I Corinthians 11:25), which associated it with the last will or "testament" of Christ, and hence to any last testament. The two divisions of the Bible were called in Greek *palaia diatheke* and *kaine diatheke,* which were translated into Latin as *vetus testamentum* and *novum testamentum,* and these became in thirteenth-century English the *Old* and *New Testaments.* Although *testament* is etymologically related to TESTIS or *testicle,* both at root involving "witnessing," the popular story that they are related by an old tradition that had men swearing solemn oaths while holding on to their private parts is very doubtful, if not outright apocryphal.

MONEY (c. 1290). Originally the protector and patron goddess of women, Juno became a great deity of the Roman state, worshiped at the temple on the Capitoline Hill. In 384 B.C., Camillus built a large temple to her in her aspect as Juno Moneta ("the Adviser") and attached the first Roman mint to it. Thereafter, Juno was represented on medals with minting tools, hammer, anvil, pincers, and dies. *Moneta* was her cult title and may derive from an Etruscan family name or more likely from Latin *monere* (to warn, advise), ultimately from the root **men-* (to think). The close connection between her title and the minting of money gave Latin *moneta* (coinage) and Old French *moneie,* the immediate source of English *money.* English, however, had already encountered *moneta,* when in the eighth century it adopted the word directly from Latin and altered it to *mynet* (coin, money). This became in Middle English *mynt* and eventually *mint.* The Old English sense of "coin," "money" survived as late as the nineteenth century ("You'll want money . . . You must take some of the *mint* I've got laid by in the old tea-pot," 1848, Elizabeth Gaskell, *Mary Barton*). By the Middle English period, *mynt* had also developed its most commonly used sense, which harks back to the Roman temple, "place where money is coined."

TRAVEL (c. 1290). With roads that were barely footpaths through forests infested with bandits and highwaymen, travel in medieval England was arduous, if not downright torturous. Torture in fact is at the root of *travel.* The *trepalium* was a Roman instrument of torture and had three stakelike prongs, its name deriving from *tres* (three) and *palus* (stake). The Latin word became the verb **trepaliare* (to torture) and eventually Old French *travailler,* which thirteenth-century English adopted as *travail. Travail* first meant to "torture," "afflict," "trouble," "weary" ("They were wery and sore *traveyled* by the waye which was longe," 1483, William Caxton, trans. of *Golden Legend*), and then "to toil or labor" ("Who *travaylleth* wel, he hath ever brede [bread] ynough for to ete [eat]," 1484, Caxton, trans. of *Fables of Aesop*), and finally it meant "painful effort," "suffering." In this evolution of meanings, the specialized sense "to journey" developed in allusion to the inevitable trouble and weariness of medieval travel, and became a separate word distinguished by the shift from the accent on the last syllable of *travail* [trə vail'] to the accent on the first syllable and the shortening of the second vowel, to give *travel* [tra' vəl].

NIGHTMARE (c. 1290). If you have ever been wakened by a feeling of suffocation, as though someone or something were sitting on your chest, you have had a *nightmare* in its etymological sense. A nightmare was thought to be a flying female goblin or ogress, sometimes called the *night hag,* who settled on a person, creating the sensation of suffocation ("Like an eyeless *nightmare* grief did sit upon his being," 1817, Percy Bysshe Shelley, *Prince Athanase*). So persistent was the belief that not until the mid-sixteenth century was the meaning of *nightmare* transferred to the real cause of the suffocating feeling: a distressing dream. *Nightmare* is a compound of *night,* deriving more or less directly from Indo-European **nekw-* (night), and *mare* (incubus), the *mare* being the supposed monster perched on the sleeper's chest ("The verie cause is, liyng or slepyng on their backe. And not through the *mare,* or night spirit, as thei term it," 1562, William Bullein, *Bulwarke of Defence against All Sicknesse*). Sometimes confused with *mare* (a female horse), *mare* (incubus) has cognates in Polish *mora* and Czech *mura* and is from the Germanic root **maron,* ultimately from the Indo-European root **mer-* (to rub away, harm).

VERMILION (1296). In addition to bright red, what do *vermilion* and CRIMSON have in common? Worms. Both were originally made from kermes, a scale insect with wormlike larvae. The dried bodies of the females have been used since ancient times to produce the oldest-known red dye. The kermes dye was later found to be inferior to a dye made from another wormlike insect, cochineal. Indo-European **wermi-* (worm), from **wer-* (to bend, turn, twist), gave "worms" to both Proto-Germanic, whence English *worm,* and to Latin *(vermis),* whence English *vermin, vermicelli,* and *varmint.* The Late Latin diminutive *vermiculus* (little worm), with reference to the dye worms, became Old French *vermeillon,* borrowed into Middle English as *vermelyon* (a red dye). Vermelyon was used to make red sealing wax, artist's paint, and cosmetics. The cosmetic use survived into the nineteenth century primarily in reference to the warpaint of the American Indians ("Happy was he who could render himself hideous with *vermilion,*" 1836, Washington Irving, *Astoria*).

BAD (1297). In one of the odd coincidences of etymology, Old Persian had the word *bad* (evil) with the same meaning as in English. But it is unlikely that the English word is from Persian. Two other theories of its origin are more plausible. Old English *baeddel* (hermaphrodite) and its derivative *baedling* (effeminate man, pederast), which were used contemptuously, are from a Proto-Germanic root related to Latin *foedare* (to defile, pollute). In its evolution to *bad, baeddel* (hermaphrodite, pederast, hence "perverted man") probably became a derogatory adjective meaning "perverted" or "evil," the same way that *wretch* (a miserable, unhappy person) became the adjective *wretch,* meaning "miserable," "wretched" ("No man is more *wrecche* nothir hath more woo . . . than he that hath an yuel wif" [No man is more *wretch* nor has more woe than he that has an evil wife], 1398, John de Trevisa, trans. of Bartholomew Anglicus, *De Proprietatibus Rerum*). The *-l* ending of *baeddel* was simply dropped, giving the two-syllable Middle English word *badde* (pronounced "bad-də"). The other often purported *bad* history derives it from Old English *gebaeded* (forced, oppressed). The sense of *gebaeded* evolved into "worthless," "bad," "evil" in the same manner that Latin *captivus* (taken by force, enslaved) became *caitiff* (cowardly, despicable). And by dropping the prefix and the ending, *gebaeded* became *bad*, the same way Old English *gemaeded* (insane) became Modern English *mad*.

SLAVE (a. 1300). English had perfectly good words for "slave" and "slavery," *theow* and *theowdom*, but like many a good Anglo-Saxon word, they withered and died when French was transplanted to English soil. The French word that replaced them in the thirteenth century was *esclave* from Medieval Latin *Sclavus*. Throughout much of the so-called Dark Ages, the Slavs, the large group of peoples in eastern Europe, including Russians, Bulgarians, Serbo-Croatians, Poles, Czechs, and others, were routinely conquered and enslaved. Late Greek *Sklabos*, the name for this group of peoples, became Medieval Latin *Sclavus* (Slav), but because the name was closely associated with the servile condition of the Slavs, *Sclavus* also meant "slave." The Greek word is an alteration of Old Slavic *Sloveninu* (Slav), which is related to *slovo* (word, speech), the name originally referring to diverse peoples all speaking the same language.

BUTCHER (a. 1300). Most European words for "butcher" are derived from roots meaning "flesh," "meat" or "slaughter," "cut." In Old English, for example, a butcher was a *hyldere*, literally "a flayer," from *hyldan* (to flay), or a *cwellere* (killer), from *cwellan* (to kill). But these were dropped in favor of French *bochier* or *bouchier* (butcher). French *bouchier* and Italian *beccio* are anomalous among the European "butcher" words, because they derive from "he-goat" (French *boc*, Italian *becco*), and mean literally "one who kills he-goats," or by

extension "a dealer in goats' flesh." Except for one or two kept for breeding, young bucks were considered useless and were routinely slaughtered for their meat. In Middle English, a *bocher* or *bowcher* was also an executioner or torturer ("Whan the bysshop came unto his place of execucion, he prayed the *bowcher* to gyue to ym [him] v. [five] strokes in the worshyp of Cristes fyue [five] woundes," 1494, Robert Fabyan, *The Newe Cronycles of Englande*) and was figuratively extended to "a brutal murderer" ("Erle of Worcester whiche for his crueltye was called the *bocher* of Englande," 1529, John Rastell, *The Pastyme of People, the Cronycles of Dyvers Realmys*).

HEARSE (c. 1300). Wolves and harrows are at the root of *hearse* (a vehicle for carrying a coffin). Indo-European **gherkwos* (to bristle) is the source of Latin *hircus* (he-goat) and its Oscan cognate *hirpus* (wolf). Because a wolf's teeth resemble the teeth of a harrow, which was like a large triangular-shaped rake used to cultivate the soil, the Oscan word gave Latin *hirpex* (harrow), which became Medieval Latin *hercia* (harrow). In Old French it was called a *herce*. A triangular frame often used in church services, with toothlike candle holders, resembled a harrow, and was naturally dubbed a *herce*, which Middle English borrowed as *hers*. The name was then extended to a similar but more elaborate framework that held numerous candles over a coffin or bier and then to a pagoda-shaped structure used in the funerals of nobility, intricately decorated with banners, heraldic devices, and candles. Complimentary poems and epitaphs were also attached to this *herse*. The name was then transferred to the frame or bier itself on which the corpse was laid, and then by the mid-seventeenth century, to the carriage that bore the body, this last being the only surviving sense.

BIBLE (a. 1300). Like the history of BOOK, the meaning of *Bible* and *biblio-* (as in *bibliography* and *bibliophile*) evolved from "tree" to "book." The Greek source *byblos* (book, writing, scroll) meant literally "paper," specifically Egyptian paper or papyrus, which was the inner bark of the papyrus plant used as a medium for writing, the same function that beech bark held in the history of BOOK. The great exporter of papyrus in ancient times was the Phoenician city *Bublos* or *Byblos,* whose name in Greek became synonymous with paper. Similarly, early Latin had *liber* and **luber* (a tree's inner bark), from Indo-European **loubh,* also the root of English *leaf* (leaf of a plant, page of a book). Because writing in early times was done on *liber,* it came to refer to "paper" or "parchment" and then to "book," eventually winding up, among other lexical places, in English *library.*

FORNICATION (a. 1300). The early Christian writers who created the verb *fornicari* (to frequent brothels) would have delighted in the coincident association between the burning in hell's furnace for this sin and the origin of the word in Latin *formus* (heat) and *fornus* or *fornax* (oven), the source of English *furnace* and *fornication.* A *fornax* was an arched or vaulted brick oven. During the late republican period, the Romans constructed under their great buildings large vaulted basements resembling the arched brickwork of ovens. Around the time of Christ, the poor and prostitutes lived in these gloomy underground dwellings, the latter plying their ancient trade there. *Fornax* (oven) then became *fornix* (brothel) with reference to the prostitutes' vaulted brick hovels. Old French adopted *fornication* from the Late Latin *fornicationem,* which had shifted its meaning from the visitation of brothels to the sexual act itself ("This sin [lechery] has branches fele . . . *fornicacion* es an" (This sin has deadly branches . . . fornication is one], a. 1300, *Cursor Mundi*). The English verb *fornicate* (to have unmarried sexual intercourse) is a back formation of *fornication* and was not used until the Elizabethan era.

OCEAN (c. 1300). Because the prehistoric Indo-Europeans probably lived inland, away from any ocean, they had no word for "ocean" or "sea." After their diaspora, which took many of them to the edge of vast waters, the ancient inhabitants along the Atlantic, Baltic, and Mediterranean coasts had to make do with their old stock of words. These speakers used various root words meaning "deep," "level," "glistening," "salt," and "water" to refer to the sea. The root **mori,* for example, probably meant "lake" or "inland sea" and may have come from an earlier root meaning "glisten." From it derive Latin and Italian *mare,* French *mer,* and German and Dutch *meer.* In English, it survives in a direct line through Proto-Germanic and Old English only in *mer*maid, though it appears in *marine* borrowed from Old French in the fifteenth century. *Sea* is from the Germanic root **saiwaz,* and because it has no cognates outside of Germanic, is probably a non-Indo-European borrowing. The Greeks used *thalassa* (sea) from a root meaning "hollow" or "deep." Greek cosmologists portrayed the world as a circular disk surrounded by a mighty stream named *Okeanos,* akin to Sanskrit *asayanas* (the encompassing). As the great primeval water, Okeanos was the father of gods and men, the link between heaven and earth. Personified, he was the son of Uranus and Gaia and husband of Tethys. This encompassing sea was the original sense in

English, borrowed from French, usually in the set phrases *ocean sea, sea ocean,* or *sea of ocean.* Before the discovery of the western hemisphere, this great outer sea, in contrast, say, to the Mediterranean, was boundless and surrounded one great mass of land. By the late fourteenth century, as knowledge of geography widened, the great ocean began to be scaled down and divided into regions like the *occean of Athlant* (Atlantic Ocean).

PAIN (a. 1300). In medieval England having a great *pain* on one's head was not necessarily a headache. In fact, as often as not a *pain* (punishment for a crime or offense) meant losing one's head ("Namoore [no more], up *on payne of* lesynge [the losing] of youre heed," 1386, Chaucer, *Knight's Tale*). This expression survives today only in the phrase *on pain of death.* Middle English *payne* or *peyne* is from French *peine,* in turn from Latin *poena* (punishment, penalty), hence *subpoena,* literally "under penalty." The Indo-European root **kwoina* (to pay, compensate, atone) gave Greek *poine* (fine, penalty) and through Latin and then Old French gave English not only *pain,* but *penal, punish,* and *impunity.* The pervasively Christian society of the Middle Ages believed that our troubles and sufferings are the result of our sins, for which we must pay the "penalty" in purgatory or hell. For a time, *pain* referred specifically to the sufferings of hell ("His saule wente un-to *payne,*" c. 1400, Anonymous, *The Romance of Duke Rowland and Sir Otuell of Spayne*). Eventually the sufferings themselves became the central meaning. *Pine* (to yearn) is a "doublet" of *pain,* since it is also from Latin *poena.* But instead of developing through French, it was introduced with Christianity directly into the Germanic languages. In English it too first applied to the pains of hell ("Of Proserpyne That quene ys [is] of the derke [dark] pyne," c. 1384, Chaucer, *House of Fame*), and had essentially the same sense development as the noun *pain,* though none of these senses has survived. The verb, however, began with the meaning "to afflict with pain," with the later extension "to exhaust or kill (a person) by torture or starvation" ("Thei *pynen* hem bi the worste hungir" [They pined or tortured him by the worst hunger], 1380,

Wyclif, *Sermons*). By the late fifteenth century, this last sense was attenuated to refer to a wasting-away from intense suffering or grief ("So doeth the soule *pyne* a way for default of gostly meate" [So does the soul pine away for lack of spiritual nourishment], 1548, Hugh Latimer, *Ploughers*). From there it was a short step to its modern sense of longing or yearning ("The new-made bridegroom . . . For whome, and not for Tybalt, Juliet *pined*," 1592, Shakespeare, *Romeo and Juliet*).

CHESS (a. 1300). This royal war game originated in northern India in the sixth or seventh century, and may have been invented by Buddhists as a substitute for war, their religion eschewing any kind of killing. In Sanskrit it was called *chaturanga*, a common term in Indian epic poetry applied to real armies and meaning literally "the four *angas*." The angas were the constituents of any army: elephants, horses, chariots, and foot soldiers. When exported to Persia, the name became *chatrang*. The conquering Arabs adopted the game from the Persians and altered its name to *shatranj*, which they eventually took to Iberia, where it became Spanish *ajedrez* and Portuguese *xadrez*. But for unknown reasons this name did not catch on in the rest of Europe, and even in Spanish and Portuguese chess has the alternative names *jaque* and *xaque* respectively, which are akin to German *Schach*, Italian *sacco*, and French *echecs* or *eschecs.* This line springs from the Arabic *shah* (king), which was taken from Persian and ultimately from an Indo-European root meaning "to gain control over." *Shah* was used in the phrase *shah mat,* literally "the king is dead," and, in the game, had the same meaning as its English derivative, *checkmate.* It is also the origin of French *eschecs* (chess), originally the plural of *eschec* (a check at chess). Middle English borrowed the French word and altered it to *ches* or *chess,* in early use frequently calling it *the chess* ("They found Kyng Richard at play, / At *the chess* in his galeye," c. 1325, *Coer de Lion*). From the beginning it was a royal game. Chess was said to be the occasion of the bitter quarrel between King Canute (c. 925–1030) and Earl Ulf, leading to the death of the latter under Canute's orders. At the coronation of Richard I in 1189, six earls and barons carried a chessboard with the royal insignia representing the exchequer court. Both *exchequer* and *checker* derive from the chess term *check.*

QUEEN (in chess). After CHESS came to England, all of the names for the playing pieces were changed, except *rook,* which is from Persian *rokh* (a soldier). In Old Persian *shatranj* (chess), the queen was not a queen and was not female, but was a *farz* or *farzin* (a counselor or minister). This name was Latinized to *farzia* or *fercia,* which became in French *fierce* or *fierge* and then, through folk etymology, probably *vierge* (virgin). This lineage may have reversed the sex of this most powerful piece. Middle English adopted the French name as *fers* ("She staal on me, and tok my *fers.* / And whan I sawgh my *fers* awaye, / Allas! I kouthe no lenger playe" [She stole up on me and took my farz. / And when I saw my farz was lost, / Alas! I could no longer play], 1369, Chaucer, *Book of the Duchess*). But this name did not survive in English or in French. The rules of chess say that when a pawn reaches the eighth or last square it becomes a *farzin* (that is, a queen). In draughts or *jeu de dames,* a similar rule allows the piece that reaches the back row to become a *dame* or queen. This promotion is called *aller à dame* (to queen). Since the "queening" rule was the same in both games, and since *farzin* made no sense in French, the old name for the chess piece was discarded in favor of *dame* (chess queen). In English *queen* would have naturally replaced *dame*.

INDENTURE (c. 1300). An *indenture* was a contract between two or more parties that had teeth in it. It is from Old French *endenteure* (indentation, furnishing with teeth), ultimately from Latin *dens* (tooth). Originally an indenture was written on a single sheet of vellum or paper, which was then cut in two in a zigzag or serrated ("toothed") fashion. When the two pieces were brought together so that the edges matched, the covenant was proved to be genuine. Sometimes a word or sentence was written across the space where the sheet was to be divided, further ensuring its authenticity. Later indentures were made using two or more copies placed on top of each other, and their tops or edges uniquely indented or serrated.

WOEBEGONE (c. 1300). Though *woebegone* is a compound of *woe* (misery, sorrow) and *begone,* it does not mean "go away misery, begone!" In fact, it means nearly the opposite, "beset with woe." *Begone* is from the obsolete verb *bego,* itself a compound in Old English of *be-* (about) and *go,* and meant "to go about," extended to "go about hostilely," "beset." By about 1300, it meant "to be beset or affected by an environment of good" ("I was . . . riche and yonge and *wel begon,"* c. 1386, Chaucer, *Wife's Prologue*) or, alternatively, "by an environment of evil or misfortune" ("Absolon . . . is for love alway so *wo bigon"* [Absalom . . . in matters of love is always beset by ill-fortune], Chaucer, *Miller's Tale*). *Woe* (misfortune, misery) is among a host of related exclamations of lament found in many languages (German *weh,* Gothic *wai,* Latin *vae,* Latvian *vai*) and reaches back to the prehistoric root **wai-,* also the source of English *wail.* The expression was originally *me is woe begone* (I am beset by woe), but because *woe* and *begone* were so strongly associated, they eventually formed a single word. *Woebegone* (beset by grief or misfortune) virtually disappeared in the later seventeenth century, but was revived around 1800 to refer to a person who looks miserable or anguished ("A poor mendicant approached, old and *woebegone,"* 1837, John Lockhart, *Life of Sir Walter Scott*).

MELANCHOLY (1303). Chaucer used *melancholy* (low spirits, sadness) the way we know it today ("Bycause he wolde soone dye, / He ne eet ne dronk, for his *malencolye"* [Because he would soon die, / He neither ate nor drank, because of his melancholy], c. 1374, Chaucer, *Troilus and Criseyde*). But more often than not during Chaucer's time, *melancholy* referred to the darkest of the four HUMORS, literally "black bile," from Greek *melancholia,* compounded of *melas* (black) and *chole* (bile) ("Ther is engendrid another substaunce that is sumwhat stynkyng & is clepid [called] *malancoli,"* c. 1400, anon. trans. of *Lanfrank's Science of Cirurgie*). Excessive black bile in a person's body was thought to cause anger and sullenness, so that *melancholy* not only referred to the humor but to this menacing or dark mind state ("If she be riche, of heigh parage, / Thanne seistow it is a tormentrie To soffren hire pride and hire *malencolie"* [If she is rich, of high social rank, / Then you say it is a torment to suffer her pride and her angry sullenness], c. 1386, Chaucer, *Wife's Prologue*). This sense was then extended to "sadness, depression." In the Elizabethan period, it was fashionable to affect a melancholy pose as a sign of one's superior refinement. Washington Irving may have been satirizing this when he wrote: "There is no more *melancholy* creature in existence than a mountebank off duty" (1824, Washington Irving, *Tales of a Traveller*).

MYSTERY (c. 1325). There are two *mysteries* in English. The lesser-known *mystery* (a. 1375) has the senses "handicraft," "art" ("Thy Paynim bard / Had such a mastery of his *mystery* / That he could harp his wife up out of hell," 1872, Alfred Tennyson, *The Last Tournament*) and "trade guild." The medieval *mystery plays,* religious tableaus based on biblical stories, were produced by the various "mysteries" or craft guilds. The members of the guild acted on wheeled stages in the streets. Like French *métier* (trade, occupation), it is from Medieval Latin *ministerium* (ministry, office), which was confused with *mysterium* or *mystery* (something hidden or secret). The other *mystery* is taken from Latin *mysterium* and has its roots in ancient Greek religious ceremonies. Greek *mysterion* (secret rite or doctrine) is from *mystes* (one who is initiated into the rites), from *myein* (to shut the eyes or lips), because only the initiated were allowed to see the secret rites and were sworn never to speak of them. Its religious senses were transplanted to the medieval Christian setting (a religious truth that can only be understood by divine revelation, a Christian rite or sacrament), but almost as soon as it entered Middle English it took on the more general meaning of any "hidden or secret thing that is beyond human comprehension."

GOBLIN (a. 1327). In French folklore, homes were sometimes blessed with a helpful sprite, similar to the Celtic "brownie," which performed household tasks. Proper etiquette toward this helper, who was male, included leaving doors open and food out for him. One such spirit became so well known in the vicinity of Evreaux, France, that, according to a twelfth-century chronicler, he was popularly known by the name of *Gobelinus,* which became the generic term, *gobelin,* for all such sprites. One derivation ascribes the term to Jean Gobelin (d. 1467), a dyer of such skill that it was said he must be in league with the Devil. More plausible versions suggest that it is from German *Kobold* (an earth spirit) or more likely from Medieval Latin *cobalus,* borrowed from Greek *kobalos* (a rogue, knave) and *kobaloi* (wicked sprites invoked by rogues). Goblins were said to be especially fond of homes where wine was plentiful and the children were pretty. They were capricious and often played pranks, such as pulling the covers off sleepers or tangling the manes of horses they loved to ride during the night. A recommended method of ridding a house of a goblin that had become a nuisance was to sprinkle flaxseed on the floor. Being a first-rate housekeeper by nature, he was obliged to pick up the seeds, a task that after a time became so tedious he would leave in disgust. The English *goblin,* though borrowed from the French, was more diabolical ("Of an arowe fliynge in the dai, of a *gobelyn* goynge in derknessis," 1388, Wyclif, trans. of Psalms 90:6). In the mid-fifteenth century, a *hob* was also a goblin, specifically one known as *Robin Goodfellow, Hob* being a folk variant of *Rob,* short for *Robin,* hence the compound *hobgoblin* (1530). Yet another name for *Hob* was *Puck,* made famous by Shakespeare in *Midsummer Night's Dream.* We still hear *hob* in the phrase *to play hob* (to make mischief, to play the devil).

GUN (1339). Before *guns* or cannons came into general military use in the early fourteenth century, missiles, usually in the form of large stones, were hurled mechanically with catapults, ballistas (a crossbowlike device), and mangonels. *Mangonel* (1194) is from Old French, taken from the Medieval Latin diminutive of *manganum* (a military engine used to cast stones or other missiles), which in turn is from Greek *manganon* (love-potion, ballista). The Greek root *mang-* refers to deception by means of beauty and is akin to Sanskrit *manjus* (beautiful). Perhaps like the Trojan Horse, the first use of siege machinery was deceptive, taking the enemy totally off guard. *Gun,* in Middle English *gonne,* pronounced [gon' ə], may be a back formation of either *mangonel* or more likely modern French *mangonneau* (a mangonel). ("With grisley soun out goth the grete *gonne,* / And heterly they hurtelen al atones, / And from the top doun come the grete stones" [With awful sound out went the great gun, / And fiercely they hurtled all at once, / And from the top down came the great stones], Chaucer, *Legend of Good Women*). A more likely derivation is that it comes from the Scandinavian woman's name *Gunnhildr.* A 1330 munitions account at Windsor Castle records a variant of this name given to a ballista: "Una magna balista de cornu quae vocatur Domina Gunilda" [A large ballista from Cornwall called Lady Gunilda]. Bestowing women's names on engines of war is an old practice. The fifteenth-century mortarlike piece in Edinburgh Castle was called *Mons Meg* or *Muckle Meg, Meg* being a pet name for *Margaret* ("The great iron murderer called '*Muckle Megg,*'" 1650). In the twentieth century, the most famous gun was the experimental artillery piece known as Big Bertha. This huge World War I cannon, mounted on a railway car, was named after Bertha Krupp, heiress to the famed Krupp armament works. *Gunnhildr* was a perfect name for a war machine because, as users of the period would have understood, both *gunnr,* from Indo-European **gwhen* (to strike, hurt), and *hildr* meant "war." The pet name for Gunnhildr was *Gunna,* which is very close to the Middle English *gonne* (gun). The proper name was transferred early in the fourteenth century to the metal tube that shoots missiles using the explosion of gunpowder. Chaucer also knew this word: "Went this foule trumpes soun / As swifte as pelet out of *gonne* / Whan fire is in the poudre ronne" (This foul trumpet sound went out / As swift as a bullet from a gun / When the powder is fired), c. 1384, Chaucer, *The House of Fame*).

AMBITION (1340). Because the white-clad Roman CANDIDATE went about soliciting votes in public, Latin *ambitio,* from *ambio* (go about), developed the extended meaning "going about to canvass for votes." Inevitably, such vote seeking became a blatant effort to curry favor and soon gave the word yet a third and broader sense, "eager desire for advancement, rank, or power." It is this sense that English adopted when *ambition* and *ambitious,* through French, entered the language during the fourteenth century. Today, a candidate is expected to have ambition, or he would not be a candidate at all and certainly would not succeed. But in early usage, ambition was akin to the pride that goeth before a fall ("Cromwell, I charge thee, fling away *Ambition,* / By that sinne fell the Angels," 1613, Shakespeare, *Henry VIII*). In America, *ambition* and *ambitious* have dialect nuances. In parts of the Upper South, *ambition* means "malice," "vindictiveness" ("His friends . . . kept urging him to revenge. A woman wanted them to stop. 'Hit jes' raises the *ambition* in him and don't do no good nohow,'" 1901, *Scribner's Magazine*). In the same region, *ambi-*

tious is often used to mean "unruly," "vicious," "angry" ("The fight had made him as *ambitious* as a wild-cat," 1853, Robert M. Bird, *Nick of the Woods*), but in the Northern United States, it often means "energetic" or "industrious" ("I don't feel very *ambitious* today," 1917, *Dialect Notes*).

COMPLEXION (1340). In medieval physiology, the relative proportions of the HUMORS combined or "twined together" constituted a person's physical nature or *complexion*, from Latin *com* (together) and *plectere* (to plait, twine). The specific proportions of the complexion also determined one's disposition, a sense that both *complexion* and *temperament* (see TEMPER) acquired, though only the latter survived ("His *complexioun* is so corrageous that he may not forbere," 1386, Chaucer, *Parson's Tale;* "The Count is neither sad, nor sick, nor merry, nor well, but . . . something of a jealous *complexion,* " 1599, Shakespeare, *Much Ado about Nothing*). Because one's complexion or temperament and bodily constitution were thought to be revealed by the color and texture of the skin, *complexion* came to refer to the general appearance of the skin, especially of the face.

HUMOR (1340). *Humor* in the Middle Ages was not funny. It was serious business, going back to ancient Greek physiological theory. The human body was thought to have four primary fluids or "cardinal humors": black bile (MELANCHOLY), PHLEGM, blood (SANGUINE), and yellow bile (CHOLER). This theory was already in place when Hippocrates (c. 460–370 B.C.), the father of medicine, postulated that disease was the result of an imbalance of the four humors. So unquestioning were the medieval doctors and their successors that this physiological model persisted well into the eighteenth century. *Humor,* borrowed from French, at first had a family resemblance to *humid* and was close to its Latin root *umor* (moisture, fluid), though primarily with reference to the dampness of the air or to vapors ("To walke unbraced, and sucke up the *humours* of the danke morning," 1599, Shakespeare, *Julius Caesar*). More specifically it usually referred to the four cardinal humors, these internal elements of the body (the microcosm) corresponding to the four external elements of the universe (the macrocosm): earth, water, air, and fire. The fondness of the medieval mind for such correspondences led Wyclif, for example, to observe that "Blood is (the) moost kyndely *umour*, answeringe to the love of God, (the) thre [three] othere *umors* in man answeren to three other loves" (c. 1380, *Sermons*). The other father of medicine, Galen (c. 130–200), who served as physician to the gladiatorial school in Rome, elaborated the theory of humors by extending it to personality and temperament. The humors determined a person's temperament and mental disposition according to which humor was dominant. By the late Middle English period (c. 1475), *humor* or *humour* was extended to the general sense "temperament or mental disposition" ("Thus I'll curbe her mad and headstrong *humour,*" 1596, Shakespeare, *Taming of the Shrew*) and appears in the common expressions *ill-humored, good-humored,* and *to be in a bad (or good) humor.* This led in the sixteenth century to the extended sense "inclination," "fancy," "whim," which was so overused that Shakespeare and Ben Jonson ridiculed it mercilessly ("I like not the *humor* of lying. He hath wronged me in some *humors.* I should have borne the *humored* letter to her . . . . I love not the *humor* of bread and cheese, and there's the *humor* of it. Adieu," 1598, Shakespeare, *Merry Wives of Windsor*). English comedies of the sixteenth and seventeenth centuries often had characters who were ridiculously dominated by a single humor, making for eccentric, caricatured behavior and audience laughter. *Humor* became associated with this behavior, whimsical, fantastic, ludicrous, and by the late 1600s it developed its modern sense, "amusing or funny quality."

ABOMINABLE (1366). The pedant Holofernes in Shakespeare's *Love's Labour's Lost* abominates the "rackers of orthography," who, among a list of offenses, spell "abhominable" without the *h,* "abbominable." In Medieval Latin, French, and English, *abominable* (offensive, disgusting, odious) was spelled as if it were a compound of Latin *ab* (off, away) and *homine* (man, human), literally "away from man," that is, "inhuman or beastly" ("The frogge is venemouse and *abhomynable* therefore to men," 1398, John de Trevisa, *Bartholomeus*). This spelling with its underlying folk etymology influenced the way the word was used and in time affected its meaning, making it more emphatic, with connotations of repulsion and revulsion, than its original Latin sense of "dislike." Holofernes's orthographers were in fact getting back to the root of the word, which is Latin *abominari* (to dislike), compounded of *ab* (off, away) and *omen* (sign of the future). An omen is usually an evil sign to be dreaded, hence the Latin exclamation *absit omen!* (may the omen be away!). The literal root sense, then, of *abominable* is "to turn away from something that is a bad omen."

FEBRUARY (1373). Perhaps for lack of a better holiday in this bleak month, February is today, with a little help from the greeting-card industry, a month of valentines and chocolates and sweethearts. But it was not always regarded so lightly. In the early Roman calendar, February was the twelfth month and was devoted to ceremonies of purification and the cult of the dead in anticipation of the new year. The most important festival of the month was Lupercalia, held on the fifteenth, probably in honor of the ancient god Lupercus, a god of the shepherds, the "wolf averter," later associated with the Greek Pan or Faunus. This festival was conducted by priests or Luperci originally chosen from herdsmen, but later from among patrician youths. Their faces were painted and they dressed only in goatskin loin cloths. The ceremony began with the sacrifice of two goats and a dog—animals associated with strong sexual urges—after which the foreheads of two Luperci were smeared with the bloody knife and then wiped with a piece of wool dipped in milk. This bizarre ritual required that they then burst into laughter. The two priests then cut the skin of the goats into strips called *februa,* the Sabine word for "purifiers" or "purgatives," from the verb *februo* (purify). They then ran through the streets striking women with the februa, which were supposed to make them fertile. From this ritual, February fifteenth was known as *dies februatus,* the day of purification, and this month of purification was called *Februarius* or *Februarius mensis,* which Middle English adopted through Old French.

JEOPARDY (c. 1374). A difficult problem in chess was a *jeopardy* ("Wolde I had . . . knowe the *jeupardyes* / That kowde the Grek Pithagores! I shulde have pleyd the bet at ches" [Had I known the jeopardies / That cowed the Greek Pythagoras! I should have played the bet at chess], 1369, Chaucer, *Book of the Duchess*). The special difficulty of a jeopardy was its pivotal importance in the outcome of the game, the move of a single piece deciding victory or defeat. The original French *jeu parti,* from Latin *jocus* (jest, play, game) and *partitus* (divided), meant literally "divided play," that is, an even and thus uncertain game, or simply "uncertainty" ("For myn estat lith now in *jupartie,* / And ek myn emes lif lyth in balaunce" [For my condition now lies in jeopardy, / And also my own life lies in the balance], c. 1374, Chaucer, *Troilus and Criseyde*). In English *-parti* became *-pardy* due probably to the influence of Old French *jeu perdu* (a lost game). Where there is uncertainty there is risk of loss, the sense (peril, danger) that survives today ("For Troye is brought in swich a *jupartie* / That it to save is now no remedye" [For Troy is brought to such jeopardy / That there is no possibility of saving it], c. 1374, Chaucer, *Troilus and Criseyde*).

BROKER (1378). The first brokers, the fourteenth-century counterparts to today's stockbrokers, were essentially tapsters or tavern keepers. At root is the Old French verb *brokier* or *broquier,* which meant "to broach or tap (a cask of wine),"

also the root for the English word *broach* (to pierce, to tap a cask). A *brokour* or *broker,* then, retailed wine "from the tap," buying it cheaply in quantity and selling it at a profit. This meaning was extended to include any retail dealer who bought goods to sell over again or who, buying for someone else, acted as a middleman or agent. Initially, like usury, this was considered immoral—making money with money, as opposed to earning money from one's labors. This gave *broker* an underlying derogatory sense, making it a natural term for a procurer or pimp, a female procurer sometimes referred to as a *brokeress. Marriage brokers,* however, were quite legitimate. The *pawnbroker* came later, probably sometime in the seventeenth century, but *pawning* (giving something as security for a debt) was an old practice. The word *pawn* or *pan* first arrived in England with the Normans, to whom it meant not only "a pledge" but also "booty or plunder taken from an enemy." This may in turn be an extension of the Old French *pan,* a "cloth" or "pane," from the practice of holding a nobleman's garment as security ("We haue no store of monie . . . but you shall haue good *pawnes* . . . this Iewell [jewel], and this gentlemans silke stockins," 1598, Ben Jonson, *Every Man in His Humor*). The latest incarnations of *broker* appeared in the 1960s in America, transferred to the political domain: *broker* used as a verb (as in "to broker a nominating convention") and *power broker,* coined by Theodore White in *The Making of the President 1960* to refer to those behind-the-scenes individuals who wield political power and influence ("By extending Syria's security role beyond the western part of Beirut, Assad reinforced his position as Lebanon's leading *power broker,*" 1988, *Time*).

SANGUINE (1378). If one is cheerful and optimistic it is because, according to medieval physiology, blood is the dominant HUMOR, the best of the four, or as Chaucer put it, "natures freend [friend]" (c. 1386, *Squire's Tale*). Chaucer's Franklyn, with his ruddy COMPLEXION and lust for life was the very picture of the *sangwyn* man. Borrowed from French, *sanguine* is ultimately from Latin *sanguis* (blood), which is itself of unknown origin. Because a person dominated by this humor had a hopeful or confident disposition, by about 1500 it was extended to the qualities themselves ("*Sanguine* groundless hopes, and . . . lively vanity . . . make all the happiness of life," 1712, Mary Wortley Montagu, *Letters*). A *sanguinary* man, however, is a man of a different color; he is bloodthirsty, a usage that entered English in the early 1600s from the same Latin root. Sanguinary laws are also bloodthirsty, because they freely impose the death penalty ("Lay then the axe to the root, and teach governments humanity. It is their *sanguinary* punishments which corrupt mankind," 1791, Thomas Paine, *The Rights of Man*).

GARTER (1382). *Garters* (bands to hold up stockings) have been around almost as long as stockings have been sliding down. But not until after the French invasion of England were they called *garters.* The earliest use of this sense in English appears in Wyclif's unusual translation of Genesis 14:23: "Fro a threed of the weeft unto a *garter* of a hoos" [From a thread of the weft unto a garter of a hose (stocking)]. (The King James version has "From a thread even to a shoelatchet.") The Old French form was *gartier* or *jartier* from *garet* or *jaret* (bend of the knee), itself probably a borrowing from Celtic, such as Breton *gar* (ham or leg bone). Its earlier history is lost. The first-known appearance of *garter* in English does not refer to the item of apparel but to the Order of the Garter (c. 1350). The name of this highest order of English knighthood has its origin in the Countess of Salisbury's garter, which slipped off her leg while she was dancing with Edward III probably sometime in 1344. The English king quickly fetched it, and to the horror of his court, tied it on his own leg. Seeing the scandalized faces, he responded in courtly French, "Honi soit qui mal y pense" [Shamed be he who thinks evil of it]. To this incident are ascribed the institution, symbol, and motto of the Knights of the Garter. With only one or two exceptions, Sir Winston Churchill being one, membership in the Order was exclusive, limited to the royal family, twenty-five knights of the peerage, and sundry foreign royalty. Members wore a dark-blue velvet garter below the left knee with Edward's words embroidered in gold. ("I vow'd, base knight, when I did meet thee next, / To tear the *garter* from thy craven's leg . . . because unworthily / Thou was installed in that high degree," 1591, Shakespeare, *I Henry VI.*)

STORY (a. 1384; floor of a building). A *history* is a kind of *story* told with as much fidelity to the facts as possible. Both words are rooted in Indo-European **weid* or **widtor* (to see), which became in Greek *histor* (wise, learned man). This gave Greek *historia* (knowledge from inquiry, a record, account), and through Latin, Old French borrowed it as *histoire* or *estoire.* In Middle English the senses of the two were at first not distinguished. In the mid-fourteenth century, a *story* sometimes referred to a painting or sculpture that represented a historical or legendary event. More specifically as an architectural term, it referred to a tier of stained-glass windows or to rows of sculptures on the fronts of buildings. Common on the larger buildings of the Middle Ages, these stories distinctively marked off each level, so that *story* was easily transferred to the level or floor itself.

CHOLER (c. 1386). When bile or *choler* is the dominant HUMOR, a person will have an irascible TEMPERAMENT and will typically have a tall, lean look, like Chaucer's Reeve, who was "a sclendre colerik man" with legs "ful longe . . . and ful lene." By the early sixteenth century, like SANGUINE, *choler* and *choleric* were extended to the traits, "anger," "hot-temperedness," themselves ("Infirme and *cholericke* yeares," 1605, Shakespeare, *King Lear*). *Choler,* from Greek *chole* (bile) through Latin and French, had the variant *cholera* ("This dreem . . . Cometh of greet superfluytee Of youre rede [red] *Colera,*" c. 1386, Chaucer, *Nun's Priest's Tale*). To distinguish it from the ancient disease *cholera,* described by Hippocrates and others, the disease was referred to as *disease cholera* or *cholera morbus* into the nineteenth century.

BACHELOR (c. 1386). The first bachelor or *baccalarius* was a cowherd, male or female. In Vulgar Latin *bacca* is a variant of *vacca* (cow). A *baccalia* is a herd of cows, a *baccalaria* is a grazing farm, and a *baccalarius* is a farm worker. By the eighth century, *baccalarius* referred to the men or women rustics who worked for the tenant of a feudal estate or a baccalaria. The root sense of subordination runs through all of the later senses of the word. The first English *bacheler,* borrowed from French in the thirteenth century, was a knight too young or too poor to support the responsibilities and dignity of his own banner and so followed another knight's banner ("Yong, fressh, and strong, in armes desirous, As any *bacheler* of al his hous," c. 1386, Chaucer, *Squire's Tale*). Late in the next century, *bachelor* was transferred to a junior member of a guild and then to a person who takes the lowest degree at a university, not yet being a "master" of the arts. This sense first appears in the system of degrees created in the thirteenth century at the university of Paris under the auspices of Pope Gregory IX. It came to be called a *baccalaureate* degree, from Latinized *baccalarius* altered by a pun on *baccalaureus,* that is *bacca lauri* (laurel berry), with reference to the laurel as a symbol of excellence in literature and the arts. *Bachelor* then took on its most common sense, "an unmarried man" (*"Bacheleris* have often peyne [pain] and wo [woe]," c. 1386, Chaucer, *Merchant's Tale*), perhaps extended directly from the earliest sense. Like a knight's bachelor, an unmarried man was usually young and had not yet made his fortune or become a full citizen. Occasionally *bachelor* referred to a maid ("He would keep you / A *batchelor* still . . . / And keep you not alone without a husband, / But in a sickness," 1632, Ben Jonson, *Magnetick Lady*). The paradoxical *bachelor's wife* is the ideal wife that a bachelor dreams about (*"Bachelers wives,* and maides children be well tought [taught]," 1562, John Heywood, *Proverbs and Epigrams*).

PHLEGM (1387), **PHLEGMATIC** (1340). To the medieval doctor *phlegm,* or in Middle English *fleem* or *fleume,* was more than just mucus. It was one of the four HUMORS that governed a person's character and health. *Phlegm* was the moist and cold humor, from Latin *phlegma.* Latin borrowed it from Greek *phlegma,* which means "inflammation," "heat,"

from Greek *phlegein* (to burn), seemingly the opposite sense, but heat in the form of fever and inflammation was supposed to produce the clammy, morbid humor. Having too much phlegm made a person sluggish, dull, and indolent ("A verry *flewmatike* man is in the body lustles [listless], heuy [heavy] and slow," 1398, Trevisa, *Bartholomeus*). The Middle English spelling *fleume* was discarded in the late sixteenth century in favor of the learned Greek and Latin spelling. It was also then that the sense of *phlegmatic* was extended from "sluggish," "apathetic" to "cool," "calm," "self-possessed."

TEMPER (1387). The *temper* of something in medieval thought was the proportionate mixture of its elements, earth, air, fire, and water, or its qualities, such as moist, hot, dry, and cold ("There is helthe, for the aier is in *tempre,* nother to hote nother to colde" [There is health, for the air is in temper, neither too hot nor too cold], 1387, John de Trevisa, *Higden*). Old English borrowed *temprian* directly from Latin *temperare* (to mix correctly, combine properly, regulate), which is from *tempus* (time, season, proper time or season), with ulterior origins in Indo-European **temp* (to stretch, extend). *Temper* also referred to the specific combination or balance of the four HUMORS that constitute a person's physical and mental makeup, that is, his *temperament* ("A noble *temper* dost thou shew in this," 1595, Shakespeare, *King John*). Under stress or provocation, a person's mental composure or balance of humors and emotions, especially with regard to anger, was spoken of as his *temper* ("Never could the strumpet . . . / Once stir my *temper,*" 1603, *Measure for Measure*). *To be out of temper,* then, was to be out of emotional balance, and *to keep or lose (one's) temper* was to keep or lose that balance.

MORTGAGE (1390). A pledge to forfeit something of value to ensure that a loan is paid back is a *gage,* from Old French *guage* (a pledge) borrowed from the Proto-Germanic root **wadjom*. In Middle English, a *gage* was also a pledge to do battle, such as a glove thrown on the ground, symbolically vowing to fight in support of one's honor or beliefs ("Thanne

Sire Piers, that was so dowhty [valiant] A knyht . . . Agens [against] kyng Marahaus put his *Gage,*" c. 1450, Henry Lovelich, *Grail*). As the Germanic root entered Old French, it also entered Old English as *wedd,* its meaning "a pledge or something deposited as security," surviving in Scottish and other English dialects ("I thought the chield Morris looked devilish queer when I determined he should remain a *wad,* or hostage, for my safe back-coming," 1818, Sir Walter Scott, *Rob Roy*). To *wed* was not only "to covenant or pledge something," but more specifically "to make a woman one's wife by giving a pledge" ("This maiden he gon *wedde* and nom heo to his bedde" [This maiden he is going to wed and take her to his bed], c. 1205, Layamon, *Brut, or Chronicle of Britain*). French *mort* (dead) ultimately from Latin *mori* (to die), combined with *gage,* gave *morgage* and *mort gaige,* literally "dead pledge." Such a pledge was "dead" on two accounts. On the one hand, if the loan was not paid back, the property or gage was forfeited or "dead" to the borrower, and on the other hand, if it was paid back, the pledge itself was void or "dead."

ROVER (1390, pirate). To citizens of the early twentieth century especially in America, along with *Towser, Rags,* and *Fido, Rover* was a favorite dog's name; but to fifteenth-century travelers it referred to the wild pirates that terrorized the sea, requiring the government to create a coast guard ("It shalbe nescessarie that the kynge have alway some ffloute [fleet] apon the see, ffor the repressynge of *rovers,*" c. 1460, Sir John Fortescue, *The Governance of England*). *Rover* is a borrowing from Middle Dutch *rover* or *zeerovere,* literally "sea robber," from *roven* (to rob). The proto-Germanic **raubojanan* is the source not only of this Dutch borrowing, but of Old English *reafian,* which survives in archaic *reave* (to rob) and *reaver* (robber, plunderer), also spelled *reiver* (as in William Faulkner's novel of that name), and modern English *rob* (through French). *Rover,* the dog, however, is not a pirate, but like a pirate is a wanderer. *Rove* originally meant in English "to shoot arrows at randomly selected targets or marks." This was a method of improving the archer's sense of the range of a target, as opposed to shooting at a target of fixed distance, which primarily honed the accuracy of the aim. In *roving,* one wandered through the woods or fields shooting at randomly selected marks, and *to rove* was soon generalized to its current sense, to "wander," "stray," "roam." *Rove* itself is probably an old variant of British dialect *rave* (to wander, stray), a remnant of the old Scandinavian invasion of England. By the sixteenth century, *rove* (to wander) and *rover* (a wanderer) had become confused with *rove* (to sail as pirates) and *rover* (a pirate) and were considered the same words with the same origins, since sea rovers roved on the seas robbing roving voyagers.

SWEET TOOTH (1390). Both of these are good Anglo-Saxon words, Germanic in origin, and reaching back to Indo-European roots, **swad* (sweet, hence, *suave, assuage, persuade*) and **dent* (tooth) itself from **ed* (to bite). The tooth in *sweet tooth,* however, does not bite, but tastes, teeth being associated with eating and the sense of taste ("I wol kepe [will keep] it for youre owene *tooth,*" c. 1386, Chaucer, *The Wife of Bath's Prologue*). In medieval English *to have the teeth cold* meant "to be very hungry" ("He that werketh not . . . shal have ofte at his teeth grete cold," 1484, William Caxton, trans. of *Fables of Aesop*), and *to love the tooth* was to love eating. If something is *toothsome* it is savory and flavorful. *Palate* (the roof of the mouth) underwent a similar extension in meaning (sense of taste) though somewhat later ("Let their *palats* be season'd with such viands," 1596, Shakespeare, *Merchant of Venice*), and was extended to "mental taste or liking" ("Tha have . . . the *palate* of the hart filyd with feuuyr of wykkyd lufe, qwarfor thai may not fele swetnes of hevenly Ioy" [They have the palate of a heart filled with the fever of wicked love, wherefore they may not feel the sweetness of heavenly joy], 1435, Richard Misyn, *Fire of Love*). A *sweet tooth,* then, is a liking or taste for sweet foods ("Delacacie his *swete toth* Hath fostred," 1390, John Gower, *Confessio Amantis*).

MUSCLE (1392). To the Romans a flexing muscle resembled a creeping mouse or perhaps it was the appearance of certain exposed muscles that resembled the shape of a mouse. They called a muscle *musculus*, literally "little mouse," the diminutive of *mus* (mouse). Since English borrowed the word directly from Latin, learned speakers probably knew its origin. This may explain why *mus* (mouse) also meant "muscle" ("Binde the garlicke upon the wrest [wrist] of the arme . . . so that it do not touche the *mousse* of the hande," 1561, John Hollybush, trans. of *Braunschweig's Most Excellent Homish Apothecarye*). It also applied to certain parts of meat, a usage that survives in English dialect.

MUSK (1398). The mouse has been an unwitting participant in word creation (see MUSCLE). From the likeness to the furry little creature, the ancient northern Indians referred to the testicles or scrotum as *muska,* from Indo-European **mus* (mouse). The Persians borrowed the word from Sanskrit as *mushk,* the Greeks took it from the Persians as *moschos,* and the Romans took it from the Greeks as *muscus.* They used the word to refer to musk, the glandular secretion of the male musk deer used in perfumes and medicines. Musk is not obtained from the deer's testicles, however, but from an abdominal sac about the size of a small orange behind its navel. The gland is removed and dried. Middle English borrowed *musk* from Old French *musc,* taken from Late Latin.

CRIMSON (a. 1400). Though VERMILION, both the original dye and the word, is from worms, *crimson* is from a semantic "worm" of a different color. Indo-European **kwrmi-* (worm) became Sanskrit *krmi-,* which when compounded with *ja-* (produced) was the ancient Indian word for the red dye *krimja,* literally "worm produced." The Arabs, whose empire in the ninth to the eleventh centuries stretched from India to Spain, borrowed the Sanskrit word and modified it to *girmizi* (the red color of the kermes insect). Old Spanish then adopted the Arabic word, altering it in the process to *cremesin,* which then found its way into Middle English via commerce in fine dyed fabrics ("The most costyous cloth of *crenseyn,*" a. 1400, *Coventry Mysteries*). *Carmine* (a vivid red color and pigment) is a late

Middle English borrowing of Medieval Latin *carminium,* which is a blend of the Arabic *girmiz* (kermes) and Latin *minium* (cinnabar, red lead). Today vermilion and crimson dyes are synthetically produced, often of mercuric sulfide.

MIGRAINE (c. 1400). Headaches have been around as long as heads, but a *migraine* is only a "half head" ache. In Latin, it was called *hemicrania,* borrowed from Greek *hemi* (half) and *kranion* (skull), since a migraine headache is usually felt only on one side of the head. In French, the first and last sounds of the Latin word were dropped, and it became *migraine,* which was borrowed into Middle English as *mygrane* (pronounced "mee-grain"), later altered to *megrim.* The Middle English *mygrane* pronunciation survives in England, but in America was altered to "my-grain," perhaps due to folk etymology, an attempt to make sense of the word by analyzing it (incorrectly) as *my* plus *grain.* Replaced by *migrain, megrim* (headache) died out except in dialect. However, before it disappeared it was extended in the sixteenth century first to mean "vertigo" or "dizziness" and then a "whim" or "fancy" ("Hee is troubled with a perpetuall *migrim;* at sea hee wisheth to bee on land, and on land at sea," 1631, Richard Brathwait, *Whimzies*). It was further extended to mean "low spirits or the blues" ("If these *megrims* are the effect of Love, thank Heaven, I never knew what it was," 1754, Samuel Richardson, *Sir Charles Grandison*).

PEDIGREE (a. 1410). In charting family trees, to denote succession the genealogist drew a vertical line that divided into three branches, which the French thought resembled the toes of a crane's foot. This three-toed line was so characteristic of old genealogical charts that they named it *pied de grue* (foot of a crane). Middle English borrowed the term as *pedicru* or *pedegru* (genealogical table), which was soon transferred to the lineage itself. *Grue* is from Latin *grus* (crane, battering ram), ultimately from the Indo-European root imitative of the bird's sound **gero* (to cry hoarsely, a crane), which also gave English *crow, crack,* and *croon.* The root **ped* (foot) gave not only French *pied,* but is present in dozens of English words, including *foot, fetter, trivet,* and *pioneer.* Another version of the pedigree of *pedigree* claims it is from the French *par degrés* (by degrees); yet another suggests *père degrés* (descent by the father). But neither of these have any credence.

ADMIRAL (c. 1425). An *admiral* in the Middle Ages was a Saracen commander or Arab ruler under the Caliph or Sultan ("Where that an heathen *admiralle* Was lorde," 1393, John Gower, *Confessio Amantis*). The Middle English spellings varied greatly, but those without the *d,* such as *amyral* or *amerayl,* were closest to the Arabic source, *amir* (commander), which also appears in English as *emir* or *amir* (Arabian chief or leader), from *amara* (to command). Since commanders are in command "of" something, *amir* was usually accompanied by *-al-* (of the), as in *amir-al-ma* (commander of the water) and *amir-al-bahr* (commander of the sea). Mistaken to be a single word, *amir-al* was then Latinized as *amiralis* and borrowed in Old French as *amiral,* the source of the English word. Another derivation says that the *-al* ending is from *-ald,* a common French masculine suffix denoting character and power, affixed to *amir.* The insertion of *d* happened in Medieval Latin, *admiralis,* influenced by the older Latin *admirabilis* (admirable), admirals being an admirable lot. When the Arabs created the office "Emir of the Sea" in Spain and Sicily, first the Genoese and French, and then the English under Edward III adopted the title "Amyrel of the Se" or "admyrall of the navy" ("The Erl of Arundel, Richard, was mad [made] *amyrel of the sea,*" 1460, John Capgrave, *Chronicles of England*). The original use (commander, Arab prince) died out about 1500, as did the qualifier "of the Sea," leaving only the modern word in its naval sense.

QUINTESSENCE (c. 1430). In ancient thought, the world was made up of four irreducible elements: earth, air, fire, and water. Traditionally, Empedocles was supposed to have introduced this world view in the fifth century B.C. But it was probably much older. In Sanskrit, for example, there are five elements or *bhutas,* the usual four plus a fifth. Aristotle held that this fifth element was an immaterial substance or ether, purer and subtler than fire, and called it *pempte ousia,* literally "fifth essence," from *penta* (five) and *ousia* (being, essence) from *einai* (to be). It composed all heavenly bodies, but also permeated all things. One of the great objects of medieval alchemy was to discover a method of distillation or some other mysterious process that would extract the *pempte ousia,* translated into Medieval Latin as *quinta essentia* and then borrowed into French as *quinte essence.* English, of course, took *quyntessense* from the French and by the mid-sixteenth century extended it to "the essential part or principle of anything."

TALENT (c. 1430). A *talent,* from Greek *talanton* (balance, weight) from the root *tal* (to lift, bear), was an ancient unit of weight originating with the Babylonians. It was used as a measure of gold or silver and became a specific denomination of money, whose value varied depending on the historical period and place. In Middle English, *talent* was figuratively extended from "balance" to "inclination" of the will ("To what thyng the saule has *talent,* / To that the body salle, ay, assent" [To whatever the soul has a talent (inclination), / To that the body shall also assent], 1340, Richard Rolle de Hampole, *The Pricke of Conscience*). These early meanings (balance, inclination) have died out, leaving only *talent* (a special ability or aptitude), which, however, is not an extension of them, but was derived whole cloth in the fifteenth century from the parable of the talents in the New Testament (Matthew 25:14–30). In it, the master gives to each of three servants a different number of *talents* (coins or money), "to every man according to his several ability." The greater the natural gifts or capacities of the man, the more talents he was given. A person with much *talent,* then, is one with God-given or, later, special natural abilities.

BELLWETHER (c. 1440). First recorded in the ninth century, a *wether* was a castrated sheep, and ultimately derives from the Indo-European root *wet-* (year), because the ram was castrated when it was a yearling. A *bellwether* is a wether that wears a *bell* to lead the flock ("He that steals a *Bell-weather,* shall be discover'd by the Bell," 1718, Peter Motteux, trans. of *Cervantes' History of Don Quixote*). Not surprisingly, when by the fifteenth century a chief or leader was called a bellwether, it was with derision. As the original meaning faded from general and increasingly urban usage, the derogatory connotations died away, and *bellwether* came to mean anything that, like a leader, is in the forefront of a trend.

NICKNAME (c. 1440). Surnames were not common in England before the thirteenth century, so it was customary to give an additional informal name to a person. This name was originally called an *eke name,* literally "an additional name," from *eke* (additional, increase), having a Proto-Germanic root, ultimately from Indo-European *aug-* (to increase), also the root of English *augment, auction,* and *auxiliary.* The indefinite article, *an,* of course, was used with the expression: *an eke name.* But the *n* of the article was confused as being a part of *eke,* speakers hearing *a neke name.* The mistake was so pervasive that by the fifteenth century *neke name* appeared in writing, and by the following century it was pronounced and spelled *nick* or *nyck name.* This confusion, where a word beginning with a vowel *(eke)* is preceded by a word ending in *n* (usually *an*), creating a new word *(eke* becoming *neke* and *nick),* is called "misdivision." Other nouns have been altered or misdivided in the same way, such as *ninny* (from *an innocent*), *nonce* (from *for then anse* "for the one"), *notch* (*an otch,* from French *oche* "notch"), and *newt* (*an ewte,* from *eft,* "small newt"). The reverse process, removing the *n* from the noun and attaching it to the article, occurred in the histories of *apron* (*a napron,* from Old French *naperon*), *umpire* (Middle English *noumper,* from Old French *nonper*), *adder* (Old English *naedre*), *auger* (Middle English *nauger, nawger*), and *orange* (Arabic *naranj*).

MOCK (a. 1450). *Mock* (ridicule, deride) makes a bit of mockery at etymologists who have tried to find its origins. One derivation says that it is from German *mucken* or *mucksen* (to growl, grumble), probably of imitative origin, the idea being that to move the mouth in a mumbling, grumbling manner at someone is to "mock" or deride them. Another interesting but more fanciful version suggests that it is ultimately related to the Greek god of ridicule and censoriousness, *Momos,* who could find defects to criticize in everything, except, to his chagrin, when it came to Aphrodite. The best he could do was to criticize the sound that her feet made. *Momos* may be akin to Greek *mokos* (a mocker), ultimately giving Old French *mocquer* (to deride, jeer). Most authorities agree that the Middle English *mokken* or *mocque* is from Old French *mocquer,* which, however, is probably not from Greek. A colloquial Latin word, **muccare* (to wipe the nose), from Latin *mucus* (mucus), gave French *moucher* and Italian *moccare* (to wipe or blow the nose). From this came *mocquer,* because to wipe or thumb the nose at someone is to jeer at or mock them. A vestige of this survives in the Modern French reflexive expression, *se moquer de quelqu'un* (to make fun of some-one), literally "I wipe my nose at someone."

GAMUT (c. 1450). "She ran the whole *gamut* of the emotions from A to B," Dorothy Parker was supposed to have said about Katharine Hepburn's performance in a Broadway play. This now well-known sense of *gamut* (range), current since the death of Shakespeare, is the figurative extension of *gamut* (the entire series of musical notes). The medieval musical scale, sometimes called the "great scale," was invented in the eleventh century by an Italian Benedictine monk, Guido d'Arezzo. He revolutionized musical notation by adding two lines to form the standard four-line staff, using both the lines and spaces. As the most famous music teacher of his time (Pope John XIX asked him to explain his system), he developed solmization or "sol-fa" in which the single syllables representing the notes of the scale are sung. His scale was a hexachord system of six tones, which replaced the Greek tetrachord. To help students sing the notes, he composed a melody to an eighth-century hymn for the feast of St. John the Baptist, each line beginning with a tone of the scale in ascending order.

> *Ut* queant laxis
> *Re*sonare fibris
> *Mi*ra gestorum
> *Fa*muli tuorum;
> *Sol*ve polluti
> *La*bii reatum,
> *S*ancte *I*ohannes.

He used the first syllables of each phrase (ut, re, mi, fa, sol, la) as the names of the notes of the hexachord (c, d, e, f, g, a), sometimes called the *Aretinian scale* after the Latin form of his surname, Guido Aretinus. The seventh degree of the scale, *si,* was added in the sixteenth century and named from the initial letters of "Sancte Iohannes." A century after that, the more singable *do* (probably from *dominus*) replaced guttural *ut.* In this notation *gamma,* the Greek letter corresponding to "g," was the name of the lowest note on the stave preceding *ut,* the first note of any scale. *Gamma-ut* or *gamut* became the name for the first or lowest tone in the medieval music scale, then was transferred to the scale itself, and then to the whole series of notes.

RIFFRAFF (a. 1470). The riffraff have always been with us, but *riffraff* (low class, common people, rabble) was first used in the late Middle English period ("Many a man was mortheryde [murdered] and kylde [killed] in that conflycte, I wot [know] not what [to] name hyt for the multytude of *ryffe raffe,"* a. 1470, William Gregory, *Chronicle of London*). It is shortened from *riff and raff,* meaning "every scrap, everything, everyone" ("Thei tok alle *riffe & raf"* [They took everything, riff and raff], 1338, Robert de Brunne, *Langtoft's Chronicle*). This phrase, borrowed in the main from Old French *rif et raf,* is probably a complex blend of several words having coincidentally similar pronunciations and negative meanings. It was also partially formed under the influence of reduplication, as in *hodgepodge* and *razzle-dazzle. Rif* or *riff* may be from French *rifler* (to spoil, strip), also the source of English *rifle* (to plunder, rob). *Raf* is from *rafler* (to carry off), originally a dicing term, probably of Germanic origin, and related to Middle English *raffle* (a dicing game), extended in the eighteenth century to a kind of lottery. Originally, then, *rif et raf* meant literally "to plunder and carry off," that is, "to take every last scrap," hence the early English *riff and raff* (every scrap, everything). To complicate the history of the English phrase, *raff* is also a fourteenth-century Scottish term meaning "plenty, abundance," extended a hundred years later to "trash, rubbish," probably under the influence of a Scandinavian word, such as Swedish *rafs* (rubbish, ragtag).

RIBALD (c. 1500; scurrilous, crude, irreverent). In the armies of the French kings in the twelfth and thirteenth centuries, the *ribaldi* were light-armed soldiers whose unenviable task was to be the first in a military assault. They were a lowly lot, considered only worthy to be cannon fodder. It was at about this time that Middle English adopted *ribald* or *ribaude.* A few centuries later, *ribalds* in France and England were employed as irregular retainers who performed the most menial tasks in royal or baronial households, hence the meaning "a menial" or "person of low birth," extended by about 1300 to "a base, good-for-nothing fellow" ("Wherfore the Scottes chosen to bene her kyng, William Walis, a *rybaude,* an harlot, comen up of nought" [Wherefore the Scots chose to be their king, William Wallis, a ribald, a HARLOT, raised up from nothing], c. 1400, *The Brut, or Chronicles of England*). Almost from its beginnings, the name was associated with dissolute or licentious behavior. In the French royal household, the *Rex Ribaldorum* or *king of the ribalds* was an officer whose duties were to conduct judicial inquiry into crimes committed within the confines of the court and to control vagrants, prostitutes, brothels, and gaming houses. In the late fourteenth century, the connotations of wantonness were tempered somewhat, and *ribald* took on its current sense (a person who uses indecent humor or offensive or crude language). It was not used as an adjective (coarse, crudely irreverent) for almost another two centuries ("The busie day, Wak't by the Larke, hath rouz'd the *ribauld* Crowes," 1602, Shakespeare, *Troilus and Cressida*). Despite its immediate French source, the *-ald* ending indicates that it is of Germanic origin, Old French often using this as a depreciatory masculine ending. The French word probably derives from a Germanic root meaning "to rub," which is the source not only of modern German *reiben* (to rub), but also of Old High German *hripa* (prostitute) and *riban* (to rub, to paint, to put rouge on the face).

❧ III ❧

THE RENAISSANCE
and
SHAKESPEARE

The Early Modern English Period
(1500—1800)

BACKGROUND

By the sixteenth century English was recognizably "modern." Spelling reform and the influence of the printing press made written English of the time essentially readable for us today. Shakespeare's pronunciation of English would also be relatively easy for a modern listener to understand, in contrast to Chaucer's English, which would be almost incomprehensible. The difference is that by this century the so-called "Great Vowel Shift" had taken place, which systematically altered the pronunciation of English vowels toward their present-day sounds. While Shakespeare pronounced *five, meed, name, goat, root,* and *down,* for example, essentially the way we do today, Chaucer pronounced them respectively, *feef, maid-a, nam-a, gott-a, rote-a,* and *doon.*

During the Early Modern period, Latin and Greek were the most important sources of new words, followed by French, Italian, and Spanish. From Latin came *censor* (the title of the Roman magistrate whose duties were to take the census and oversee public morals); *placebo* (I shall please); *preposterous* (the last comes first); *proletarian* (Roman citizen of the lowest class); *orchestra* (place where the senate sat in a theater); and *larva* (ghost, mask).

Most Greek borrowings in English have come through Latin or French. But with Renaissance England's renewed interest in Greek studies, many Greek words were adopted firsthand, such as, *anonymous, catastrophe, criterion, ephemeral, idiosyncrasy, misanthrope, ostracize, polemic,* and *tonic.* Also from Greek came *proboscis* ("forward" plus "to graze"); *troglodyte* ("cave dweller," "one who creeps into holes"); *cynic* ("dog-like," with reference to a group of ancient Greek philosophers); *irony* ("dissembler"); *laconic* ("person from Laconia," whose capital was Sparta); *museum* ("shrine of the Muses"); *mausoleum* (from King Mausolus, whose enormous tomb was one of the seven wonders of the ancient world); *oxymoron* ("sharp" plus "stupid"); *sarcasm* ("sneer," literally "to strip off flesh"); and *pantheon* ("shrine of all the gods").

Most of the Latin and Greek borrowings of this period were self-conscious attempts by sixteenth- and early seventeenth-century writers to enrich the English vocabulary. It was an effort to take the lexical resources of "high" Latin, such as *alacritas, catalogus,* and *rumino* and convert them into English *(alacrity, catalogue, ruminate)* in order to raise or elevate "low" English. George Puttenham in Queen Elizabeth I's reign dubbed these deliberately transfused Latinisms "inkhorn terms." Shakespeare satirized the overenthusiastic coiners of Latinisms in his pedantic schoolmaster, Holofernes, in *Love's Labour's Lost.* But to such writers as Sir Thomas Elyot and Sir Thomas More we owe hundreds of learned borrowings that we commonly use today, including *absurdity, acceptance, analogy, animate, compatible, contradictory, dissipate, exhaust, explain, exterminate, exasperate, frugality, irritate, modesty,* and *monopoly.*

Despite Holofernes, Shakespeare was himself responsible for introducing and using many newly minted inkhorn terms. But usually these new words were used with their etymological meanings in Latin and not in the senses we know today. For example, when Shakespeare uses *to communicate* he means it in its original Latin sense *(communicare),* "to make common to many," "share," and not its current sense "to exchange information" ("Thou are an elm, my husband, I a vine, Whose weakness married to thy stronger state / Makes me with thy strength to *communicate,"* *Comedy of Errors*).

Many inkhorn terms lived for a time, but did not survive beyond the seventeenth century. For example, *anacephalize* (Greek "to sum up") died out in favor of the Latinism *recapitulate*. *Deruncinate* (to weed), *adminiculation* (aid), *illecebrous* (delicate, alluring), *expede* (to accomplish), *eximious* (excellent), *assate* (to roast), *suppeditate* (furnish, supply), *temulent* (drunk), and many others did not survive, probably because there were already perfectly good words with these meanings.

French continued to be an important source of borrowings, though nothing like the former flood after the Norman Conquest. Sometimes French words that were borrowed in earlier periods and had become full-fledged English terms were re-borrowed in this period with different forms and meanings, such as *assay* (1338) and *essay* (1597); *forge* (1279) and *fabricate* (c. 1450); *gentle* (a. 1200) and *genteel* (1599) or *jaunty* (1662); *hostel* (c. 1250) or *hospital* (1300) and *hotel* (1765); *recognize* (1414) and *reconnoitre* (1707); *suit* (a. 1300) and *suite* (1673); and *ticket* (1528) and *etiquette* (1750).

From Italian came *ballot* (from "little ball," used as counters in voting); *ruffian* ("pimp"); *regatta* (from the name of a gondola race held in Venice on the Grand Canal); *zany* (a variant of *Giovanni*); and (through French) *brigade* and *brigand* (both from *brigare,* to "brawl," "fight"). Spanish gave English of this period *cigar* ("grasshopper") and *flamingo* and *flamenco* (the Spanish name for the ruddy-complexioned Flemish).

English was additionally enriched by words adopted from more than fifty other languages. This was largely due to the expansion of the British Empire, which enabled English to adopt words from all parts of the world, such as *pariah* (from Tamil, meaning "drummer," drumming at festivals and funerals being the hereditary duty of members of a low caste in southern India); *pagoda* (ultimately from Sanskrit meaning "goddess" or "blessed"); and *fetish* (from Portuguese "charm" or "sorcery" as applied to West African worship of charms and talismans). Dutch gave *foist* (from "fist," that is, to cheat by "palming" dice), and *maelstrom* ("to grind" plus "stream"). *Compound* (enclosure) is from Malay. *Bungalow* ("Bengal") and *seersucker* ("milk and sugar") are from Hindi, as is the later *juggernaut* (from the name of the huge wagon that bore the image of the Hindu god Krishna in an annual procession and beneath the wheels of which many devotees threw themselves to be crushed as a sacrifice to the god). Arabic gave *mohair,* from the word meaning "selected," or "choice," and *popinjay* from the word for "parrot." *Pal* is from Romany, the Gypsy language. *Taboo* is from Polynesian.

The printing press in Renaissance England had a profound influence on English. In about 1476 William Caxton introduced into England the art of printing, which he had learned on the continent. Books were now relatively cheap compared to the expensive handwritten manuscript books of earlier times, making them available to greater numbers of readers. This greatly increased communications and opened the way for the rapid spread of literacy and with it the growth of social consciousness. It also encouraged writing in the vernacular and, in the case of English, expanded its currency and respectability as a written language. On the continent by 1500, already there were over 34,000 printed titles, but most were works written in Latin. But by 1640 in England, there were over 20,000 titles printed in English.

Printed books unlike manuscript books could also be reproduced in thousands of copies all exactly the same. This pushed English toward a standard form, both written and spoken. And because nearly all of the publishing in England was done in London, beginning with Caxton, London English was further assured of becoming the standard form.

The latter part of this period, from about 1650 to 1800, sometimes called the Augustan Age or the Age of Reason, is characterized by a strong sense of order and the value of regulation and standards. Correctness became an ideal, along with the rules and formulas for defining correctness. Attempts were made throughout the period to standardize, refine, and fix or stabilize the language. This was, after all, the age when the dictionary came into its own as the authority on correct English and the purveyor of new words.

PASSION (c. 1175, 1588). *Patience* and *passion* (love, ardent sexual affection) seem dramatically opposed to each other, but are, etymologically speaking, really the same thing, both deriving from Latin *pati* (to suffer). English *passion* was taken directly from Late Latin *passionem* (suffering) in the twelfth century and was used primarily in Christian theology to refer to the sufferings of Christ on the cross ("Gods *passion,* and I had twise so many cares, as you have, I'ld drowne them all in a cup of sacke," 1601, Ben Jonson, *Every Man in His Humour*). It was then extended to "the sufferings of martyrs," then "suffering" generally, and by the fourteenth century, "suffering from a painful disorder of the body" ("It is of ryght good effecte in the *passions* of the joyntes [joints]," 1563, Thomas Gale, *An Antidotarie*). Once established in English, *passion* was influenced by its source word, *passionem,* in its use as a translation of Greek *pathos* (experience, emotion, an affection of the mind), broadening the English reference to "strong or overpowering emotion" ("Of all base *passions,* feare is most accurst," 1591, Shakespeare, *Henry VI*). This opened the way for the common modern use, "strong feelings of love or sexual desire" ("My sword . . . shall plead my *passions* for Lavinia's love," 1588, Shakespeare, *Titus Andronicus*).

NICE (c. 1290–1769). *Nice* has not always been a nice word. Despite its nebulous modern senses of varied approval ("She was the first *'nice'* girl he had ever known," 1925, Fitzgerald, *The Great Gatsby*), its early history covers such disapproving and derisive senses as "stupid," "lascivious," "slothful," and "unmanly," all now obsolete. Its earliest sense, "foolish," "stupid," "senseless," appears in the thirteenth and fourteenth centuries ("He made the lady so mad and so *nyce* that sche whorshipped hym as the grettest prophete of God Almighty," 1387, John de Trevisa, trans. of Higden's *Polychronicon*), and is from Old French *nice* (silly), from Latin *nescius* (ignorant), literally "not to know," a compound of *ne* (not) and *scire* (to know). From there it is difficult to trace the convolutions of its senses, the next apparently being "wanton," "lewd" ("These are complements, these are humours, these betraie *nice* wenches that would be betraied without these," 1588, Shakespeare, *Love's Labour's Lost*), followed by "strange," "rare," "uncommon" ("For there be straunge wonderous workes, dyverse maner of *nyce* beestes and whall fishes," 1535, Coverdale Bible) and "slothful," "lazy." This latter seems to have been extended to "effeminate," "unmanly" (laziness being unmanly?) to "delicate," "overrefined," "coy." Once we get to "delicate" it becomes easier to see the extensions to "fastidious" or "dainty" with regard to food or cleanliness (1551), then, on the one hand, to "particular," "precise," "requiring great precision" (1513) and, on the other hand, "appetizing" with regard to food again (1712). Something that is appetizing is "agreeable" or "delightful" (1769) and from there come the myriad gradations on approval or commendation, ranging from "good," "kindly" to "attractive" to "sexually modest" to "cheerful" or "congenial."

INOCULATE (c. 1420, 1722). To the ancient Roman horticulturist, a grafting shoot or bud looked like an eye, so to engraft or implant was called *inoculare,* from *in-* (into) and *oculus* (eye, bud). English borrowed the Latin word in the fifteenth century and used it to mean "to propagate by inserting a bud into a plant," a specialized sense still in use ("A dextrous Hand *inoculates* a Rose-tree Bud upon an Apple-Stock," 1707, *Curiosities in Husbandry and Gardening*). Though Edward Jenner's experiments with vaccination did not begin until about 1796, *inoculate* (to implant a germ or virus into a person) is first recorded in 1722 with reference to implanting the smallpox virus to prevent smallpox ("The Experiment of *inoculating* the Small-Pox upon . . . Criminals," 1722, London *Gazette*). Inoculation had been used from ancient times in China, India, and Persia, but it took Dr. Jenner using cowpox virus or *vaccine,* from Latin *vacca* (cow), to demonstrate its feasibility to the West.

NUPTIAL (1490). "Methinks a father / Is at the *nuptial of his son* a guest / That best becomes the table," wrote Shakespeare in *A Winter's Tale.* But etymologically speaking, the bard is not quite correct, because *nuptial* (marriage, wedding), from Latin *nuptiae* (wedding), is ultimately from the root word *nubere,* which was used strictly from the woman's point of view (to marry a man, take a husband). Because from ancient times it was the custom for the bride to wear a veil, Latin *nubere* (to marry) meant literally "to cover with a veil," and is closely related to *nubes* (a cloud) and *nebula* (a little cloud). It is also related to Greek *nymphe* (bride, nymph) and is the origin of *nubile,* meaning "of marriageable age" ("Buckingham's Neece was not yet *Nubile* in yeares," a. 1642, George Eglisham, *Forerunner of Revenge*) or, more broadly, "physically mature enough to be suited for or desirous of sexual activity."

OBSESSION (1513, 1680). When Sir Thomas More wrote in 1513 in his *History of King Richard III* that "They which were in the castell [castle] . . . sent also to the Earle of Richemonde to advertise [advise] hym of their sodeine [sudden, unexpected] *obsession,*" he was not talking about the people in the castle suddenly becoming neurotically preoccupied with some passion or irrational idea. Rather the *obsession* is the unexpected siege of the castle by an enemy. This earliest sense of *obsess* (to besiege) is from Latin *obsidere* (to besiege), literally "to sit at or opposite to," that is, "to sit down before a fortress or the enemy," from *ob-* (opposite to, against) and *sidere* (to sit). Just as an army can besiege a castle, the devil or a demon can besiege or beset a person ("A man is said to be *obsest,* when an evill spirit followeth him, troubling him at divers times and seeking opportunity to enter into him," 1616, John Bullokar, *An English Expositor*). *Obsession,* being harassed by a demon from without, was distinguished from *possession,* being inhabited by a demon, the castle walls of a person's self having been breached. Then gradually *obsession* was taken out of the realm of superstition and demonology and transferred to psychology, a preoccupying fixed idea or feeling replacing the obsessing or besieging demon. This development of senses was completed by about 1680. Shortly afterward, however, *obsess* and *obsession* disappeared from use altogether, essentially becoming obsolete, only to be mysteriously revived in the nineteenth century.

PARAGRAPH (1525). A break in a narrative or discourse where a new idea or argument begins was marked in ancient Greek manuscripts with a short horizontal stroke, also used to mark off the different speeches in a play. Because it was written in the margin or beside the running text, this mark was called a *paragraphos,* from *para* (by the side of, beside) and *graphos* (written). The Greek word passed into Medieval Latin and from there either directly or through French into six-teenth-century English, where it referred to the paragraph symbol itself. Besides a horizontal stroke, the Greek scribe sometimes used a wedge-shaped mark, the ancestor of the reversed *P* indicating a paragraph break, sometimes called a *pilcrow.* This symbol had been in common use in Middle En-glish manuscripts and was retained by early printers before indenting the first line of a paragraph became standard prac-tice. *Pilcrow* is probably a folk etymology ("pilled crow," a bald or peeled crow) for Middle English *pylcrafte* and *pargrafte,* a modification of Latin *paragraphus.*

IMP (1526). In Old English an *impa* was a young shoot or sapling, a sense that only survived into the seventeenth cen-tury ("About the foot of the tree it bears many young *imps,* which are such suckers of the sap, that they draw away all the goodnesse," 1601, Philemon Holland, trans. of *Pliny's Natural History*). Through a Germanic source, *impa* derives from Latin borrowed from Greek *emphyein* (to engraft), a compound of *em-* (in) and *phyein* (to make grow). In Middle English, it was extended first to "a slip used in grafting" (1377) and then (c. 1412) to "offspring" or "a male scion" (*scion* itself originally meant "a shoot used in grafting"), especially a scion of a noble house ("That his sonne prince Edward, that goodly *ympe,* maie long reigne over you," 1548, Edward Hall, *Chronicle*). By the 1500s, the devilish reputation of male children gave *imp* its next sense, "child of the devil," and then in the following century, it was weakened to "a mischievous child," the same way that "little devil" is playfully used of children ("I once caught a young male [Yahoo] of three years old . . . but the little *imp* fell a squalling, and scratching, and biting," 1727, Jona-than Swift, *Gulliver's Travels*).

PORCELAIN (c. 1530). In the thirteenth century, Marco Polo brought white, translucent ceramic ware, subsequently called *porcelain,* from China, where fine pottery had been perfected to a high art. To the Italians the hard, glazed surface resembled the shiny cowrie shell or *porcellana,* from Latin *porcellus,* the diminutive of *porcus* (pig). The undecided question in *porcelain*'s history comes down to what part of the pig's anatomy *porcellana* ultimately refers to. One explanation derives it from *porcella* (a young sow), the feminine of *porcellus,* claiming that the cowrie shell's opening resembles the sow's vulva. A variation on this cites *porcus* as Latin slang for pudenda. Another version holds that the Italian name derives from the shell's curved outer surface, which was thought to resemble the raised back of a little hog, and adds that toy pigs were made using the shell as the body and putty or other materials to form appendages. In addition, a pig's color is similar to the shell's.

FARCE (1530). When an eighteenth-century cookbook enjoins the cook to "make a *farce* with the livers minced small," it is not calling for a low comedy of livers, but is using the old word for forcemeat or stuffing, from Old French *farcir* and ultimately Latin *farcire* (to stuff). In Middle French a *farce* (a broadly satirical comedy), like savory stuffing, was filler, ad lib gags and buffoonery that actors inserted in religious dramas or MYSTERY plays. Earlier the Medieval Latin form *farsa* or *farsia* referred to the various phrases "stuffed" or inserted in litanies between the words "kyrie" and "eleison" and to other expansions of liturgical formulas. This also gave the sense "to pad or spice up a speech or literary piece" ("With what stuffe our old historiographers have *farced* up their huge volumes," 1577, Holinshed, *Chronicles*).

ARTICHOKE (1531). This plant with its edible globelike flowers is native to the Mediterranean region and as early as the 1450s was known in northern Italy, where it was called variously *arcicioffo, arciciocco,* and *articiocco.* Ultimately it is from an Arabic word *al-harshuf,* which in Spanish-Arabic became *al-harshofa.* Popular attempts to make etymological sense of this strange-sounding name for the strange-looking plant has created a confusion of different forms of the word

in most of the European languages. In Italy, it was confused with *arci-* (arch-, chief), *cioffo* (horse collar), and *ciocco* (stump), all of which influenced the northern Italian version borrowed by the English. In France, it sounded like an odd combination of *chou* (cabbage), *chaud* (warm), and *hault* or *haut* (high), giving the French variants *artichau, artichou,* and *artichaud.* The sixteenth-century Latinized version, *articoccus* or *articactus,* associated it with cactus. In English, the last syllable was often interpreted as *choke* or *chock,* and the first sounded like either *horti-* (garden, as in *horticulture*) or *hearty,* giving such strange explanations for the name as "choking the garden" *(hortichoke)* and "choking the heart" or "having a choke or chock in the heart" *(heartychock).* Other odd spellings abounded, each with its own implicit "etymology" *(archecokk, archichoke, archychok, artochock, hortichock, artychough, hartichoake, hartechooke, horty-chock),* until by the nineteenth century a standard spelling and pronunciation were finally established.

ALOOF (1532). The windward side of a sailing ship, the side toward the wind, was called *luff,* and to luff was to steer the head of the ship closer into the wind. *Luff,* and its variant *loof,* is from Middle Dutch *loef,* cognate with Old Icelandic *lofi* (palm of the hand), with reference to the flat oar or rudder used to steer a ship, and is ultimately from the Indo-European root **lep* (to be flat, palm), hence English *glove*. To be *on luff* or *on loof* meant "windward." The preposition *on* was reduced to the prefix a- (as in *afoot, asleep, aground*), giving *aloof* ("But surely this anker lyeth too farre *aloufe* fro [from] thys shyppe, and hath neuer a cable to fasten her to it," 1532, Sir Thomas More, *Works*). A ship naturally drifts toward the shore or objects that are leeward, that is, downwind or away from the direction of the wind. Sir Thomas More's "shyppe" has drifted leeward, so that the anchor is too far upwind or "aloufe" to be reached. Because the ship's head must be kept into the wind or "kept aloof" to prevent drifting toward the lee shore or anything else downwind, *aloof* became a steersman's order *("Aloofe, aloofe* then cryed the master out," a. 1577, George Gascoigne, *Works*). From the nautical sense of keeping aloof in order to stay away from leeward objects comes the general meaning of "distant, apart, removed" ("I stand *aloofe,* and will no reconcilement," 1602, Shakespeare, *Hamlet*).

EXPLODE (1538). Theater critics can be cruel but rarely are they homicidal as a modern reader might think reading Henry Fielding's *Tom Jones* (1749): "In the playhouse . . . when he doth wrong, no critic is so apt to hiss and *explode* him." This is the original sense of *explode,* adopted from Latin *explodere* (to drive off by clapping or hissing), originally theatrical jargon meaning to deride or "boo" an actor off stage, from *ex* (out) and *plaudere* (to clap), hence English *applaud* and *plaudit.* It was extended more generally to "scornfully reject" ("Not that I wholly *explode* Astrology: I believe there is something in it," 1696, Thomas Tryon, *Miscellanea*). The British scientist Robert Boyle was the first to use it with the meaning "to drive out with sudden noise and violence" ("The inspired Air . . . when 'tis *exploded,* carrys them away with it self," 1660, *New Experiments Physico-Mechanicall*), the precursor to the now most common sense, "to go off with force and noise, like a bomb," first appearing in American English ("All Europe is like a mine ready to *explode,*" 1790, Gouverneur Morris in Jared Sparks *Life of Gouverneur Morris*).

PARASITE (1539). Shakespeare alluded to the etymology of *parasite* when he wrote (1607) in *Timon of Athens:* "May you a better feast never behold, / You knot of mouth friends! . . . Most smiling, smooth, detested *Parasites.*" A parasite is indeed a "mouth friend" at a feast, from Middle French *parasite,* ultimately of Greek origin in *parasitos* (a person who eats at another's table, a toady earning meals through flattery). It is constructed of Greek *para* (beside, at the side of) and *sitos* (food), literally "feeding beside." In ancient Greece there were no connotations of reproach in being called a parasite, of which there were two classes, religious and civil. The religious parasites were assistants to the priests, whose duties included providing food for temple visitors and arranging sacrificial banquets. It was the civil parasites, however, that gave rise to the modern sense of the word. This class of persons received invitations to dine in certain official settings, such as the prytaneum or townhall, as distinguished from officials who had a right to dine there by virtue of their office. It was not until the parasite appeared in Greek comedy that the word took on the meaning of "sponger," "freeloader." The parasite's main objective in these comedies was to get a good dinner, for which he was willing to endure every kind of humiliation, often relying on a stock of witticisms and flattery to use at the patron's table. *Parasite* was not used in the biological sense (an animal or plant that lives on another organism) until about 1720.

PROTOCOL (1541). The revival of nationalism in the Baltic states in 1989 and the belated protest against the secret protocol signed by Hitler and Stalin allowing the Soviet Union to annex Lithuania, Latvia, and Estonia put *protocol* (a pact or treaty between countries) in the news. Although such pacts have been concluded since the invention of writing, and probably before, they have been called *protocols* only since about the sixteenth century. The English term is borrowed from Middle French *prothocole* (the draft of a document or record of a transaction), in turn from Medieval Latin *protocollum,* which had the same meaning, but additionally had the older Greek sense of *protokollon* (the first sheet or flyleaf of a manuscript). That word is a compound of *proto* (first) and *kolla* (glue) and referred to a sheet "glued" to the outside of a manuscript or papyrus roll. It recorded the date and described the contents and origin of the unbound document, and allowed a reader to get a sense of the document without having to unroll the whole thing. *Protocol* was used in English only with regard to documents of international diplomacy, and until about 1950 did not gain general currency in English the way it had in French, where it has many extended senses. In the mid-nineteenth century, it was an official record of procedures in an autopsy or a scientific experiment. By the 1940s this sense had been extended to the rules of conduct and etiquette in affairs of state ("[Truman] felt that it would not be good *protocol* for him to be out hobnobbing with an Englishman out of office at the very time that the man now in charge of Britain's foreign affairs is in Washington," 1949, Washington *Post*). From there it was a short extension to any code of proper conduct, including the Emily Post variety.

ALCOHOL (1543). *Alcohol* has an unlikely origin in eye makeup, a fine metallic powder, usually of antimony, used by Arab women to line the eyes and stain the lids ("They put betweene the eye-lids and the eye a certaine black powder . . . made of minerall brought from the kingdome of Fez, and called *Alcohole*," 1615, George Sandys, *A Relation of a Journey Begun 1610*). The Arabic name for this powder is *al-koh'l*, literally "the powder," from *al* (the) and *koh'l*, hence English *kohl*, borrowed from Hebrew *kakhal* (to paint, stain) as in Ezekiel 23:40 ("Lo, they came: for whom thou didst wash thyself, paintedst thine eyes, and deckedst thyself with ornaments"). Alchemists adopted the word and broadened it to refer to any powder produced by sublimation, that is, by heating it until it vaporized and then condensing it into a very fine powder. Raw sulfur, for example, was refined in this way to give *alcohol of sulfur*. By the mid-seventeenth century, it had been extended to liquids whose essence or "spirit" ("Intense selfishness, the *alcohol* of egotism," 1830, Samuel Taylor Coleridge, *Lectures on Shakespeare*) was obtained by distillation, a process happily used on wine to give *alcohol of wine*. A century later the phrase *alcohol of wine* was shortened to *alcohol* and soon referred to any distilled liquor. Although *alcoholic* as an adjective was in use as early as 1790, it did not become a noun denoting a person addicted to alcoholic liquor until the end of the nineteenth century. The disease itself, *alcoholism,* was not identified as such until about 1850.

ROUND ROBIN (1546). Originally *round robin* and *Jack-in-the-box* were sacrilegious nicknames for the communion host or wafer ("Rayling biles agaynst the sacramente, termynge it *'Jacke of the boxe,'* 'sacramente of the halter,' *'round Robin,'* with like unseemely termes," 1555, Bishop Nicholas Ridley, *Works*). The host was a *round robin* because of its round shape, the same reason that English dialect used this expression for a pancake. And it was a *Jack-in-the-box* because it was reserved, like the springy puppet, in a small container or box. The latter expression probably did not survive much beyond the sixteenth century, but *round robin* reappears two centuries later in sailors' jargon. Then it referred to a mutinous document of protest on which the petitioners signed their names in a circular pattern to disguise the order of signatures. With no name heading the list, this sly method prevented anyone from being named as leader and destined to hang, few British captains being willing or able to hang their whole crew. The reference to *round* in *round robin,* of course, refers to the circle of signatures, but why *robin?* It may be an alteration of an originally idiomatic French expression, *rond* (round) and *ruban* (ribbon), ribbons often being used to tie up documents. Whatever the ulterior origin, the modern senses are from the sailor's expression, first being extended to any petition or statement signed by several persons, often in alphabetical order, all of whom take responsibility for its contents. And then by the 1890s in America, because all members of a *round robin* are involved, it was used for a tournament in which every player or team meets each of the others in turn.

GAUNTLET (c. 1420, glove; *throw down the gauntlet,* 1548; *run the gauntlet,* 1676). *Gauntlet,* the glove worn as part of medieval armor, made of leather and steel plates ("These hands, that wont to wave a dreadful sword, / Instead of iron *gauntlets* now must wear / Perfum'd gloves!," 1658, Sir Aston Cokaine, *Trappolin*), was borrowed from French *gantelet,* the diminutive of Old French *gant* (glove), probably of Germanic origin. *To cast (fling* or *throw) down the gauntlet* (to challenge) comes from the custom of throwing a glove or gauntlet on the ground in challenging an opponent ("Makynge a proclamacion, that whosoever would saie that kynge Richard was not lawefully kynge, he woulde fighte with hym at the utteraunce, and *threwe downe his gauntlet,"* 1548, Edward Hall, *Chronicle*). During the Middle Ages a gage (see MORTGAGE) or pledge was given in a court of law as a promise to fulfill the judgment handed down. Originally the gage was property of value deposited by the defendant as security. The glove became a formal symbol of the deposit, standing for the hand that would deliver the pledged property. This was transferred to the wager of battle. The glove, instead of being handed to the adversary, was thrown down by the defendant as security that he would defend his cause in arms. The *gauntlet* in the expression *run the gauntlet* ("They stripped them naked, and caused them to run the *Gauntlet,"* 1676, Increase Mather, *The History of King Philip's War*) has nothing to do with gloves or wagers, though *gauntlet* (glove) influenced the way the original word *gantlope* was altered. A *gantlope* was a military punishment in which the culprit was stripped to the waist and made to run between two rows of men, who beat him with sticks or knotted ropes. English soldiers in the Thirty Years' War picked it up from the Swedes as *gatlopp* and brought it to England. It is a compound of Swedish *gata* (lane), which also appears in *gattooth* and is akin to English *gate* and *gait,* and Swedish *lopp* (course), akin to English *leap* and *lope.*

PARAGON (1548). English may have borrowed *paragon* (model of excellence or perfection) from Spanish *paragon,* which may be from *para con* (in comparison with), all things suffering by comparison with a true paragon ("Thys prince was almost the Arabicall Phenix, and emongest his predecessors a very *Paragon,"* a. 1548, Hall, *Chronicle*). *Paragon,* however, first appears in Italian, and is shortened from *pietra di paragone,* meaning "comparison stone" or "touchstone," a hard, flintlike stone used to test gold and silver by rubbing them against it, the streak left on the dark stone indicating the quality of the metal. It is probably ultimately from Greek *parakonan* (to rub against, sharpen, or whet), compounded from *para* (beside) and *akone* (whetstone) from *ake* (point). A slightly different derivation suggests that the Italian *paragone* (model) is from Medieval Greek *parakone* (polishing stone), also from *parakonan* (to rub against). The underlying metaphor of this version is "polishing" something to perfection, rather than testing the excellence of something.

IMMOLATE (1548). In the ritual sacrifices of ancient Greece, before the sacrificial animal, usually a goat, was clubbed to death and its throat cut, its neck was sprinkled with barley meal. The Romans adopted this practice and called it *immolare* (to sacrifice), from *im-* (upon) and *mola* (meal), or in full *mola salsa* (salted meal), the sacrificial meal sprinkled on the victim. Renaissance English borrowed the Latin term, most often using it in a broader sense (to sacrifice, to kill as a victim) than its original ritual context ("The horrible custom of *immolating* the captives of war at the tombs of those who had been slain in battle," 1794, Richard Sullivan, *A View of Nature*).

MANURE (1549). When Sir Thomas Smith wrote: "To speake of the Common wealth . . . of England, it is governed, administered and *manured* by three sortes of persons" (a. 1577, *The Commonwealth of England and the maner of Government thereof*), he was not vulgarly claiming that the English government was spread with dung or compost, the sense of *manure* that today we know best. *Manure* was originally a verb meaning "to hold or manage land or property, to administer," extended from the Anglo-French *maynoverer* (to work with the hands), from Medieval Latin *manoperare,* a compound of *manus* (hand) and *operari* (to work, operate). Borrowed into English in the fourteenth century, the most important responsibility of *manuring* or managing land was "to till or cultivate" it, a sense that was often used figuratively (*"Manure* your heart with diligence, and in it sow good seed," 1645, Z. Boyd, *Holy Songs*). This was extended to mean "to cultivate or train the mind or body," a usage that sounds very odd to modern ears ("Those Scotts which inhabit the southe, beinge farre the beste parte, are well *manured,*" c. 1540 translation of Vergilius' *English History*). From the sense "to cultivate," it naturally developed the meaning "to enrich the land with fertilizer," giving the noun *manure* (dung or compost used as fertilizer). The Medieval Latin word that became *manure* in the fourteenth century became in the eighteenth century *manoeuvre* or *maneuver,* when English reborrowed it through Old French, using it in the sense of "a planned movement of troops," as though miniature soldiers "moved about by hand," literally, "hand operated," were used in the strategic planning.

CUE (1553). Shakespeare spells *cue* (signal to an actor to enter or begin) as *Q* ("Had you not come upon your *Q* my Lord, William Lord Hastings had pronounc'd your part," 1594, *Richard III*), because there was a tradition that *Q* or *q* was an abbreviation for Latin *quando* (when) supposedly written in the actors' copies of the play at the points at which they were to enter stage or begin speaking. However, no such marked scripts have ever been found. Another explanation places *cue*'s origin in French *queue* from Latin *cauda* (tail), the "tail" or ending of one speech marking the beginning of the next. In English, *queue* and its variant *cue* were used in the nearly literal sense, "a long plait of hair, pigtail" in the eighteenth century ("Those *cues* or locks . . . look like a parcel of small strings hanging down from the crown of their heads," 1772, Captain James Cook, *Voyages*). Almost contemporary was the extended meaning referring to the tapering tail-like billiard cue, which earlier in French referred specifically to the small end of the stick then called the *billard.* Not until the early nineteenth century did *queue* refer to a line of people waiting their turns to proceed ("That talent . . . of spontaneously standing in *queue,* distinguishes . . . the French People," 1837, Thomas Carlyle, *French Revolution*). The problem with the "tail" derivation is that *queue* or *cue* (tail, plait) first appeared in English almost two centuries after *cue* (signal for an actor). Moreover, *queue* is not used with the stage meaning in French, which uses *replique* instead. Without more or better evidence, the origin of *cue* remains a mystery, or as a lexicographer would put it, "origin obscure."

CANNIBAL (1553). When Columbus made his historic landing in the West Indies, he encountered the ferocious warlike Caribs, a native South American people that called themselves *Galibi* (brave men), from *caribe* (brave, daring), akin to Tupi *caryba* (valiant man, hero). About a century before Columbus arrived, the Galibi or Caribs, who criss-crossed the Caribbean in their canoes, had invaded the Lesser Antilles and driven out the Arawak Indians. They practiced cannibalism and fasting, as well as scarification (ritual scarifying of the skin). To Columbus their tribal name sounded like *Canibal* or *Caniba*, which he associated with the *Gran Can* (Grand Khan), the ruler of the Far East, whose dominions he believed were nearby. Their outrageous (to the Europeans) anthropophagic habits were quickly associated with their name, which in Spanish became *caribal* or *canibal*, borrowed into English in the mid-sixteenth century with specific reference to the Caribs ("Columbus . . . sayled toward the South, and at the [sic] lengthe came to the Ilandes of the *Canibals*. And because he came thether on the Sundaye called the Dominical day, he called the Illand . . . Dominica," 1553, Richard Eden, *A Treatyse of Newe India*). It soon denoted any human eater of human flesh ("And of the *cannibals* that each other

eat, . . . This to hear / Would Desdemona seriously incline,"
1604, Shakespeare, *Othello*). Shakespeare's *Caliban,* the name
of the savage character in *The Tempest,* is a variant of *cariban*
(a Carib or cannibal).

HALO (1563). A *halo,* an ancient sign of divinity, has its
origin beneath the hooves of oxen. Long before the industrial
age oxen were used to thresh grain. They were tethered to the
end of a pole that pivoted about an axis, treading the grain
in an endless circle and in the process wearing a path on the
wooden threshing floor. The Greeks called the threshing
floor with its circular path *halos,* itself of unknown origin.
They then transferred the word to the disk of the sun or moon
and then to the ring of light sometimes seen through a mist
or haze around these brightest of astral bodies. English borrowed the word in this latter sense from Latin *halos,* and in the
mid-seventeenth century extended it to the nimbus or aureole
around a holy personage in religious art. The halo itself pre-
dates Christianity. The Roman emperors, who were considered divine, were often portrayed with halos, as was the Greek
mythical figure Proserpine. Christian artists, however, raised
halos to an intricate symbolic art form. The Virgin Mary, for
example, had a circlet of stars, while Christ sometimes had a
cross-shaped nimbus; God was portrayed with rays radiating
in triangular directions, and mere mortals, if their portraits
were made while they were still alive, had square halos. So
popular were halos in art that English has two other words for
them. *Aureole* was borrowed in the fourteenth century through
Old French from the Latin phrase *aureola corona* (golden
crown), ultimately from *aurum* (gold) going back to Indo-
European **auso-* (gold). *Nimbus* is contemporary with *halo*
(1616) and like *halo* was borrowed directly from Latin, *nimbus*
(cloud), ultimately from Indo-European **nebh-* (cloud).

INNUENDO (1564, 1678). There were doubtless times
when barristers nodded off during the monotonous drone of
Renaissance English law thickly laced with Medieval Latin.
But if they were doing their jobs, they often "nodded to"

something by means of *innuendo,* literally "by giving a nod to," from Latin *innuere* (to nod to, signify). The thing nodded to was a point that required explaining. But before the lawyer launched into his explanation, usually in legal documents, he prefaced it with *innuendo,* a formula that simply meant "namely, that is to say" ("What-soever thinge it is, that knave your sonne—*innuendo* this deponentes sonne—made it, & brought it to the church," 1564, *Child-Marriages, Divorces, etc. in the Diocese of Chester*). The interpolated clarification itself then became known as an *innuendo,* and by about the mid-seventeenth century it was extended to something merely hinted at or suggested indirectly.

PETTIFOGGER (1564). Lawyers have never been liked overmuch and have garnered many derogatory nicknames, including the ever-popular *pettifogger* and its synonym SHY-STER ("We must all turne *pettifoggers,* and instead of gilt rapiers, hang buckram bags [lawyers' brief cases?] at our girdles," 1612, Thomas Dekker, *If It Be Not Good Works, the Devil Is In It*). Around 1600, *pettifogger* was broadened to "one who quibbles over trivia," often used as the adjective *pettifogging,* meaning "quibbling, petty" (" 'You are,' continued Mr. Pickwick, 'a well-matched pair of mean, rascally, *pettifogging* robbers,' " 1837, Charles Dickens, *Pickwick*). *Pettifogger* is probably related to *pettifactor* (a petty, underhanded lawyer), and may even derive from it, a compound of *petty* (insignificant, small-minded), from French *petit* (small), and *factor* (an agent or representative), also of French origin, ultimately from Latin *facere* (to do, make). More likely, *pettifogger* is a compound of *petty* and *fogger* (an underhanded person, especially a low-class lawyer, a huckster). *Fogger,* which is obsolete except in dialect, is from *Fugger,* the name of a famous and powerful family of merchants and financiers of Augsburg in the fifteenth and sixteenth centuries. The Fuggers were, among other things, bankers to the Hapsburgs and were instrumental in the rise of Charles V to the imperial throne in 1519. The Fugger name was widely known and was synonymous in several European languages with money and finance. In German, for example, *fugger, fucker,* or *focker* meant "monopolist," "great merchant," "usurer," and in certain dialects "huckster" or "peddler." A *petty Fugger* would be a small businessman who uses the same dishonorable means popularly attributed to the great financiers for making a profit, but on a petty scale. It was then probably used of lawyers in the sense of "a *petty fogger* of the law," which then gave rise to the specific sense, "a shyster lawyer."

JADE (1569, ornamental stone; 1620, to become exhausted). The Spanish conquistadors brought back from Mexico and Peru a greenish-blue stone that they called *piedra de ijada* (colic stone) from *ijada* (the side or flank of the body), ultimately from Latin *iliata* or *ilia* (flanks, groin). It was so called because when applied to the side it was supposed to cure colic and renal diseases. For the same reason this stone was also known in medieval Latin as *lapis nephriticus* and later *nephrite*, from Greek *nephros* (kidney). *Piedra de ijada* was shortened to *ijade* and then borrowed into French as *l'ejade,* altered eventually to *le jade,* the form borrowed by English, *jade.* To ride a *jade* or a worthless, wornout horse ("This same philosophy is a good horse in the stable, but an arrant *jade* on a journey," 1768, Oliver Goldsmith, *The Good-Natured Man*) has nothing to do with green stones or kidneys, though some etymologists claim that the Old Spanish *ijada* and its derivative *ijadear* (to pant, hence a broken-winded horse) are also the origin of this word. *Jade,* the horse, however, is doubtless a different word altogether, deriving from a Scandinavian source, like Old Norse *jalda* (mare), probably ultimately from a Finnish, and therefore non-Indo-European, root. It was transferred disparagingly to women ("When I could not thrive by all other trades, I became a squire to wait upon *jades,* " 1584, R. Warde, *Three Ladies of London*), and then around 1600, it became a verb meaning "to make (a horse) a jade," then more generally to "fatigue," "wear out," "become tired" ("As an horse that is good at hand, but naught at length, so is the Hypocrite; free and fiery for a spurt, but he *jadeth* and tyreth in a journey," 1620, Robert Sanderson, *Sermons*) and finally to the most common form today, *jaded* (worn out, dull, or sated by continual use or indulgence).

HAPHAZARD (1575). This Renaissance word is a compound of two older words: *hap* from the late twelfth century, and *hazard,* first used about 1300. At the time of its coinage in the sixteenth century, *haphazard* (mere chance) was redundant, having components both meaning "chance." *Hap* (chance, luck, fortune) can be traced back to its Indo-European root **kob-* (to suit, succeed), which became Proto-Germanic **hapan,* passing into a Scandinavian language, probably Old Norse, and then to early Middle English ("His *hap* wes tha wurse" [His hap (fortune) was the worse], c. 1205, Layamon, *Brut*). *Hap* is itself the root of *mishap* (bad luck); *hapless* (without luck); *happen* (to occur by "hap" or chance); *happy* whose meaning evolved from "good fortune," "lucky" to "very glad"; and the portmanteau Americanism *happenstance* (a chance circumstance), coined in the late nineteenth century by combining *happen*ing and circum*stance. Hazard* (risk, peril) is from Old French *hasard* (a dice game of chance) from Old Spanish *azar* (an unlucky card or throw of dice, game of chance), probably borrowed from Arabic *az-zahr* or *al-zahr* (the dice). A contrary but less-likely history says that the game *hasard* took its name from a castle in Palestine, *Hasart* or *Asart,* where it was invented during a prolonged and apparently tedious siege. The castle's actual Arabic name was *Ain Zarba.* Hazard, known in America as *craps,* was very popular in England in Shakespeare's time ("Who will go to *Hazard* with me for twentie Prisoners?," 1599, Shakespeare, *Henry V*) and was played for high stakes in the famous gaming rooms Crockford and Almack in London. From a game of chance, *hazard* was extended to refer simply to "chance" itself ("Slave, I have set my life upon a cast, / And I will stand the *hazard* of the Dye," 1594, Shakespeare, *Richard II*), the sense compounded in *haphazard.* And, as in the development of JEOPARDY, out of this high-stakes game, in which there is a chance of great loss, came the sense of "peril," "danger." In the seventeenth and eighteenth centuries to take a chance or risk was to be *hazard-*

ous (venturesome), but like *hazard, hazardous* took on the sense of danger and came to mean "risky."

CANARY (1576). Pliny the Elder mentions a Roman expedition in 40 B.C. to the Canary Islands or *Canaria insula* "so called from the multitude of dogs of great size," literally "Isle of Dogs," from Latin *canis* (dog). Though the indigenous dogs have long been extinct, the native bird the *canary*, whose name in the twists of etymology means "dog," has thrived, especially after its domestication in Italy early in the sixteenth century. *Canary* is from Spanish *Canaria*, the islands having been a colony of Spain since the fifteenth century. The earliest English sense of *canary* is "a lively Spanish dance" ("I have seen a medicine / That's able to breathe life into a stone . . . and make you dance *canary*," 1601, Shakespeare, *All's Well That Ends Well*). Before the devastating grape blight of 1853, *canary* was also a well-known wine exported throughout Europe ("I' faith, you have drunk too much *canaries*," 1598, Shakespeare, *2 Henry IV*).

CURMUDGEON (1577). This is a favorite chestnut of professional and amateur etymologists, everyone taking a stab at its history. Until the twentieth century, a *curmudgeon* was a nasty-tempered, avaricious fellow ("Why do covetous *cormogions* distill the best substance of their braines to get riches?," 1601, Thomas Wright, *Passions of the Minde*), perhaps best embodied in Dickens's Ebenezer Scrooge. More recently the miserly connotations have been dropped and a *curmudgeon* is a blunt but honest, albeit cantankerous, person, usually an older man, a sense perhaps popularized by Harold L. Ickes, Interior secretary under FDR, in his *Autobiography of a Curmudgeon.* For a time, the earliest-known citation for *curmudgeon* spelled it *cornmudgin* (1600), which gave etymologists, notably the eminent Walter Skeat, what they thought was surely the origin of the word. They argued that it was a compound of *corn* (grain) and *mudgin,* either from Middle English *muchen* or *michen* (to pilfer, steal) or from Norman French *muchier,* a variant of Old French *mucier* (to conceal, hide away). A *cornmudgin* in this scenario is literally "a hoarder or hider of corn." Since Skeat proposed this etymology in 1882, however, several earlier written examples have come to light, spelling it *curmudgen* and *cormogeon.* It is now clear that the writer of *cornmudgin* was using a play on words, attempting an English equivalent of Latin *frumentarius* (corn dealer). Dr. Johnson's dictionary offered the erudite folk etymology *coeur méchant* for French *méchant coeur* (evil or malicious heart), but there is no evidence to support this anywhere. Others have noted that the first syllable may be *cur* (dog), while the ending is that of *bludgeon* or *dudgeon.* Another word buff suggests that it is *cur* plus the obsolete Hertfordshire dialect *mudgel hole* (dunghill), hence *cur-mudgel* (dunghill dog), but even he notes that there is not a shred of evidence for this imaginative history. Yet another etymologist suggests that it is akin to Scottish *curmurring* (grumbling, murmuring), or perhaps Shetlands and Orkney dialect *curmullyit* (an ill-tempered person), but all of these derivations are primarily stabs in the dark.

CALLOW (1580). A *callow* youth may be immature and shallow, but he is rarely bald, as *callow* literally implies, deriving from Old English *calu* ("A man of whos heed heeris fleten awei, is *calu*" [A man whose head hair has fallen off, is bald], 1388, Wyclif, Leviticus 13:40). By about 1600, it was transferred to young birds that are unfledged or featherless, that is, "bald." As soon as this sense was established, it was figuratively applied to youth ("The *callow* Down began to cloath my Chin," 1697, John Dryden, trans. of *The Works of Virgil*), taking on its most prevalent meaning, "inexperienced," "immature." Although *callow* and *calu* strongly resemble Latin *calvus* and Gaelic *calbh* (bald), they are from a Germanic root, ultimately from Indo-European **galwo* (bald, naked). In English dialect *callow* land is bare, and in Irish it is marshy.

OSTRACISM (1588). *Ostracism* (banishment) is usually considered a painful punishment, but some writers in ancient Greece spoke of it as an honor. Instituted in 508 B.C., ostracism was a political device supposed to protect the Athenian democracy from the undue influence of a single person who might threaten the harmony of the country. Each year if an ostracism was deemed necessary, the citizens of Athens met to record their votes, which was done by placing in urns fragments of pottery on which they had written the name of the person they wanted banished. These potsherds or tile fragments, which functioned in the ancient world as scrap paper, were called *ostraca,* from the stem **ostr-* also found in *ostreion* (the origin of *oyster*) and akin to *osteon* (bone). If at least six thousand votes were cast against a person, he or she was banished for ten years. Because such a person was not considered a criminal or traitor, but merely one whose power was potentially harmful to the state, there was no disgrace involved and all property and citizen's rights could be reclaimed. By contrast, the Roman practice of ostracism was exile for life, all property reverting to the state.

HARLEQUIN (1590). Perhaps best recognized today from Picasso's early paintings, the clownish *harlequin* of pantomime and comedy ("A man of sense acts a lover just as a Dutchman would a *harlequin,*" 1728, Henry Fielding, *Love in Several*

Masques), with his catlike mask and particolored costume, was one of the stock characters in the improvised medieval plays known in Italy as *commedia dell'arte.* In the Italian productions, he was known as *Arlecchino* and carried a bat or wooden sword, the ancestor of the slapstick. Unlike his stage pals *Pantalone* (see PANTS) and the *Zanni,* two or three servant-types whose function was to plot and scheme and arouse laughter (hence *zany* "crazy"), *Arlecchino* was not born in Italy, but in old England, where he was known as *Herla cyning* (King Herla), a mythical character probably related to the Germanic god Woden. In a rare reversal, Old French borrowed this Old English figure as *Hellequin* or *Harlekin,* who appears in the folk literature as early as 1100 and was a ragamuffin leader of demons who rode through the air on horses. In medieval French plays he is portrayed as an "invisible" spirit of the air. The Italian *Arlecchino,* then, was probably borrowed from the French character. Though the name itself is ultimately of Old English origin, the childlike and amorous Arlecchino probably influenced the character of the Renaissance English harlequin.

LOOPHOLE (1591). Castles and fortress walls were usually designed with narrow vertical openings or windows called *loopholes* ("Thou that makest a heart thy Tower, / And thy *loop-holes,* Ladies eyes," a. 1625, John Fletcher, *Nice Valour*). Arrows and other missiles could be shot through the loophole ("Incessant volleys were securely discharged from the *loop-holes,*" 1781, Edward Gibbon, *Decline and Fall of the Roman Empire*) with little worry that the foe could shoot back through the opening, which was very narrow on the outside of the wall but considerably wider on the inside. Earlier it was called simply a *loop,* from Middle Dutch *lupen* (to lie in wait, peer), not the same word as *loop* (a curve or bend in a cord, leaving an opening), which is of unknown origin. A narrow loophole could also be a means of sly escape, either literally or figuratively ("It would be much below You and Me . . . to have such *loop-holes* in Our souls, and to . . . squeeze Our selves through our own words," 1663, Andrew Marvell, *Correspondence*). Though *loopholes* in architecture have gone the way of medieval castles, they are still found in laws and contracts ("What *loop-hole* they will find in the case, when it comes to trial, we cannot foresee," 1807, Thomas Jefferson, *Writings*).

BROTHEL (a. 1593). A *brothel* in the fourteenth century was not a place but a person, specifically a "scoundrel" or "low-life" ("The holy Lenton faste, whiche these *brotheles* so boldly take upon them to breake," 1532, Sir Thomas More, *Confutacyon of Tindales Answere*). It is from Old English *brothen* (ruined, degenerate) from Proto-Germanic **breuthanan* or **breutanan* (to break), the source also of *brittle*. By the beginning of the Early Modern English period, it was extended to "a woman of ill-repute or a prostitute" ("Why doeth a common *brothel* take no shame of hir abhomination?," 1535, Bishop John Fisher, *Works*). A house of prostitution was a *brothel's house*, which became confused with *bordel house*. *Bordel* (house of prostitution) had been adopted from Old French *bordel* (cabin, hut, brothel) as early as the thirteenth century. It is the diminutive taken from Medieval Latin *borda* (hut, cottage), itself a Germanic borrowing, such as Middle High German *bort* (board, plank), referring to the boards in the construction of a hut or cottage. *Brothel's house* became *brothel house*, then by the Elizabethan era just *brothel* ("Keepe thy foote out of *Brothels*," 1605, Shakespeare, *King Lear*).

ADDLE (a. 1593). A rotten egg has been called an *addle egg*, literally "a stinking urine egg," since the thirteenth century. In Old English, *addle* or *adela* meant "urine," "mire," "liquid filth," and though its distant history is lost, it is probably of Germanic origin since it has several cognates in the Germanic languages, such as Old Swedish *-adel* "urine" (as in *ko-adel* "cow piss") and Middle Low German *adele* "liquid manure." Although rotting eggs and foul urine have putridness in common, the original connection between the two is rooted in bad Latin. *Addle egg* is a translation of Medieval Latin *ovum urinae* (egg of urine), which is a mistaken rendering of classical Latin *ovum urinum* (wind egg), itself from Greek *ourion oion*. An egg fertilized by a cock became a baby chicken, but one impregnated by the wind became rotten. The similarity between *addle* and *idle*, both connoting abortiveness and uselessness, presented an opportunity for word play that few seventeenth-century writers could resist ("Pan. He esteemes her no more than I esteeme an *addle egge*. Cre. If you love an *addle egge* as well as you love an idle head, you would eate chickens i' th' shell," 1606, Shakespeare, *Troilus and Cressida*). Such punning contributed to the development of *addle*'s next sense, "idle," "vain," and with allusion to an addle egg's decomposed condition, "unsound," "confused" ("Their brains were *addle*, and their bellies as empty of meat as their heads of wit," 1621, Robert Burton, *Anatomy of Melancholy*). The natural likeness between eggs and heads gave the phrases *addle-brained*, *addle-headed*, and *addle-pated* ("Let every idle *addle-pated* gull / With stinking sweet Tobacco stuffe his skull," 1630, Jeremy Taylor, *Works*). From these it was a short step to *addled* (muddled, confused).

WISEACRE (1595). The ACRE of *wiseacre* (a person who thinks he is wise, a know-it-all) has nothing to do with the measurement of land, even though that confusion or pun has been made almost from the beginning. Instead, *wiseacre* is a loan translation of Middle Dutch *wijsseggher* (soothsayer), compounding *wise* and *seggher*, an old version of *sayer*, "one who says," "a braggart" ("This *Wiseacre* was reckoned by the Parish, who did not understand him, a most excellent Preacher," 1711, Sir Richard Steele, *Spectator*). The Middle Dutch is probably an altered borrowing of Old High German *wizzago* (prophet), from *wizzan* (to know).

LEAVE IN THE LURCH (1596). *Lurch* was originally the French game *lourche*, exported to England and popular there during the seventeenth century. It was probably similar to backgammon, but just how it was played has been lost in time. The French word is borrowed from Middle High German *lurz* (left, wrong), the sense of leftness or wrongness being extended to "utter defeat." In the game, to incur a "lurch" (the French would have said *demeurer lourche*) meant to be soundly beaten, a meaning that is still used in other games, especially cribbage. Used figuratively in the seventeenth century, *lurch* meant "discomfiture" or "predicament," the effect of being skunked or lurched in a game ("If heereafter thou fall into the lyke *lurch* . . . so then I will accompt of thee as a reprobate," 1584, Thomas Lodge, *Alarum*). This sense survives only in *to leave someone in the lurch*, that is, to leave someone in a state of discomfiture or in a difficult situation without assistance.

SCAVENGER (1596). The first *scavengers* were tax collectors. But despite the ancient aversion for the taxman, this was not a derisive epithet. Originally pronounced *scavager* before the insertion of *n* sometime during the 1500s, as happened also with *harbinger, passenger* and *messenger,* a *scavager* was an inspector who collected *scavage* (a duty levied on goods). Borrowed in the late fifteenth century from Old French *escauwage* (inspection) from *escauwer* (to inspect), in turn from the Germanic root that gave English *show, scavage* was the tax assessed through the "inspection" of goods. The responsibilities of the *scavager* were extended sometime around 1500 to include cleaning the streets, and some thirty years later the taxing duties were limited to refuse removal ("A *scavenger*'s cart happening to stand unattended . . . Mr. S. found it impossible to resist the temptation of shooting Mr. Silas Wegg into the cart's contents," 1865, Dickens, *Our Mutual Friend*). By the end of that century, *scavenger* referred more broadly to "a person or animal that removes dirt or decaying matter" ("The Swine . . . is the Husbandmans best *scavenger* . . . for his food and living is by that which would else rot in the yard," 1614, Gervase Markham, *Cheape and Good Husbandry*). As if to underline the heartless indifference toward child labor, in the nineteenth century a *scavenger* was a child employed to gather up the loose cotton lying on the floor and machinery in a spinning mill.

BALDERDASH (1596). When the Elizabethan playwright and pamphleteer Thomas Nashe wrote in a 1596 tract *Have with You to Saffron-walden,* "Two blunderkins [blunderers,

fools] having their braines stuft with nought but *balder-dash,"*
he was using *balderdash* in its earliest recorded sense, "froth
or a frothy liquid." From this, *balderdash* was extended to any
vile mixture of liquors ("Beer or butter-milk, mingled together . . . It is against my free-hold . . . to drink such *balderdash,"* 1629, Ben Jonson, *New Inn*). From liquors jumbled and
adulterated, *balderdash* was transferred to language that is
jumbled and nonsensical, the only extant sense, first used by
Andrew Marvell, one of the great Elizabethan poets and
dramaturges: "Did ever Divine rattle out such prophane *Balderdash!"* (1674, *The Rehearsal Transprosed*). If this is the actual
order of sense development, then the prehistory of *balderdash*
is problematic. One derivation may be that it is, at least in
part, from *balductum,* the fifteenth-century name for posset, a
sweetened and spiced hot drink of curdled milk and ale or
wine. *Balductum* was then transferred from "a posset" to
"nonsense" or "balderdash" ("The stalest dudgen or absurd-
est *balductum* that they or their mates can invent," 1593, Ga-
briel Harvey, *Pierce's Supererogation*). Most etymologists, however, treat the surviving sense of *balderdash* (nonsense) as the
earliest or original, despite the dating of the known citations.
This approach says that it is from a Scandinavian word akin
to Swedish dialect *ballra* (to bellow, prattle, tattle), Icelandic
baldrast and Norwegian *baldra* (to make a clatter), and Danish
balder (noise, clatter), which also gave English dialect *balder*
(to use coarse language), compounded with *dash* (to mix or
adulterate by adding something of a different quality). Like
slapdash, the original compound expressed a quick or confused sound, extended to a hodgepodge of sounds and then
generally to any mixture. Yet another derivation argues that
balderdash is from Welsh *baldorddus,* an adjective formed from
baldordd (idle chatter).

CLUE (1596). The Indo-European root **gel-* (a compact
mass or lump), through Proto-Germanic, gave English such
words as *cloud, clod, clot,* and *klutz,* and Old English *cleowen* (a
globular body or ball). The latter evolved into *clew* (a ball
formed by winding thread or yarn), a sense that Shakespeare
uses figuratively: "If it be so, you have wound a goodly *clewe"*

(1601, *All's Well That Ends Well*). But the most important literary event in this history is the Greek legend of Theseus, who was guided out of the Minotaur's Labyrinth by a ball of thread held by Ariadne. This notion of "threading" one's way out of a maze or labyrinth permanently changed the sense of *clew* ("By a *clewe* of twyn as he hath gon / The same weye he may returne a-non ffolwynge [following] alwey the thred as he hath come," 1385, Chaucer, *Legend of Good Women*) and its variant *clue* ("Having lost the *Clue* which led us in, / We wandered in the Labyrinth of Lust," 1596, Michael Drayton, *The Tragicall Legend of Robert Duke of Normandy*). Once the literal and literary senses were forgotten, the standard meaning of "something that indicates a solution," "a key" was left to stand on its own ("Seeking in the movements of the heavenly bodies for a *clue* to the accidents of life," 1628, Sir Kenelm Digby, *Voyages into the Mediterranean*).

PETARD (1598). We know this word almost exclusively from Shakespeare's original metaphor in *Hamlet:* "Let it work; / For 'tis the sport to have the enginer / *Hoist with his own petar,* " that is to say, harmed with his own weapon, caught in his own trap. Shakespeare's spelling is how the French pronounced *petard,* the word borrowed into English and the name of an explosive military device used to blow in a door or gate or to breach a wall. The petard was a metal or wooden case, originally bell-shaped, but later cubical, charged with powder and fired with a fuse that was unreliable enough to make a military engineer worry about being hoisted in the air from a too sudden detonation. The French word is a bit of soldiers' basic humor, from *peter* (to break wind, in Italian *petto*), in Old French *pet* (fart), borrowed into English ("Though all their cunning scantly be worth a *pet,* " 1515, Alexander Barclay, *Egloges*), and ultimately from Latin *pedere* (to break wind).

BIGOT (1598). In the twelfth-century French romance of Girard of Roussillon, *bigot* appears as the name of certain tribes of southern Gaul. This may be an Old French variant of *Wisigothus* (Visigoth), the Medieval Latin form being *Bigo-thi*. The Visigoths of southern France were Arians, followers of the doctrines of Arius (fourth century), which held the heretical view that Christ was separate from and lower than God. The Franks, on the other hand, were Catholic and would have considered the Arian Visigoths "despicable foreign heretics," the meaning they would have attached to *Wisigothus* or *Bigothi*. This more or less jibes with the earliest English sense of *bigot* (a religious hypocrite), but this derivation is more conjectural than proven. Another explanation suggests that *bigot* derives from Spanish *bigote* (beard, mustache), as in the expression *hombre de bigote*, which means not only "bearded man," but "spirited or fiery fellow," hence a zealot or *bigot* (a person who unreasonably and intolerantly espouses a particular religious creed or opinion). This history has even less evidence to support it. The most plausible etymology cites the work of the twelfth-century Anglo-Norman chronicler Wace: "The French have much insulted the Normans, both with evil deeds and evil words, and often speak reproaches of them, and call them *bigots* and dreg-drinkers." The French insult probably derives from the profane exclamation "by God!" and is popularly supposed to have its origin in an encounter between Charles III ("the Simple"), king of the West Franks, and Hrolf or Rollo, duke of the Normans. When the king commanded the duke to kiss his foot, the brave duke was said to have responded, "Ne se, *bi got*" (No, by God!). More likely the Norman soldiers, like all soldiers, were fond of profanity and adopted the English oath "by God!," in Middle English *bi god* (compare *begad*), which the French naturally associated with the Normans, eventually calling them **bigods* or *bigots*. Precedent for this is in Middle French *godon* (an Englishman), which is how the French heard the profanity *God damn* during the English occupation of France. The problem with this derivation of *bigot* is that it is not clear how its use as a derogatory term for a Norman developed into its first sense, "religious hypocrite." One possibility is that *bi god* or *bigot*, being a meaningless expression to a Frenchman, was confused with *beguin* (a religious devotee), thereby altering its meaning.

MACARONI (1599). When Yankee Doodle stuck a feather in his cap and called it "macaroni," he was not calling the feather a piece of hollow pasta; rather he was calling his appearance, his demeanor and pose that of a *macaroni* (a dandy, fop). Borrowed in the late sixteenth century from Italian *maccaroni* (a type of pasta, originally a mixture of flour, cheese, and butter), its ulterior origin is obscure. It may be from Italian *maccare* (to bruise, crush) referring to the crushing or milling of wheat into pasta flour, from Latin *macerare* (macerate). Or it may derive from Greek *makaric* (a sort of barley broth). In the mid-1700s, the *Macaroni Club* in London took its name from the members' affected penchant for continental fashion and taste, including a preference for foreign foods, macaroni being a novelty in England at the time ("The *Macaroni Club* which is composed of all the travelled young men who wear long curls and spying-glasses," 1764, Horace Walpole, *Letter to Earl Hertford*). *Macaroni* was transferred to the members themselves and then to any young man who mimicked continental dress and manners, something that parents and "the establishment" had difficulty abiding ("I wanted you to be a man of spirit; your ambition was to appear a first-rate *Macaroni;* you are returned fully qualified, and determined, I see, to shew the world what a contemptible creature an Englishman dwindles into, when he adopts the follies and vices of other nations," 1773, C. Hitchcock, in *Macaroni*).

COFFEE (c. 1600). Coffee, a plant indigenous to Abyssinia, was brewed there at least as long ago as the fifteenth century. Though there is no evidence to confirm it, some etymologists

trace *coffee* (French and Spanish *café,* German *Kaffee*) to the name of the Abyssinian province, *Kaffa,* where the trees grow wild. From Abyssinia, coffee spread throughout the Arab world, gaining great popularity there for its ability to dissipate drowsiness during long Moslem religious services. In Arabic it was called *qahwah* and in Turkish *kahveh* from a root meaning "wine." Considered an intoxicating beverage, it was proscribed by the *Koran;* yet it became to Arabia what tea was to China. Coffee did not arrive in Europe until the seventeenth century, and when it did, its name was probably taken directly from the Arabic or Turkish word (*"Coffee,* which makes the politician wise, / And see through all things with his half-shut eyes," 1712, Alexander Pope, *The Rape of the Lock).* The important social institution the coffeehouse soon appeared in Europe, the first one in England opening in London in 1652. Until about 1700, the world's limited supply of coffee came almost exclusively from Yemen, where the choice coffee known as *mocha* originated, named after the southern Yemen seaport from where it was exported.

CANDIDATE (1600). Political candidacy, like the word itself, is very old, dating back to Rome at least four centuries before Christ. The Roman office seeker campaigned in a toga, whose whiteness was intensified by rubbing chalk into it, the color being symbolic of the stainless integrity of the wearer. Latin *candidatus,* literally "clothed in white," from *candidus* (white), was transferred to the person seeking office. Not until the seventeenth century did English adopt it as *candidate,* by which time it had lost the original color symbolism of "fairness," "forthrightness," "honesty," that is still implicit in the related terms *candor* and *candid.*

SPENDTHRIFT (1601). *Spendthrift,* one who spends profusely or wastefully ("Fie, what a *spend-thrift* is he of his tongue," 1610, Shakespeare, *The Tempest*), sounds like an oxymoron: how can one spend profusely and be thrifty at the same time? But it is compounded with the archaic sense of *thrift,* "savings," "earnings" ("He . . . spends his *thrift* at dice," 1605, *The Famous Historye of the Life and Death of Captaine T. Stukeley*), and literally means "[one who] spends thrift or earnings." *Thrift* is from *thrive,* of Scandinavian origin, combined with the *-t* suffix that similarly formed *drift, gift,* and *rift.* A competing term in the sixteenth and seventeenth centuries was *dingthrift* ("Wilte thou therefore, a drunkard be / A *ding thrift* and a knave?," 1567, Thomas Drant, *A Medicinable Moroll*), from *ding* (to strike, beat, dash), literally, "to dash or ruin earned money." But before the end of the 1600s, *spendthrift* had thoroughly dinged its rival word.

GAZETTE (1605). The first *gazette,* or in the original Italian, *gazzetta* (news sheet), was published in Venice about 1536, and supposedly sold for a *gazet,* "a certain Venetian coin scarce worth our farthing" (1660, Randle Cotgrave, *A French and English Dictionary*). The value of the coin was so small that it could not have paid for the sheet itself, whether printed or handwritten, so if *gazet* is the source of *gazzetta,* the coin must have been the price paid merely to read it. Or there may be a completely different origin. An observer of the time noted the *gazzetta*'s decidedly yellow slant, typically containing "running reports, daily news, idle intelligences, or flim flam tales" (1598, John Florio, *A Worlde of Words, or Most copious and exact Dictionarie in Italian and English*). In short, it was a kind of tattle sheet, a late Renaissance version of the *National Enquirer* or similar modern tabloids. This suggests that *gazzetta* may be the diminutive of *gazza* (magpie) in the sense of "gossip," "idle chatter," the same notion behind the English newspaper titles *The Tatler* and *Town Talk.* In England, the name was transferred to the official government journal, *The Oxford Gazette*, first published in 1665 when the court was located in Oxford, becoming *The London Gazette* the following year. It appeared every Tuesday and Friday and listed announcements of pensions, government appointments and promotions, bankruptcies, and other public notices. The derivative, *gazetteer*, originally meant "one who writes in a gazette," but now only refers to a geographical dictionary, from the name of the first such work, written for gazette newswriters or gazetteers (1693, Laurence Echard, *The Gazetteer's: or, Newsman's Interpreter: Being a Geographical Index*).

WILLY-NILLY (1608). The original sense of *willy-nilly* was "willingly or unwillingly" and comes from the contraction of "will I, nill I" or "will he (she, you), nill he (she, you)," literally "with or without the will of the person concerned." For a time there was a competition over which would come first, *will* ("Will you, nill you, I will marry you," 1596, Shakespeare, *Taming of the Shrew*) or nill ("Your name will be inserted among the other authors—'Nill ye, will ye,' " 1787, Robert Burns, *Letters*). In the long run, *will* won willy-nilly. The archaic *nill* (to be unwilling) itself is a contraction of *ne*, a simple negative, and *will*, in Old English *nyllan*, from *ne* and *wyllan*. *Ne* is an ancient negating word that goes back practically unchanged to Indo-European **ne-* ("The lady . . . asked whi [why] he *ne wolde* [would not] with her speke," a. 1450, *The Book of the Knight of La Tour-Landry*). When combined with a verb, it is usually reduced to *n-* as in the Latin counterpart to *willy-nilly: nolens volens*. Today *ne* is obsolete, though it lives in words like *never, neither, naught,* and *no*. Over time *willy-nilly*, probably influenced by *shilly-shally*, a reduplication of *shall I*, acquired the meaning "vacillating" ("The *willy-nilly* disposition of the female in matters of love is as apparent in the butterfly as in the man," 1883, Francis Galton, *Inquiries into Human Faculty and Its Development*).

GHETTO (1611). The origin of *ghetto* is much disputed, but the first *ghetto* was a section probably of an Italian city, most likely Venice, where the Jews were required by law to live separately. The word first appears in sixteenth-century Italian and was adopted in English the following century ("Walking in the Court of the *Ghetto,* I casually met with a Iewish Rabbin that spake good Latin," 1611, Thomas Coryat, *Crudities*). One history of its origin dates it from 1516, when the Jews of Venice were expelled to an islet called *Gheto* or *Geto,* so named from a foundry, or *getto,* situated there. Another version argues that it is from *Egitto,* borrowed from Latin *Aegyptus* (Egypt). In eleventh-century documents, the Jewish ghettoes of Venice and Salerno were called *Judacaria,* and in the fourteenth century there is mention of the ghettoes "San Marino ad Judaicam" and "San Nicolò ad Judaicam." *Judaicam* may have become Italian *Giudeica,* eventually altered to *ghetto.* These explanations, however, are problematic because the pronunciations of *getto* (jātō), *Egitto* (ājētō), and *Giudeica* are so different from *ghetto* (getō). Some etymologists seek the origin in Yiddish or Hebrew *get* (deed of separation). The simplest version, favored by the *Oxford English Dictionary,* is that it is an abbreviation of *borghetto,* the diminutive of *borgo* (borough).

INVEST (1613). In the sixteenth century, the Dutch East India Company, which had a monopoly on the Spice Islands trade, made a fatal business mistake by nearly tripling the price of pepper. For the British, this was the last straw. To compete with the Dutch merchants, Queen Elizabeth incorporated the East India Company by royal charter in 1600, thereby institutionalizing capital investment. The 125 happy shareholders in the company reaped profits that rarely dropped below a hundred percent. At that time, *invest* was already in use in its borrowed Latin sense, "to clothe or envelop in a garment" ("They held the Universe to be a large suit of clothes which *invests* every thing," 1704, Jonathan Swift, *Tale of a Tub*), from *in* (in) and *vestire* (to dress, clothe), also the root of English *vest, travesty,* and *transvestite.* Its figurative meaning, "to clothe or endow with certain qualities," first appears in Shakespeare's *Othello* ("Nature would not *invest* her selfe in such shadowing passion, without some

Instruction," 1604). But it took the East India Company to make current its financial sense, "to commit money in order to receive an expected profit," as if one's capital were given a new form, clothed in a new way. This sense was adopted from Italian *investire* when another English trading company, the Levant or Turkey Company, picked the word up. It then passed into East India Company use ("To *invest* itt in Indico [indigo] to bee in Surrat before the raynes [rains]," 1615, T. Elkington, *Letter to the East India Company*) and from there into general English usage.

PITUITARY (1615). The anatomy of the *pituitary body* or *gland* has been known for centuries, but its function has been a mystery until relatively recently, with the discovery that all the other endocrine glands depend on it for stimulation, making it the "master gland." Because it is situated behind the nasal passage at the base of the brain, it was originally thought to have the lowly function of secreting the mucus of the nose, and was accordingly sometimes called the *phlegmatic gland* (see PHLEGM). This is in fact the earliest meaning of *pituitary*, "of or secreting phlegm or mucus," from Latin *pituita* (slime, phlegm), which also gave English *pituitous* ("Forth creeps the ling'ring snail; a silvery line . . . Marks his *pituitous* and slimy course," 1800, James Hurdis, *The Favorite Village*). Originally the Latin word meant "the moisture or resin exuded from trees" and is closely related to *pinus* (pine tree), that is, a tree yielding resin, hence English pine and *piñon*.

MUMMY (1615). The embalming recipe of the ancient Egyptians included large amounts of pitch or asphalt known in Persian as *mumiya,* from *mum* (wax). Arabic borrowed the Persian word and used it to refer to the embalmed body itself. Pitch or mumiya was also a key ingredient in the prescriptions of Greek and Roman medical authorities. Medieval physicians took this one step further, reasoning that the bituminous embalming formula that preserved or mummified human bodies would have even greater efficacy than mere pitch. This led in the Middle Ages to a brisk trade in Egyptian mummies,

which were shipped to Europe, where the asphaltic and fatty "exudations" in the wrappings were mixed in an unctuous or liquid medium, and used as a salve or taken as a medicine. The Arabic *mumiya* became Medieval Latin *mumia,* borrowed into English around 1400 as *mummy,* not, however, referring to the embalmed body itself but to the disgusting medical prescription ("And these dead bodies are the *Mummie* which the Phisitians [physicians] and Apothecaries doe against our willes make us to swallow," 1599, Richard Hakluyt, *Voyages*). This medical practice soon involved the use of ground fragments of the mummified bodies themselves. Eventually the whole rationale was lost and the prepared or dried flesh of executed criminals became one of the standard recipes of mummy in the pharmacopoeia, a practice that survived into the eighteenth century. It was not until about 1600 that *mummy* in English denoted the embalmed body itself.

IGNORAMUS (1616). The official report for 1631 of court cases brought before the Star Chamber, as the English court of justice was called in the fifteenth through seventeenth centuries (from the stars painted on the ceiling of the chamber), records that "At the precedent Assizes the Grand Jury found an *ignoramus.* " Contrary to appearances, this does not mean that they found an ignorant and foolish person wandering about the chamber. Prior to about 1800 *ignoramus* was strictly a Latin legal term meaning literally "we do not know," from *ignorare* (not to know), from *in-* (not) and *gnarus* (aware, knowing). It was the word that grand juries wrote on the bill of indictment when they found insufficient evidence to warrant a trial; otherwise, they wrote *Billa vera*, "a true bill." Today English grand juries use "not a true bill," or "not found" or "no bill," instead of *ignoramus*. The close association of *ignoramus* with law and lawyers was made explicit in a Latin play called *Ignoramus,* written by George Ruggle in 1615, his stated purpose being "to expose the ignorance and arrogance of the common lawyers." *Ignoramus* was the name of the main character and was intended to savage one Francis Brakin, the recorder or principal legal officer of the town of Cambridge. A tract published a few decades later, titled *The Case and Argument against Sir Ignoramus of Cambridge,* attempted to rebut Ruggle's play. We cannot say whether this little skirmish was ever resolved, but one outcome was that *ignoramus* had entirely shifted its meaning from the judgment passed by a grand jury to "a person of utter ignorance."

ACCOLADE (1623). In addition to a slap on the shoulder with the flat of a sword blade, the ritual of being knighted included a kiss and an embrace. Beginning in the seventeenth century, this ritualized salutation was called an *accolade,* from French *accolade* (an embrace around the neck), ultimately from Latin *ad-* (toward, before) and *collum* (neck). Though the name is relatively recent, the ceremony itself is much older. William the Conqueror is said to have initiated the tradition of slapping the shoulder when he gave his son Henry a blow when conferring knighthood upon him. For a time, this accolade was delivered with the bare fist, amounting to a box on the ear, but was eventually replaced with the gentle tapping of the sword. The current meaning of *accolade* (praise, award) is a late-nineteenth-century extension of the honor bestowed upon someone being knighted.

HOCUS-POCUS (1632). *Hokos Pokos* or *Hocas Pocas* was the alias of a famous conjuror ("Iniquity came in like *Hokos Pokos,* in a Iuglers [juggler's] jerkin, with false skirts," 1625, Ben Jonson, *The Staple of News*). He took his name from the gobbledegook formula that he intoned when working his "magic." In 1655 Thomas Ady, a chronicler of witches and witchcraft, described Hocus Pocus's stunts this way:

> I will speak of one man . . . that went about in King James his time . . . who called himself, The Kings Majesties most excellent Hocus Pocus, and so was called, because that at the playing of every Trick, he used to say, *Hocus pocus, tontus talontus, vade celeriter jubeo,* a dark composure of words, to blinde the eyes of the beholders, to make his Trick pass the more currantly without discovery. *(Candle in the Dark: or a treatise concerning the nature of witches and witchcraft)*

Hocus pocus or simply *hocus* came to refer to any conjuror or juggler ("Epitaph . . . On *Hocas Pocas*. Here *Hocas* lyes with his tricks and his knocks, Whom death hath made sure as his Juglers box," 1640, *Witt's Recreations with a Thousand Outlandish Proverbs*). Hocus Pocus may have taken his sham Latin formula from the Roman Catholic mass, *Hoc est corpus meum* ("This is my body"). Or he may have been playing on the Latin word *jocus* (joke, jest). As a popular formula of mock conjuring, it is first recorded in 1632 (*"Hocus-pocus,* here you shall have me, and there you shall have me!," Thomas Randolph, *Jealous Lovers),* and a decade or so later it appears in its most common sense, "trickery," "deception." Like rabbits out of a hat, *hocus-pocus* has produced several new words, mostly in American English and slang, including *hokey-pokey* (1847, deception, nonsense, ice cream sold by street vendors) and *hanky-panky* (1841, mischief, trickery). Abbreviated to *hocus* (deception), it produced *hoax* (1796) and, either blended with *bunkum* (nonsense) or merely as the mock Latin neuter *hocum* it became *hokum* (1917, pretentious nonsense), originally theater slang, which in turn became *hoke* (1928, fake) and *hokey* (1945, corny, mawkish).

QUACK (1638). Like the poor, quackery has always been with us and, except for one other, is the oldest profession. But its practitioners have been known as *quacks* (ignorant pretenders to medical knowledge and skill) only since the seventeenth century. The origin of this word is a minor etymological puzzle. It is generally agreed that *quack* is an abbreviated form of *quacksalver* with the same meaning, and that this in turn was adopted from Dutch *quacksalver,* now spelled *kwakzalver.* The origin of the Dutch word is in dispute. The second element, *salver,* probably derives from Dutch *salf* or *zalf* (ointment, salve) or *salven* (to salve). And most etymologists agree that the first element is the English word *quack* (to croak or quack), formed onomatopoeically from the sound that a duck makes (Dutch has *kwakken* and German *quacken*). Hence, a quacksalver is one who "quacks" or boasts of the virtues of his salves, a tradition continued in America by itinerant tonic or "snake-oil" salesmen barking their wares from wagons. Other etymologists do not agree with the quacking metaphor. Instead they derive the first element from Middle Dutch *quac* (unguent), which is related to *quagmire* and *quaver,* the Indo-European root having the basic meaning "sliminess." But such a redundant compound, "unguent" and "to apply salve," seems unlikely. Another derivation claims *quacksalver* is from *quicksilver* (mercury), which was used extensively in folk medicine but with results that would have brought the doctor's competence into question. *Quicksilver,* from *quick* (alive, living), was then modified by the quacking metaphor and the verb meaning "to salve."

SELFISH (1640). *Selfish* was coined by the Presbyterians during the mid-1600s, the period of their greatest influence in England ("A carnal *selfe-ish* spirit is very loathsome in what is spirituall," 1640, W. Bridge, *True Souldiers*). It replaced two perfectly good contemporary synonyms meaning "selfish or devoted to one's own interests exclusive of others," *self-ended* and *self-ful.* The *end* of *self-ended* means "aim" or "purpose" ("Publique spirits delight in their worke more then [than] their wages, but *self-ended* men love their wages better than their worke," 1645, W. Goode, *The Discovery of a Publique Spirit*), and *self-ful* means literally "full of self." *Self* itself was originally a pronoun going back to Old English and Proto-

Germanic, and did not acquire its full philosophical sense, "ego," until the seventeenth century ("A secret *self* I had enclos'd within, / That was not bounded with my clothes or skin," a. 1674, Thomas Traherne, *Poetic Works*). *Self* was celebrated in that self-same century with the creation of a large portion of the compounds that we use today, such as *self-abasing, self-abnegation, self-accusation, self-centered, self-conceit, self-concern, self-confidence, self-conscious, self-contained, self-contempt, self-defense, self-destruction, self-determination, self-esteem, self-evident, self-flattery, selfhood, self-interest, selfish, self-knowledge, self-made, self-regard, self-respect, self-righteous, self-seeking,* and *self-sufficient.*

LAMPOON (1645). Visiting a typical seventeenth-century French pub, one would probably hear a drinking song satirizing a famous person. Sometimes it was a scurrilous satirical poem instead, but both song and poem often had the refrain or chorus: "Lampone, lampone, camerada lampone," that is, "Guzzler, guzzler, my fellow guzzler," or some similar refrain with *lampone* or *lampons* (let us drink or guzzle), from *lampere* (to guzzle), a nasalized variant of *laper* (to lap), ultimately of imitative origin. So regular was the refrain that the song itself became known as a *lampon,* borrowed into English as *lampoon* (a harsh satire directed against a person).

BAGATELLE (c. 1645). "Vive l'amour! et vive la *bagatelle!*" wrote Laurence Sterne with typical verve and sentiment in a letter from Paris. *Bagatelle* in both English and in its French source means "a trifle," but its disputed history roots the French word in Italian *bagatella* (trifle). The Italian is the diminutive of the Parmesan dialect *bagata* (a tiny property), which may be from Lombard *baga* (a wine skin). The Lombard word is cognate with English *bag* and *baggage*. The fact that from the sixteenth century *baggage* meant "a trifle" supports this version of *bagatelle*'s history ("May decke her selfe simply . . . neither have these little trifling *bagages,*" 1579, Laurence Tomson, *Calvin's Sermons*). A more widely accepted history derives Parmesan *bagata* from Italian dialect *baga* (berry), a single berry being an insignificant bit of fruit. It in turn is from Latin *baca* (berry, pearl), borrowed from some non-Indo-European language, and akin to the name of the Thracian wine god *Bacchos*. In the early nineteenth century, *bagatelle* was extended to a short piece of light music, a trifling composition, usually for piano.

ELECTRIC (1646). In the Middle English era, *electrum* was amber, a hard fossil resin ("Of the pyne appyll tree cometh droppynge and woosynge [oozing] whyche is made harde . . . and soo tornyth [turns] in to a precyous stone that hyghte [is called] *Electrum,*" 1398, John de Trevisa, *Bartholomeus*), from Latin and Greek *elektron,* which also referred to an alloy of gold and silver, bright and yellow like amber, from *elektros* (gleaming, shining) and akin to *elektor* ("the shiner," the beaming sun) and Sanskrit *arka* (a sunbeam), ultimately of unknown origin. The British scientist William Gilbert, in his important treatise written in Latin *On the Magnet, Magnetic Bodies and the Great Magnet, the Earth,* used *electrica* (1600) to denote substances that had the same property as amber or *electrum* to attract or repel objects when rubbed. The property itself was not a new discovery, having been described centuries earlier by Thales of Miletus. From this scientific Latin term came English *electric* and *electricity.*

WHIPPING BOY (1647). The cruel and unusual punishment of whipping is very old, *whip* going back to Indo-European **weib* or **weip* (to turn, vacillate). The Romans considered it a humiliating punishment and the law forbade Roman citizens to be scourged. Similarly in medieval England, freemen could not be punished with the whip, though villeins and servants could be flogged almost at will. A young English prince, of course, could not be touched with the lash, even though he could misbehave as badly as the next boy. For this reason every prince had his own personal *whipping boy,* who was educated along with him and was flogged in his stead whenever the royal personage misbehaved and earned a whipping. The broadened sense of a SCAPEGOAT does not appear until about 1840.

PARAPHERNALIA (1651). In Roman law *parapherna* were the articles of property owned by a wife that were not part of the dowry she brought to her husband, literally "beside or beyond her dowry," from *para* (beyond) and *pherne* (dowry). The latter word of this Latin borrowing from Greek is related to *pherein* (to carry), in Latin *ferre,* the root of many English words, such as *fertile, confer, defer, offer, suffer,* and *transfer.* The concept of parapherna, or in Medieval Latin *paraphernalia bona* (paraphernal goods), abbreviated to *paraphernalis,* was transferred to legal systems based on Roman law, including the English, which borrowed the abbreviated form as *paraphernalia.* In English law, however, paraphernalia was restricted to the wife's personal belongings, such as clothing and jewelry. Early in the eighteenth century it was extended to "personal belongings or trappings," then to "furnishings, mechanical articles, or accessories," and finally to "appurtenances in general."

ALIMONY (1655). A man—or these days almost as likely a woman—paying *alimony* (a money allowance given to a former spouse as maintenance) may not feel particularly nourishing, but that is the root sense of the word. Jeremy Taylor used this earliest sense (nourishment) figuratively when he wrote, "These men will allow the Sacraments to be . . . spiritual *alimony*" (1660, *The Worthy Communicant*). English borrowed *alimony* in the seventeenth century directly from Latin *alimonia* (nourishment), from *alere* (to nourish) and *-monia* (state or condition). Ultimately from Indo-European **al* (to grow, nourish), the Latin word is also the root of *adolescent, aliment, alumnus,* and *coalesce.* In English, at least, there was a perfectly good word for "nourishment," namely *nourishment,* but there was no specific word referring to the support or maintenance payments made to an ex-spouse. And so the word survived only in this latter sense.

BUCCANEER (1661). *Buccaneers* were seventeenth-century swashbuckling adventurers and pirates of various nationalities united only in their antagonism toward Spain. They sailed primarily in the Caribbean, provisioning themselves on the islands of the West Indies, notably Santo Domingo, where immense herds of wild cattle wandered the hills. The Caribbean natives who had survived the Spanish extermination were skilled in preserving meat by drying and smoking it on a wooden frame called in French a *boucan,* borrowed from a Caribbean language such as Tupi, which has the word *mocaem* (a wooden frame for drying or smoking meat). From *boucan* came *boucaner* (to dry or jerk meat) and *boucanier* (one who dries and smokes meat on a *boucan*). The name was first applied to the French hunters of Santo Domingo, who prepared the meat of wild game in this way. Robinson Crusoe considered himself a *buccaneer* for a time ("Having been an old Planter at Maryland, and a *Buccaneer* into the bargain," 1719, Daniel Defoe, *Robinson Crusoe*).

AMUCK (1663). In the seventeenth century, Europeans returning from Malaya brought back stories of homicidal natives running berserk and attacking anything that got in their way. The Portuguese word for a frenzied Malayan was *amouco* or *amuco,* borrowed directly from Malay *amok* (in a murderous rage). The English subsequently adopted it, usually in the set phrase *to run amuck* ("Jealousy of the women is the usual reason of these poor creatures running *amock*," 1772, Captain James Cook, *Voyages*). Whatever the reason for such behavior—jealousy, religious frenzy, mushroom-induced hallucinations, or some other cultural propensity for running amuck—the references to Malayan society quickly died out and the word became a solid addition to English, usually meaning "wildly," "headlong" ("I might have run *'amok'* against society, but I preferred that society should run *'amok'* against me," 1854, Thoreau, *Walden*). For a time it was confused with *muck* ("And runs an Indian *muck* at all he meets," 1687, John Dryden, *The Hind and the Panther*).

TRUE-BLUE (1663). Blue has long been the color of unchangingness or constancy ("To newe thinges your lust is ever kene. / In stede of *blew,* thus may ye were al grene [green]," a. 1500, *Balade against Women Unconstant*), perhaps in reference to the unchanging color of the sky or to some special fast dye. The emphatic, rhyming expression *true-blue* ("*True blue* will never stain," 1672, William Walker, *Phraseologia*) originally referred to the Scottish Presbyterian or Whig party in the seventeenth century, the members having adopted blue as their color in contrast to the royal red.

SPICK AND SPAN (1665). Originally *spick and span* meant "new," literally new as a "spike and spoon," before it came to mean "like new," "clean and neat" ("My Lady Batten walking through the dirty lane with new *spicke and span* white shoes," 1665, Samuel Pepys, *Diary*). *Spick and span* is from earlier *spick and span new* ("They were all in goodly gilt armours, and brave purple cassocks apon them, *spicke, and span newe,*" 1579, Sir Thomas North, trans. of Plutarch's *Lives*), which is an emphatic extension of *span-new* (quite new). The emphasis is created by reduplicating the sound of *span* (spoon, chip) with *spick,* a similar process occurring in the Scottish variant *spank span-new* and in the Dutch and Flemish version *spikspeldernieuw,* literally "spick-and-spill-new," *speld* being a "spill or splinter." *Spick* is a dialectal variant of *spike* (nail) and complements the sense of *span* (spoon). *Span-new* itself is from a Scandinavian source, probably Old Norse *span-nyr,* literally "chip-new," fresh and clean as a chip newly chiseled from a wood block, compounded of *nyr* (new) and *spann* (chip), cognate with English *spoon,* the first spoons being wooden and flat like a large chip or spatula. The same metaphorical meaning of freshly cut wood also appears in Scottish *splinter-new* (in German *splinterneu,* Dutch *splinternieuw*). Similarly, something *brand new* (1570) is as if fresh and glowing like a "brand" (a burning coal of wood) on a hearth fire, an image that also gives *fire new* ("Your *fire-new* stampe of Honor is scarce currant," 1594, Shakespeare, *Richard III*).

MAROON (1666). When the Spanish transported slaves to the West Indies in the sixteenth century, some managed to escape and head for the hills, especially in Jamaica. These fugitives were called in American Spanish *cimarron* (a runaway), originally an adjective meaning "wild," "untamed," literally "living in the mountain tops," from Spanish *cima* (summit). French adopted the word in the clipped form *marron,* which also became the English word ("They will run away and get into the Mountains and Forests, where they live like so many Beasts; then they are call'd *Marons,* that is to say Savages," 1666, John Davies, *History of the Caribbee Islands*). Descendants of these escaped slaves are still called *maroons* in Jamaica. The word was current in the antebellum American South, where people escaped from their daily routine to go on *maroons,* camping trips or pleasure parties similar to a picnic but lasting longer ("On Monday we form a *maroon* party to visit some saw mills," 1785, *South Carolina Historical Magazine*). From the sense of a fugitive in the wilderness, *maroon* was extended to "lost in the wilds," with the piratical usage "to abandon someone in the wilds, especially on a desolate island or coast." *Marooner* then became a synonym for a pirate or BUCCANEER. The color *maroon* is of a completely different origin. A large sweet chestnut, native to southern Europe, is called in French *marron,* from a French dialect word predating Roman influence, perhaps a Ligurian word. The color sense of *marron,* borrowed into English in the eighteenth century, comes from the claret color of the chestnuts.

SALIENT POINT (1672). All *salient points* have a tendency to leap out at one (from Latin *salire* "to leap"), but in at least three different ways. The oldest *salient point* is an archaic medical term from Latin, *punctum saliens,* literally "the leaping point," but referring to the "leaping" point-size heart of an embryo (*"Punctum Saliens,* a little Speck or Cloud that appears in a Brood-egg, and seems to leap before the Chicken begins to be hatch'd," 1706, Edward Phillips, *The New World of English Words*), and going back to the writings of Aristotle. From this literal medical reference ("His end was not unlike his beginning, when the *salient point* scarce affords a sensible motion," 1672, Sir Thomas Browne, *A Letter to a Friend*), it was extended to "the starting point of anything" ("That was the *salient point* from which all the mischiefs . . . of the present reign took life," 1769, *Junius Letters*). This sense is now rare, but *salient points* are not. Like its Latin root, *salire* (to leap), the earliest (1646) sense of *salient* is "jumping or leaping upwards" ("Do beating hearts of *salient* springs Keep measure with thine own?," 1830, Alfred Tennyson, *Adeline*), which was extended to "jutting out," "prominent." A *salient point* could be a prominent bit of land ("The town is on a *salient point,"* 1844, Alexander Kinglake, *Eothen*), which has no direct relationship to the old medical expression, or it could be an "outstanding" idea or concept ("Some few *salient points* emerge full of eternal significance," 1863, Arthur Penrhyn Stanley, *Lectures on the History of the Jewish Church*), which is probably an extension of the medical jargon, the embryonic heart or starting point being the most significant and prominent.

MALL (1674). The recent custom in America of young people promenading—"hanging out" or "cruising" in the current vernacular—at the suburban *mall* is a tradition that goes back to at least seventeenth-century England, when the word was first current ("We see them in the *Maul* and in the Park walking, giggling, with their sparks [lovers]," 1706, *Reflexions upon Ridicule*). *The Mall,* with the definitive "the," was located in St. James's Park, London, and was a beautiful tree-lined promenade. The time of day when the throng of dandies and fashionable ladies was at its peak was called *high mall.* Originally, the St. James's Park mall was a long alley in which the game of *mall,* short for *pall-mall,* was played ("No sooner has he touched the flying ball / But 'tis already more than half the *Mall,*" 1661, Edmund Waller, *St. James's Park*). *Pall-mall,* a game in which a wooden ball was to be hit through a suspended ring at the end of the alley, was borrowed from French *pallemaille,* in turn taken from Italian *pallamaglio,* literally "ball-mallet," being a compound of *palla,* a variant of *balla* (ball), and *maglio* (mallet), from Latin *malleus* (hammer). In English, the *mall* originally referred to the mallet or *maul* used in the game ("Noe persons shall after play carry their *malls* out of S. James's Parke without leave of the said keeper," 1662, *Order-book*).

BLOODY (1676). When in George Bernard Shaw's *Pygmalion* (1912), unpolished Liza Doolittle uses the exclamation *bloody,* her genteel auditors are positively shocked: "Walk! Not *bloody* likely. *(Sensation)* I am going in a taxi." In the seventeenth and eighteenth centuries, however, *bloody* (very, exceedingly) was used by virtually everyone in colloquial speech ("He is *bloody* passionate. I saw that at the Hall," 1740, Samuel Richardson, *Pamela*), and no one was thought the worse for saying it. But in the nineteenth century and after, as the thoroughly Victorian *Oxford English Dictionary* puts it, *bloody* was

> constantly in the mouths of the lowest classes, but by respectable people considered "a horrid word," on a par with obscene or profane language, and usually printed in the newspapers (in police reports, etc.) "b——y."

The earliest appearances of the word are in the phrase *bloody drunk* ("The doughty Bullies enter *bloody drunk,*" 1684, John Dryden), which is to say "drunk as a blood," or in the old stock phrase *drunk as a lord,* a *blood* being an aristocratic rake or rowdy ("As many and as well-borne *bloods* as those," 1595, Shakespeare, *King John*). *Blood* is a reference to a well-born person's "good blood" or parentage ("They be worthy men of *blood,*" 1393, John Gower, *Confessio Amantis*) and may additionally allude to the old idea of the blood's being the seat of emotion or passion, as in *it stirs the blood, it makes the blood run cold, my blood boils,* and the phrase *in cold blood* (not in the heat of passion, deliberately). *Blood,* the bodily fluid, can be traced back to a Proto-Germanic root, **blothan,* but no further, since surprisingly Indo-European has no word meaning "blood." Once *bloody drunk* became current, it was extended to similar expressions like *bloody angry,* the natural association with bloodshed ("a bloody battle," "a bloody butcher") fixing it in the public's imagination. An alternative history, or perhaps a concurrent one, suggests a connection with the oath "'s blood!" *("'Sblood!* An arrant traitor as any is in the universal world," 1599, Shakespeare, *Henry V),* which, like *zounds!* (from *God's wounds*) and *gadzooks!* (from *God's hooks,* a reference to the nails on the Cross), is a profane allusion to the blood shed at the Crucifixion *("God's blood,* the King set me in the Tower," a. 1541, Sir Thomas Wyatt, *Defence).* Another less convincing version claims that *bloody* is a contraction of the mild oath "By our Lady."

CULPRIT (1678). At the murder trial of the 7th Earl of Pembroke, the earl is addressed as *culprit,* the first-known instance of the word: "*Clerk of Crown.* Are you guilty, or not guilty? *Earl.* Not guilty. *Cl. of Cr.* Culprit, how will you be tryed? *Earl.* By my Peers. *Cl. of Cr.* God send you a good deliverance" (1678, *State Trials).* The clerk, however, is not calling the Earl a guilty offender, the usual meaning today of *culprit,* but is acting out his part in the standard formula at the beginning of a felony trial. Formerly when the accused pleaded "Not guilty," the Clerk of the Crown replied in judicial French "Culpable: prest d'averrer nostre bille" (Guilty: ready to aver our indictment), that is, he stated that he was ready *(prest)* to begin the prosecution. Old French *prest,* and later variants *pret* or *prit,* are from Latin *praesto* (ready, hence *presto),* from earlier **prai* (at, before) and **hestos* (hand). The words *culpable prit,* abbreviated to *cul. prit,* were then entered on the record as showing that issue had been joined. Later when French was no longer used as the language of law, the formula *cul. prit* or eventually *culprit* was mistaken for a term of address to the accused. It did not imply guilt of an offense until the mid-eighteenth century, when it was confused with Latin *culpa* (fault, offense).

ALBATROSS (1681). In Portuguese, "pelican" is *alcatraz,* a name used by early seventeenth-century English voyagers to refer to the black frigate bird. Modified in English to *alcatras,* it was then mistakenly applied to the albatross. But because the albatross is a white bird, folk etymology, using Latin *albus* (white), altered the name to *albatross. Alcatraz* itself is a variant of Portuguese *alcatruz* (bucket of an irrigation waterwheel), with reference to another odd belief, that the pelican uses its large bucketlike beak to carry water to its young in the desert. *Alcatruz* is from Arabic *al-gadus* (the water jar), borrowed from Greek *kados* (jar), itself borrowed from either Phoenician or Hebrew *kad* (water jar). Arabic also calls the pelican *sagga* or *saqqa* (water carrier). The sailor's superstition that it is fatal to kill an *albatross,* the largest of webfooted sea birds, formed the basis of Samuel Taylor Coleridge's poem (1798) *Rime of the Ancient Mariner* ("Instead of the cross, the *albatross* / About my neck was hung"). The albatross of that poem then provided the metaphor for the extended sense of "a moral, emotional, or political burden" (Senator Bob Dole, referring to the slow-moving response of the Bush Administration to bailing out the savings and loan industry: "This thing could be an *albatross* in 1992, which happens to be an election year").

ACUPUNCTURE (1684). Although we think of *acupuncture* (the insertion of a needle into the skin for therapeutic purposes) as one of the "new age" therapies borrowed from the Chinese, England discovered it in the seventeenth century

("They have a two-fold method of Cure [in gout] . . . *Acupuncture,* and burning with their Moxa," 1684, *Bonet's Mercurius Compitalitius*). The Oriental word for the technique was not adopted, however; a new word was coined from Latin *acus* (needle), also the source of *acumen, acute,* and *eglantine,* and English *puncture,* itself ultimately from Latin *pungere* (to prick, pierce), hence also *point, poignant, compunction,* and *pungent.* For a time, the awkward *acupuncturation* was also used ("The famous Operation of the Chinese and Japonese, termed *Acupuncturation,"* 1743, Lorenz Heister, *General System of Surgery*).

BULLY (1688). When Pistol in Shakespeare's *Henry V* (1599) says of the young King Henry, "I kiss his dirty shoe, and from heartstring / I love the lovely *bully,"* he is in no danger of offending the king, whom he unknowingly addresses. This is *bully*'s earliest and, to us, most surprising use—as a term of endearment similar to "sweetheart" or "darling," and applied to either sex. The positive connotations of the noun were then extended as an adjective meaning "worthy," "admirable," "excellent" ("The cook will give you a *bully* dinner," 1855, William Carleton, *Willy Reilly*). Borrowed in the sixteenth century from Dutch *boel* (lover, brother), it is perhaps from Middle High German *buole* (lover, friend, relative), but cannot be traced back any further. The underlying sense, "lover," was transferred to "one who lives by protecting prostitutes" ("Mars the Celestial *Bully* they adore, / And Venus for an Everlasting Whore," 1706, Daniel Defoe, *Jure Divinio, a Satyr*), and then to the more general current sense, "one who is cruel or abusive to a weaker person." Or it may have gotten to this last meaning along a different path, beginning with *bully boy* (fine fellow), which became the pattern for later combinations such as *bully ruffian* (a tough) and *bully-huff* (a bullying boaster). *Bully* was then extracted from these phrases to stand on its own with the new meaning "an abusive or cruel person."

BEAR/BULL (c. 1700). In the early eighteenth century *bears* were sold at the stock exchange ("Being at that General Mart of Stock-Jobbers called Jonathans . . . he bought the *bear* of another officer," 1709, Sir Richard Steele, *Tatler*). A *bear* in this earliest sense is a stock sold but not turned over to the purchaser until a later date. In the meantime, the seller expects the price of the stock to fall below the rate he has contracted to sell it for, so that he can make a profit ("Instead of changing honest staple for Gold and Silver, you deal in *Bears* and *Bulls*," 1714, C. Johnson, *Country Lasses*). Such a speculator was called a *bearskin jobber* ("Every secret cheat, every *bear-skin jobber*," 1726, Daniel Defoe, *The Political History of the Devil*). The original phrase was probably *to sell the bearskin*, an allusion to the well-known saying recorded since the 1500s: "To sell the bear's skin before one has caught the bear," which, of course, is what the bear speculator does. *Bear* was then transferred from the stock to the speculator himself, and then to a falling market. *Bull* (a buyer of stocks who expects them to rise in value, originally the stocks themselves), just the opposite of a *bear*, was probably adopted as a contrasting animal that tosses upward with its horns, whereas the bear pulls down with its paws ("And all this out of Change-Alley? Every Shilling, Sir; all out of Stocks, Tuts, *Bulls*, Rams, Bears, and Bubbles," 1721, Colley Cibber, *Refusal*).

TOAST (1700). From at least the fifteenth century, it was a culinary custom to put *toast*, spiced bread browned over a fire, into wine or other beverages ("Go, fetch me a quart of Sacke, put a *toast* in 't," 1598, Shakespeare, *Merry Wives of Windsor*). A drunk or "soak," like toast soaking in wine, was sometimes called a *toast* ("Bring my father a Quart; I'll be hang'd if 'twill do the old *Toast* any hurt," 1709, *Rambling Fuddle-Cups*). The word itself is borrowed from Old French and is ultimately from Latin *torrere* (to parch), also the root word for *thirst* and *tostada*. Drinking to a person's health is an old custom, but the English word for it, *toast*, is supposed to have originated with an incident that took place at Bath, England, during the reign of Charles II (1660–84). One of the reigning belles of the season was observed standing in a bath, whereupon all but one of several admirers drank to her health from the water.

The dissenting wag instead requested the toast, alluding to the woman herself, as if she were the spiced toast flavoring the drink. Whether the incident actually occurred or not, the metaphor of the woman as the spiced toast in a drink is probably the origin of this usage ("More censorious than a decayed Beauty, or a discarded *Toast,*" 1700, William Congreve, *Way of the World*). By about the mid-1700s, the word was broadened first to refer to any person, event, or institution whose well-being or honor is drunk to, and then to the custom itself.

TESTIS (1704). Both this word and *testicle,* which is considerably older (c. 1425), were borrowed directly from Latin *testis* (male sex gland), a special use of *testis* (witness), also the source of *testify, testimony,* and TESTAMENT. The testes are so called because they bear witness to a man's virility. The same thing is true in French *temoins,* literally "witnesses." English also borrowed (c. 1480) Latin *testis* as a legal term meaning "witness" ("The saide Edward Hall, your great maister and *testis,* was about the compiling of his storie," 1563, John Foxe, *Actes and Monuments*). But because of the inevitable mirthful ambiguity between the two uses of *testis,* the legal sense died out.

CONDOM (1705). With the scourge of AIDS, *condom* has virtually become a household word. The earliest reference occurs in a 1705 letter claiming that the Duke of Argyll, when he entered the Scottish Parliament in that same year, "brought along with him a certaine instrument called a *Quondam,* which occasioned ye debauching of a great number of Ladies of qualitie, and our young gentlewomen." Eighteenth-century English also referred to it as "armor," "machine," "Cundum shield," and "preservative," its original purpose not being as a contraceptive, but as a shield or preservative against disease. The origin of *condom* has evaded etymologists for over two centuries. The most popular and long-lived derivation claims that it comes from the name of the supposed inventor, a physician, one Dr. Condom (or Condon or Cundum). But *Condom* and *Cundum* are not British names, and, although *Condon* is, the rules of English phonology cannot account for a switch in the pronunciation of the final "n" to an "m." In any case, more than a few scholars have searched in vain for evidence of Dr. Condom, who now keeps company with the London plumber Thomas *Crapper,* the American distiller named BOOZE, and the artistic sailor *Scrimshaw.* The French, famed for their amorous propensities, have lent their name to several terms associated with illicit love-making, including *French pox* (syphilis) and *French letter* (condom). It is understandable, then, that the town called Condom in southern France be proposed as the origin of *condom.* But there is no evidence connecting the town with the prophylactic. Moreover, the French pronunciation of Condom (kõ dõ) is too different from the pronunciation of *condom* to have been its origin. Another derivation resorts to Latin *condum* from *condus* (that which secures, preserves, reserves), probably through Greek from Persian *kondü* or *kendü* (an earthen vessel for storing grain); but this version is also questionable. For now at least, the history of *condom* remains a conundrum.

NINCOMPOOP (1706). Samuel Johnson in his famous dictionary suggests with his usual learnedness that *nincompoop* (fool, simpleton) is from Latin *non compos* in the phrase *non compos mentis,* literally "not of sound mind" ("Fashion, though a goddess, is a fool, and all her worshippers . . . are *nincompoops,*" 1807, Eaton S. Barret, *Rising Sun*). Later etymologists embellished Johnson's claim by proposing that *non compos* was influenced by *ninny* (silly fellow, simpleton), *ninny* itself probably abbreviated from *"an inno*cent." But Johnson's etymology does not jibe with the earliest forms, *nicompoop* and *nickumpoop.* A more plausible history argues that *nincompoop* was formed in the same manner as *tomfool,* a compound of a proper name, *Tom,* and *fool.* The name or first element in *nickumpoop* is *Nick* from *Nicholas* or *Nicodemus,* which is used in French for "a fool." The last element is probably English slang *poop,* "to deceive, cozen, befool" ("We shall . . . trumpe and *poope* him well enough if . . . he will needes fall a comedizing [ridiculing] it," 1596, Thomas Nashe, *Saffron Walden*), probably related to Dutch *poep* (fool, clown). Compounded with *noddy* (fool), *poop* (to befool) is found earlier in the nincompoop synonym *poopnoddy* (blockhead, fool), literally "to befool or cozen a simpleton." It has the variant *noddypoop* (a fool, to befool).

GNOME (1712). Short, stocky, and bearded, *gnomes* were supposed to be the inhabitants of the interior of the earth and guardians of veins of precious metals and other subterranean treasures. Each of the four elements (air, earth, water, fire) had natural inhabitants ("According to these Gentlemen [the Rosicrucians], the four elements are inhabited by Spirits, which they call Sylphs, *Gnomes,* Nymphs, and Salamanders. The *Gnomes* or Daemons of Earth delight in mischief," 1712, Alexander Pope, *Rape of the Lock*). Gnomes are so thoroughly at home in the earth that they can move through their element as easily as fish do through water and birds through air. The name may derive from Greek *gnome* (intelligence, thought), since gnomes were said to be intelligent and could provide intelligence about the secret treasures of the earth. The Swiss alchemist and physician Paracelsus (1493–1541), who refers to *Gnomi* as a synonym of Pygmaei in several of his works, may have invented the word, perhaps whole cloth or perhaps with Greek *gnome* in mind. Another possibility is that it is from quasi-Greek **genomos* (earth dweller), patterned after *thalassanomos* (dwelling in the sea).

WHISKEY (1715). Although the practice of distilling fermented liquor is very ancient in the Far East, perhaps as old as 2000 B.C., a method for distilling wine was not discovered in Europe until the twelfth century, probably by alchemists working in Salerno, Italy. The distilled liquor was called in Medieval Latin *aqua vitae* (alcohol, spirits), literally "water of life," which, translated into Irish-Gaelic, became *uisge beathadh, uisge* (water), rooted ultimately in Indo-European **wed-* (whence also English *water, wet, wash,* and *otter*), and *beatha* or *bethu* (life), cognate with Greek *bios* (life). Elizabethan English borrowed the Irish word as *usquebaugh* ("She filles them then with *Uskebeaghe,*" a. 1581, John Derricke, *The Image of Ireland*) altering it to *whiskybae,* and then shortening it to *whisky.* The Russians chose not to translate the Latin *aqua vitae,* but called distilled liquor "little water" or *vodka,* which also derives from the Indo-European root **wed-* but on the Slavonic branch *(*wod-a).* English borrowed *vodka* in the nineteenth century to refer specifically to liquor distilled from potato mash.

RIGMAROLE (1736). In the medieval French game of chance called *rageman* or *ragman,* strings were attached to verses or other items on a written roll and players drew a string at random. In one version of the game, amusement was the sole object and the verse corresponding to a player's string described a personal characteristic of the player. Other versions were probably gambling games. The name of the game is probably from Anglo-French *Ragemon le bon,* literally "Ragemon the good," which was the title of one set of verses and the name of one of the characters. The list or roll of verses itself was called, not surprisingly, the *ragman's roll* or *ragman roll.* Another derivation notes that a set of rolls, called the *ragman rolls,* recorded the instruments by which the Scottish kings and nobility were compelled to subscribe their allegiance to Edward I of England in the 1290s. These rolls, which were preserved in the Tower of London, had numerous seals with dangling pendants, giving the documents a "ragged" look, which at least one etymologist claims is the origin of *ragman.* Another history connects it with *Ragman,* a nickname for the Devil, probably of Scandinavian origin, such as Icelandic *ragmenni* (a craven person, coward) or Swedish *raggen* (the Devil). In this version, a *ragman roll* was the Devil's list of names. Because a list of items is often long and rambling, in the 1500s *ragman roll* came to refer to any roll or catalogue of items ("All the heresies that they have in all theyr whole *raggemans rolle,*" 1532, Sir Thomas More, *Confutacyon of Tindales Answere*), while in Scottish, perhaps in allusion to the lists recording fealty to King Edward, *ragman* referred to "a long or rhapsodic and usually pointless discourse." By the early eighteenth century, *ragman roll* was altered to *rigmarole* and essentially had the same meaning as the Scottish term two centuries earlier, "a long-winded, unimportant harangue" ("His speech was a fine sample, on the whole, Of rhetoric, which the learn'd call *'rigmarole,'*" 1818, Lord Byron, *Don Juan*). Since the 1930s, we usually hear *rigmarole* used in its most recent extended sense, "a foolish and lengthy procedure or activity" ("The Government set up . . . the whole *rigmarole* of scheduling, listing, and building preservation orders," 1955, London *Times*).

NAMBY-PAMBY (1745). In the petty battles perennially fought in the literary world, the skirmish between the great English poet Alexander Pope, aptly nicknamed "the Wasp of Twickenham," alluding to his venomous pen, and Ambrose Philips, a forgotten pastoral poet, is one of the few to have enriched English with a new word, *namby-pamby*. In 1713 Philips, who was a Whig and held various appointed government posts, was praised by the influential Whig newspaper, *The Guardian,* as being the only worthy successor of Spenser, subtly implying a comparison with Pope's pastorals. Incensed by this silly criticism, the Tory Alexander Pope went on the attack, writing an anonymous article for *The Guardian* in which he compared his poetry with Philips's and with supreme irony gave preference to his rival. With the publication (1725–26) of Philips's childish adulatory poems, dripping with sentiment and addressed "to all ages and characters from Walpole steerer of the realm, to miss Pulteney in the nursery," Pope's friend and fellow poet Henry Carey joined the squabble by parodying Philips and writing: "So the Nurses get by Heart *Namby Pamby's* Little Rhimes." Carey coined the nickname by playing on the diminutive of *Ambrose, Amby,* and adding the alliterative *P* from *Philips*. His parody captured the weakly sentimental and insipid character of Philips's poetry that became the definition of *namby-pamby:* "*Namby-Pamby*'s doubly mild, / Once a man and twice a child . . . / Now he pumps his little wits / All by little tiny bits." Pope struck the fatal blow in 1733 by using Carey's coinage in his satiric and popular poem *The Dunciad:* "Beneath his reign shall . . . *Namby Pamby* be prefer'd for Wit." The name caught the public's fancy, and to Philips's horror, it became a common term for a weak and wishy-washy person.

SERENDIPITY (1754). It is relatively rare in word history that a consciously invented word becomes an established part of the language. But when there is a need for a new word—a kind of semantic hole or void that needs to be filled—and when the proposed word is able to catch the fickle and mysterious public fancy, then it will take root. *Serendipity* (an ability to make happy or valuable discoveries by accident) did just that. Sometime in 1754 Horace Walpole, politician and man of letters, serendipitously coined it from the title of the Persian fairy tale "The Three Princes of Serendip." The heroes of the tale, as Walpole explained, "were always making discoveries, by accidents and sagacity, of things they were not in quest of." *Serendip* is an old name for Sri Lanka, known in Walpole's time by the old name *Ceylon,* and is from Arabic *Sarandib.* Just as English *Ceylon* is a "corruption" of *Sri Lanka,* Arabic *Sarandib* is an alteration of the Sanskrit name of the island, *Sinhaladvipa,* from *sinhala* (resplendent land).

NICKEL (1755). Niccolite, the copper-colored ore from which the Swedish mineralogist Baron Axel von Cronstedt first extracted nickel in 1751, was known in German as *Kupfernickel,* literally "copper demon," *Kupfer* or *copper* coming ultimately from Greek *Kypros,* Cyprus, where the metal was mined in ancient times, and *Nickel* (dwarf, goblin, mischievous demon), originally a nickname for *Nickolaus.* The ore earned its name because it was deceptive and tricky, having little or no copper despite its appearance. Cronstedt named his newly discovered metal *nickel,* which he shortened from *kopparnickel,* a partial Swedish translation of *Kupfernickel.* In the United

States, nickel was used in minting coins and became the name of a one-cent piece (1857) and then a five-cent piece (1883).

BOOZE (1768). *Booze* is a variant of *bouse* or *bowse,* "to drink deeply," "to guzzle" ("Hail ye holi monkes . . . depe cun ye *bouse* that is all yure care," c. 1300). It also meant "liquor" ("Drynke to hym deorly of fol god *bous . . .* / When that he is dronke ase a dreynt mous" [Drink to him dearly of full good booze . . . / Until he is drunk as a drowned mouse], c. 1300, in Wright, *Specimens of Lyric Poetry*). After these early citations in Middle English, *bouse* went underground for a couple of hundred years and reemerged as thieves' and beggars' cant in the sixteenth century, then passed into general colloquial use ("They lye *bowzing* and beere-bathing in their houses every after-noone," 1592, Thomas Nashe, *Pierce Pennilesse*). *Bouse* is probably a borrowing of Middle Dutch *buisen* (to drink deeply) and *buise* (large two-handled drinking vessel). The root of the latter is *buis* (tube, pipe) or *bus* (box, urn), akin to English *box* and German *buchse,* from Late Latin *buxis,* ultimately from Greek *pyxis* (box), in allusion to its construction from *pyxos* (wood of the box tree). Another version traces the Dutch borrowing *buisen* or *busen* to an old, lost root that was also the source of English *bosom* and *boast,* the underlying sense being that a drunk or boozed-up person typically boasts and puffs up his chest. Another story, probably apocryphal, derives it from E. G. Booze, an American distiller who sold his whiskey under his own name in log-cabin-shaped bottles. If there really were cabin bottles labeled with this name, it is likely that the name derives from the older English *bouse,* and not from a distiller's name. *Boozer* (a drunk or tippler) did not appear until the early nineteenth century. At the end of that century, in England it also meant "a pub."

BOUDOIR (1781). A *boudoir* (a woman's dressing room) to the French, with their highly refined sensibilities and corresponding accouterments, was a room where one could retire after being offended to sulk or pout. It is from French *bouder* (to pout, sulk), whose ulterior origin is lost in obscurity, though some guess it to be of imitative origin (the sound of a pout?), while others speculate that *bouder* is from the same root as *pout, b* and *p,* and *d* and *t,* being expected substitutions of sounds in Indo-European word development. The French in this were not being sexist, since the *boudoir* was originally not for women only, but was also a man's private apartment, where he too could go and pout.

❋ IV ❋

THE
INDUSTRIAL REVOLUTION
and the
VICTORIANS

The English of the New Middle Class

BACKGROUND

Even though English had more or less become standardized by the end of the Early Modern English Period, its vocabulary continued to grow. The language responded to the need for thousands of words to describe the new knowledge resulting from advances in science and industry. Technological advances brought railroads and led to factories and machines and products that required naming.

Consequently the language mirrors the "progress" of this century as seen in words like *horsepower, concrete, refrigerator, lithograph,* and *photograph* and *photography,* this latter pursuit contributing a significant vocabulary of its own, including *camera, film, enlargement, emulsion, shutter,* and *focus.* Progress in the last quarter of the nineteenth century is captured by many new words and meanings, such as *apartment house, aeroplane* or *airplane, battery, blueprint, drop forging, feminist, fundamentalist, marathon, motorcycle, oilfield, telephone,* and *typewriter.*

The nineteenth century saw the English vocabulary expand with discoveries in chemistry, which gave new words like *acrylic, amino,* and *protein.* Biology and medicine contributed *aerobic* (coined by Louis Pasteur); *bacterium* (from Greek "stick," "rod"); *nuclear* and *nucleus* (from Latin meaning "little nut"); *botulism* (from Latin for "sausage"); *poliomyelitis* and *polio* (from Greek "gray" plus "marrow"); and *vaccine* (from Latin *vacca* "cow"). From physics came *cathode* (from Greek "way down," that is, the path the electric current was supposed to take from the electrolyte into the negative pole, compare *anode* and *electrode*) and *galvanize* (from the Italian scientist Luigi Galvani).

Many of the new scientific words relied heavily on Greek and Latin, but other nonscientific words also had their origins in these two staple languages of English loan words, including *aryan* (ultimately from Sanskrit); *aegis* (Greek *aigis,* the shield of Zeus); *gorilla* (Greek *Gorillai;* the name of a group of wild, hairy creatures); *procrustean* (in allusion to the legendary Greek thief Procrustes, who stretched the bodies or cut off the legs of his guests so they would fit in his bed); and *python* (originally the name of the serpent that Apollo killed near Delphi).

French remained an important source of new words through the nineteenth century. Among the new French loans were *canard* ("false rumor," from *canard,* "duck," in the expression "to half sell a duck," that is, to not sell it at all, hence "to deceive" as by spreading false news); *cab* ("taxi," from *cabrioler,* to "caper," "leap," from its bouncing motion); *foyer* (from *foyer,* "the room for actors to rest when not on stage"); *mayonnaise* (from Mahón, a seaport of Minorca captured by the Duc de Richelieu, whose chef invented *mahonnaise* to commemorate his boss's triumph); *restaurant* (from "food that restores," from *restaurer,* to "restore," "refresh"); *rococo* (from *rocaille,* "shellwork"); *toilet* (from *toilette,* a "cloth," "bag for clothes"); *mascot* (from *mascotte,* "sorcerer's charm," "good-luck piece"); *picayune* (from the name of a coin of little value); *silhouette* (from Étienne de Silhouette, French minister of finance who was fond of amateurish outline portraits); *pari-mutuel* ("system of betting on races"); *pornography* (ultimately Greek "prostitute" plus "write"); *svelte* (ultimately Italian "slim," originally "pulled out," "lengthened"); *rhinestone* (a loan translation of French *caillou du Rhin,* "Rhine pebble," so-called because this paste jewelry was originally made in Strasbourg, a city near the

Rhine River in northeastern France); and *brouhaha* ("noisy confusion").

The expansion of the British Empire that had begun in Renaissance England reached its height during the nineteenth century. Expanded commerce with the world meant a greater variety of borrowings from virtually every corner of the globe. For example, from Spain, English borrowed *aficionado* ("a devotee of a sport or other activity," literally "fond of ") and *mascara* (Spanish "soot," "stain," "mask"), and from Italy, *tutti-frutti* ("all fruits"). From India and the Hindi language came *pajamas* (ultimately from Persian, meaning "leg clothing"). *Caddy* (a small chest) is from *catty,* a measure of weight established by the East India Company, which took the word from Malay, the measure of a chest of tea being transferred to the chest itself. From Japanese came *rickshaw* from earlier *jinrikisha* (*jin,* "man," plus *riki,* "power," plus *sha,* "cart," "carriage") and *judo* ("softness" or "gentleness" plus "way" or "art"). From China came *pidgin,* not from Chinese itself, but from the Chinese pronunciation of English *business, business English* (Pidgin English), being the mixed Chinese-English language of Chinese and English traders and merchants.

Historical events also contributed to the nineteenth-century English vocabulary. The French Revolution gave TERRORISM, *aristocrat, guillotine* (from Joseph Guillotin, a physician who advocated its use, but who was not the inventor), and *chauvinism* (after Nicolas Chauvin, a fanatical devotee of Napoleon). *Ambulance* (French, literally "walking hospital") came into use during the Crimean War, when wagons or carts were used extensively for carrying casualties. The dye *magenta* was discovered in the year of the Battle of Magenta, Italy, 1859. Militant nationalists have been around for a long time, but were not called *jingos* (hence, *jingoism*) until Disraeli sent a British fleet into Turkish waters to resist the Russian advance in 1878. The word is taken from the refrain "By jingo!" in a nationalistic music-hall song that became the theme song for those eager to fight the Russians.

Although *strike* (refusal to work to force an employer to meet certain demands) was first used late in the eighteenth century, organized strikes did not really come into their own until the nineteenth century. This sense of the word is from the lowering or "striking" of a ship's sail as a symbol of sailors' refusal to go to sea. The closely related usage *scab* (a strikebreaker) first appeared in 1806, an extension of the earlier meaning of "one who refuses to join a trade union," from *scab* (a low, mean fellow), ultimately from Latin "to scratch." A more tragic note is the entry into English of Yiddish *pogrom* (an organized massacre, ultimately from Russian "by," "through" plus "to thunder," "roar") around 1880.

Slang terms for the first time entered the general vocabulary in significant numbers, as *mooch* (to sponge off others, probably from Middle English *mychyn,* to "pilfer," "steal"); *crazy as a loon* or *drunk as a loon* (probably with reference to the bird, but also influenced by *loony* and *lunatic*); *lulu* ("a remarkable person or thing"); *lush* ("drunkard," from *lush,* "juicy and tender," "growing thick and green"); *gadget* (originally sailors' slang, perhaps from French *gachette,* "piece of a mechanism"); *wangle* (printers' slang for "faking by manipulation"); *flunkey* (of unknown origin); *fogey* (of Scottish origin); *spiffy* (of uncertain origin, but probably originally dialectal); *snob* (Cambridge University slang for a "townsman" or "local merchant"); *slob* (from Irish "mud," "slime"); and *a dead ringer* (originally a horse-racing term for "a horse entered fraudulently in a race").

During the nineteenth century the direction of linguistic influence across the Atlantic began to be reversed. Many American English terms came into wide use in Britain and its English-speaking colonies, such Americanisms as *o.k.* or *okay* (one of the most widely known and etymologized of all Americanisms); *stogie* ("cigar," from *Conestoga,* the drivers of these wagons being associated with smelly cigars); *bronco* (an American borrowing from Spanish, "a knot in wood"); *Uncle Sam* (humorous expansion of the initials "U.S." and originating during the War of 1812); *smart aleck* (after Aleck Hoag, notorious pimp and confidence man in New York City); *hoodlum* (probably originating in San Francisco and perhaps from German dialect for "ragamuffin"); *stump speech* (literally a speech given while standing on a stump); and *running mate* (originally a horse-racing term referring to the horse in a race that sets the pace for another).

In many ways the nineteenth century as a discrete period in

the history of the English language is more artificial than usual, all divisions of time in linguistic history (or for that matter in history itself) being convenient fictions. But it was a time of great events, of social and scientific changes that are to one degree or another captured in the following word histories.

CRETIN (1779). There may be *cretins* on Crete, but the original cretins were in the Swiss Alps. In the Swiss French dialect of Valais or Savoy a congenitally deformed and mentally deficient person was called a *crestin* or *crétin,* which is from Old French *Chrestien* (Christian) and Latin *Christianus.* In most European languages, the word for "Christian" was used in the sense of "human being" as distinguished from brute animals ("A fitter food for a horse than a *Christian,*" 1749, Henry Fielding, *Tom Jones*). Even a person of extreme mental and physical deformity was a human or Christian or *cretin.* A similar development occurred in French *benêt* (simpleton, idiot) from Old French *benoit* (blessed) and Latin *benedictus,* and in the use of *innocent* ("In body deformed, in minde foolish, an *innocent* borne," 1579, John Lyly, *Euphues*) and *natural* ("I own the Man is not a *Natural;* he has a very quick Sense, though very slow Understanding," 1722, Sir Richard Steele, *The Conscious Lovers*).

OXYGEN (1790). Though the English chemist Joseph Priestley was the first to isolate and describe oxygen in 1774, he gave it the unfortunate name *dephlogisticated air,* because he believed it to be common air with its *phlogiston* removed. Along with other famous chemists of the time, Priestley subscribed to the "phlogistic theory," an alchemical hypothesis formulated in 1702 by Georg Stahl. Phlogiston was believed to be a "substance" that existed in combination in all combustible materials. When something burned, phlogiston was supposed to be released, the more violent the combustion, the larger the amount of phlogiston present; hence the name *phlogiston,* from Greek *phlogistos* (burnt up), from *phlox* (flame), akin to *phlegein* (to burn). Another chemist, K. W. Scheele, working independently, announced a year after Priestley that he had isolated the element, which he called *empyreal air.* When it was discovered that oxygen in the free state was essential to all life, it was also called *vital air.* But it took the French chemist Antoine Lavoisier, to give the newly discovered gas a name that would stick. Lavoisier mistakenly believed that oxygen was essential in the formation of acids, and in 1777 he accordingly proposed the name *principe oxygine,* a few years later altered to *principe oxygène* (1785), which he intended to mean "acidifying principle," from Greek *oxys* (sharp, sour, acid) and French *gène* (that which produces). A year later, the name was shortened to *oxygène.* It was also Lavoisier's work, specifically his discovery of the composition of water, that was the *coup de grâce* to the theory of phlogiston.

URANIUM (1797). When the German chemist Martin Klaproth in 1789 isolated a yellow metallic oxide from pitchblende, he named the metal *uranium* in honor of the planet newly discovered by Herschel, Uranus. Sir William Herschel had first thought that the object in his telescope in 1781 was a comet, but after studying its movement for a few weeks, he realized he was looking at a planet. He named it *the Georgium sidus* or *the Georgian planet,* in honor of his patron King George. In England, the seventh planet from the sun was commonly called either *the Georgian planet* or *Herschel* well into the nineteenth century, but neither term was ever adopted on the continent. Instead, in keeping with the mythological names of the other planets, the German astronomer Johann Bode proposed the Greek god *Uranus,* husband of Gaia, or Earth, and father of Cronos, or Saturn, and whose name is from Greek *ouranos* (heaven, sky). When Klaproth discovered another metallic element a few years later, he called it, by analogy with *uranium, titanium* from *Titan,* one of the race of giants in Greek mythology. In the early 1940s, with the discovery of two synthetic chemical elements that follow uranium in the periodic table, they too were given planet names. *Neptunium,* the first element after uranium, was named for the planet Neptune (from the Roman god of the sea), the first planet beyond Uranus. And just as Pluto (from the Greek god of the subterranean world of the dead) is the planet after Neptune, *plutonium* is the element after neptunium.

TERRORISM (1798). We think of *terrorism* as a recent word for a recent phenomenon, but it has been used for almost two hundred years. *Terror,* of course, has been around an even longer time. Borrowed into Middle English from French *terreur,* it is ultimately from Latin *terrere* (to frighten) and Indo-European **tres-* (to tremble), hence *terrible, terrific,* and *deter.* But *terrorism* is rooted in the Reign of Terror (1793–94) during the French Revolution, also known as "the Terror" and "the Red Terror," because of the brutal and bloody murder of anyone, regardless of sex or age, whom the Revolutionary Tribunals regarded as obnoxious. The *terrorists* in this horrific time were the so-called Jacobins, the Tribunals and their agents, and the ironically named Committee of Public Safety headed by the infamous Robespierre. Both *terrorist* and *terrorism* first appear in English in reference to the French Revolution, but almost as soon were extended to their present general senses.

AMMONIA (1799). Ammonia salts or *sal ammoniac* (salt of Ammon, ammonium chloride) has been known since at least the time of Pliny (first century A.D.), who makes reference to it. It was used pharmaceutically and in the manufacture of ammonium alum used in dyes. Originally, the salts were prepared from camel dung near the temple of Jupiter Ammon in Libya, *Ammon* being the Greek form of the Egyptian deity *Amun.* In 1774, Joseph Priestley first isolated ammonia gas and called it "alkaline air," a choice as logical as his name for OXYGEN, "dephlogisticated air," and as unpopular. It took a non-English chemist, Torbern Bergman, to give it a lasting name (1782), which he took from the name of the salts used to form the gas.

HYSTERIA (1801). By the late nineteenth century, when Sigmund Freud did his pioneering work on the causes and treatment of *hysteria* (a psychoneurosis characterized by emotional outbursts and physical and sensory disturbances), the disorder had already been described millennia earlier by ancient physicians. But because it seemed to be a woman's affliction, as evident, for example, in the German name for it, *mutterweh* (literally "mother woe"), instead of placing the causes of hysteria in the psyche of the patient, the ancient doctors located them in a malfunctioning uterus or, in Greek, *hystera.* The Greek word gave the adjective *hysterikos* (belonging to or suffering of the womb), which through Latin became French *hystérique,* borrowed into English in the seventeenth century as *hysteric* (characterized by hysterical fits and convulsions). *Hysteria* was then formed as an abstract noun corresponding to the adjective *hysteric.*

DOMINO (1801). *Dominoes,* a game played with twenty-eight flat rectangular pieces or *dominoes,* was not invented until the eighteenth century, probably in Italy. The English word, however, and probably the game, are borrowed from the French. Earlier, a *domino* was a kind of hooded cloak worn by canons or priests, the French word deriving from Latin *dominus* (lord, master), perhaps in reference to the priests who wore it. Or a priest's cloak may have been called a *domino* half in jest by association with the common liturgical phrases priests used containing *Domino* (Lord), such as *benedicamus Domino* (let us praise the Lord). *Domino* was extended to the loose cloak that has a small mask covering the upper part of the face and that is worn at masquerades ("Reserve . . . is a bad *domino* which only hides what good, people have about 'em, without making the bad look better," 1836, Dickens, *Sketches by Boz*). This masked cloak is probably the origin of the name of the game: tiles or pieces made of ebony resembled the black cloak, and the pips or dots looked like the eyes of the mask.

PHANTASMAGORIA (1802). Before there were movies, TV, and videos, there was the *magic lantern,* essentially the precursor of the schoolteacher's "overhead projector," a device that uses a large magnifying lens to project on a screen or wall pictures painted on glass. Invented in the seventeenth century and exhibited in 1665 at Lyons by a "learned Dane" who called it *Laternae magicae,* the device provided much entertainment ("A *Magic Lanthorn* [sic], a certain small Optical Macheen, that shews by a gloomy Light upon a white Wall, Spectres and Monsters so hideous, that he who knows not the Secret, believes it to be perform'd by Magick Art," 1696, Edward Phillips, *The New World of English Words*). A conjuror and inventor named Philipstal modified the magic lantern so that the projected figures could be manipulated to appear to grow or shrink in size, or to dissolve and vanish. He presented his invention, which he called a *phantasmagoria,* at an exhibition of optical illusions in London in 1802. His invention's sensational name was probably intended as a bit of hype, a mouth-filling combination of Greek *agora* (assembly, place of assembly) and *phantasm,* from French *fantasme,* ultimately from Greek *phantasma* (mere appearance, image) and *phantos* (visible), which have the root *phan* of *phainein* (to show, appear), and are also the source of English *phantom.* Both the device and the name caught the public's fancy, and, alluding to the bizarre images projected on the wall, *phantasmagoria* soon meant "a shifting succession of things seen or imagined" ("Such was the *phantasmagoria* that presented itself for a moment to my imagination," 1835, Washington Irving, *Newstead Abbey*) and then more generally, "a constantly changing scene" ("The wildest frolic of an opium-eater's revery is nothing to the *phantasmagoria* of the sky tonight," 1856, Elisha Kane, *Arctic Explorations*).

PIANO (1803). *Piano* is shortened from Italian *pianoforte,* an instrument invented by the curator of Prince Ferdinand dei Medici's large collection of musical instruments, the Paduan harpsichord maker Bartolommeo Cristofori, around 1710. Although in certain gross respects the pianoforte resembles the earlier *harpsichord* (from *harpe,* "harp," and Latin *chorda,*

"string," "cord"), whose strings are plucked by quills attached to a keyboard, its true predecessor is the *dulcimer* (from Latin *dulcis,* "sweet," and *melos,* "song"), whose strings are struck with small hammers. More closely resembling the piano was the *clavichord* (from Latin *clavis,* "key," and *chorda*), popular during the sixteenth through eighteenth centuries. It used small metal wedges to strike the strings, producing a very delicate tone. But during the eighteenth century, the piano essentially supplanted these earlier instruments, when musical taste gradually favored the volume and expressiveness of the piano. Cristofori called his invention *gravecembalo col piano e forte* (harpsichord with soft and loud), which described the gradation of tone and volume that a performer could achieve in contrast to the unvarying sound of the harpsichord. This cumbersome name was soon shortened to *piano e forte* (soft and strong), then to *pianoforte* and then by the late eighteenth century further shortened to *piano.* Italian *piano* is from Latin *planus* (smooth, graceful, flat, even), ultimately from Indo-European **pelə* (flat, to spread), also the root of numerous other English words, such as *plain, plane, explain, palm, planet, plastic,* and *plaster.*

YOKEL (1812). The history of *yokel* (a stupid rustic, a country bumpkin) is made especially difficult because the several proposed versions are all plausible, except perhaps for the claim that it is a figurative use of English dialect *yokel* (green woodpecker), the implicit "green" referring lamely to the greenness or naïveté of a country lout. The woodpecker's name is itself probably an imitation of its call. Another version claims another bird, the owl, is involved. Though we usually think of owls as being wise, in the past, more often than not, this dopey, blinking, dull-seeming bird was a symbol of stupidity. Latin *ulucus* (owl), for example, is the root of Spanish *loco* (stupid, crazy), and English *goof* may ultimately be from Italian *gofo* from *guffo* (owl). In this view, *yokel* may derive from Shetland *yuggle* (owl), which is akin to Danish *ugle* (owl). Even more plausible is the version that relates it to *yoke,* this being an important farm implement used to yoke or join draft animals. In English dialect, a *yokel* is a ploughboy who does the day's ploughing or *yoking* ("Stretching their limbs with the keen zest of those who for three hours at a *yoking* have sat their saddles," 1897, Lord Ernest Hamilton, *The Outlaws of the Marches*). Finally, another interpretation claims that it is from German *Jokel,* a derogatory term for a farmer, the diminutive of *Jakob.* There is good precedent for taking a man's name and using it in a derisive way to refer to a rube or hick. *Rube,* for example, is the pet name for *Reuben,* and *Hick,* spelled *Hikke* in the fourteenth century, is an old nickname for *Richard.*

MAGNESIUM (1812). Before he discovered this silver-white metal in 1807, Sir Humphry Davy used *magnesium* to refer to manganese, another metallic element. Although it was not until a couple of decades later that another chemist isolated the metal, Davy deduced the existence of the element and derived its name from *magnesia* or magnesium oxide ("That magnesia consists of *magnesium* and oxygene, is proved both by analysis and synthesis," 1812, Davy, *Elements of Chemical Philosophy*). In the Middle Ages, *magnesia* referred to two different minerals: lodestone, a naturally occurring iron ore with magnetic properties, and a silvery stone, perhaps talc. *Magnesia* was ultimately taken from Greek *Magnesia lithos* (lodestone), literally "Magnesian stone," from Magnesia, a region in Thessaly where the stone is found. In alchemy, it was supposed to be one of the components of the philosopher's stone. But its most popular and still current use refers to hydrated magnesium carbonate, a white chalky powder used as an antacid and cathartic. This use was probably influenced by modern Latin *magnes carneus,* literally "flesh magnet," because the white powder adheres strongly to the lips, proving that it has the same attraction for flesh that the lodestone does for iron.

SHORT SHRIFT (1814). *Shrift,* or in Old English *scrift,* is a borrowing of Latin *scriptum* (script, writing). Early in its English history, it meant "penance" (c. 1030) and "confession" (c. 1175), probably from the notion of a prescribed or "written" penalty. When a convicted criminal was required to pay the ultimate penalty, he was allowed a *short shrift,* that is, a brief or *short* moment to make his *shrift* or confession, before execution ("Make a *short shrift,* he longs to see your head," 1594, Shakespeare, *Richard III*). Sir Walter Scott, who popularized many other archaisms, is given credit for the now well-known figurative meaning of *short shrift,* "summary treatment or little mercy or consideration" ("They are like to meet *short shrift* and a tight cord," 1823, Sir Walter Scott, *Quentin Durward*).

FALDEROL (c. 1820). Old songs often have meaningless refrains, such as *tra-la-la* or *fal-al-deral* ("Wildair [sings] *Fal, al, deral!,*" 1701, George Farquhar, *Sir Harry Wildair*), that become so well known that they take on a separate life of their own ("Some rough native harp / Strikes up With English *fol-de-rolling,*" a. 1847, Eliza Cook, *Happy Mind*). Because the phrase itself is nonsensical and trifling, *fal-de-ral* came to refer to "a flimsy or useless thing" ("None of your *fal-de-ral* lavender boots, but rigid, unmistakeable shoes," 1861, George Sala, *Dutch Pictures*) and then more generally to "nonsense," "balderdash" ("There was a feast, and plenty of pleasant palaver and *fol-de-rol,*" 1883, Mark Twain, *Life on the Mississippi*).

MORGUE (1821). When Matthew Arnold in a letter of 1863 referred to "an amiable family" that had "nothing at all of the English *morgue,*" he was not alluding to a place where dead bodies are housed until identified. Instead, he was using the older French borrowing, *morgue* (haughty demeanor, pride), which originally meant "a sad or solemn facial expression." Although it is tempting to relate it to Latin *mors* (death), which is the root of *mortuary* and *mortician,* it is probably from Old French *morguer* (to look at solemnly), and before that, from Vulgar Latin, **murricare* (to pout or make a face) and **murrum* (snout), ultimately of imitative origin. A section of one of the Paris prisons where the guards viewed new prisoners to establish their identity was called the *morgue,* probably because of the solemn, defiant expressions on the inmates' faces. Later *The Morgue* was the name of a small building in Paris where bodies were viewed for identification. After its adoption into English in the early nineteenth century, it became primarily an American usage.

SCAPEGOAT (1824). When William Tyndale came to *Leviticus* 16:8 in the Bible, he translated it as: "And Aaron cast lottes over the II gootes [two goats]: one lotte for the Lorde, and another for a *scapegoote*" (1530). In the great annual fast of atonement, the goat that was chosen by lots to be the Lord's was sacrificed as a "sin offering." After the sins of the people were symbolically placed upon the head of the other goat, the *scapegoat,* literally "the goat that escapes," it was released into the wilderness. Other versions of the Bible of the time gave similar interpretations. The Vulgate refers to the live goat or scapegoat as *caper emissarius* (goat that is sent out), and the Coverdale Bible (1535) calls it the "free goat." Strictly speaking, these interpretations are faulty. In Hebrew, the freed goat is called *'azazel,* which Tyndale interpreted as *'ez ozel* (goat that departs) and translated with his own coinage, *scapegoat.* But the Hebrew word is a proper name, thought to be that of a demon or devil, and probably originated with the Canaanite deity *Aziz.* The transferred meaning of "one who bears the blame for others" first appears in print in 1824.

TOADY (1826). *Toadies* don't cause warts, but in the seventeenth century their fawning, sycophantic behavior gave them a bad case of indigestion. The first *toadies,* originally called *toad-eaters,* literally ate toads as a profession ("I inquired of him if William Utting the *toad-eater* . . . did not once keepe at Laxfield; he tould me yes, and said he had seene him eate a toade, nay two," 1629, John Rous, *Diary*). A toad-eater was typically in the employ of a charlatan who sold nostrums that were said to be so powerful and universal that they could even act as antidotes to a dread poison allegedly found in toads. This was no small concern for seventeenth-century gourmands, for to mistakenly eat a toad's leg for a frog's leg, like eating toadstools instead of mushrooms, supposedly meant certain death. To prove the efficacy of his cure-all, the charlatan would put on a good show and compel his obsequious assistant to eat a toad (or pretend to eat one). The *toad-eater* would then feign convulsions and death, whereupon his master would administer a swig of the elixir and restore the *toad-eater* to health ("Be the most scorn'd Jack-pudding in the pack, / And turn *toad-eater* to some foreign Quack," a. 1704, Thomas Brown, *Works*). The pathetic sight of the cowering assistant made *toad-eater* and its abbreviated diminutive, *toady,* natural terms for similarly subservient behavior.

LIMELIGHT (1826). Thomas Drummond, a British inventor and administrator, while attending lectures given by Michael Faraday at the Royal Institution, learned that when oxygen combined with hydrogen in the presence of calcium oxide or lime a brilliant light was given off. Drummond was involved in the geological survey of Great Britain in the early 1820s, and at the front of his mind was the problem of making distant surveying stations visible. He constructed a lanternlike apparatus containing a block of lime heated with an oxyhydrogen flame, and in 1825 the *Drummond light,* as his spotlight was first called, was successfully used to measure the distance—sixty-seven miles—between Divis Mountain, near Belfast, and Slieve Snaght. In 1829, the *limelight* as it was now called ("The naked eye can detect no difference in brightness between the electric light and the *lime light,*" 1860, John Tyndall, *The Glaciers of the Alps*), was used in a lighthouse. But its best-known use in the nineteenth century was in theaters to throw a bright light on important actors ("When Shakespeare played Hamlet and Macbeth, he had neither *limelight,* footlights, scenery, costumes, nor stage machinery," 1886, Frederic Harrison, *The Choice of Books*). Its figurative use, *to be in the limelight* (to be in the full glare or center of public attention), first appeared toward the end of the century and survives today long after limelights have become defunct and forgotten.

MORPHINE, HEROIN (1828, 1898). When the German pharmacist F. W. A. Sertürner in 1816 isolated a powerful drug from opium that relieved pain and induced deep sleep, he called it *morphin* in honor of *Morpheus,* Ovid's god of dreams, the son of Sleep. Ovid coined Morpheus, literally "fashioner or molder," from Greek *morphe* (form, shape), because the god gave dreams their insubstantial forms. *Heroin,* the name and the drug synthesized from morphine were also German concoctions. Friedrich Bayer and Company registered *Heroin* as a substitute for morphine in the 1890s. Clinical trials of the drug supposedly showed that it was nonaddictive and would be useful as a cure for morphine addiction, relieving the withdrawal symptoms. Its name is probably from Greek *heros* (hero), because taking the drug makes the user feel superhuman, inflated, and euphoric. The sap of the poppy plant or *opium* has been used since ancient times. The name in English is a fourteenth-century borrowing from Latin *opium,* ultimately from Greek *opos* (juice) and Indo-European **swokwos* (resin, juice).

LUNCH (1829). Considered in the early nineteenth century a vulgar usage, *lunch* (a midday meal) was abbreviated from *luncheon,* under the influence of the older form and sense of *lunch,* a "thick piece" or "hunk" ("He shall take breade and cut it into little *lunches* into a pan with cheese," 1600, Richard Surflet, trans. of Estienne and Liebault's *Maison rustique*), a lunch or simple midday meal often consisting of a "hunk" of bread and cheese, though *luncheon* also originally meant a "piece" or "hunk" ("Eating a great lumpe of bread and butter with a *lunchen* of cheese," 1617, Fynes Moryson, *An Itinerary*).

This earliest sense of *lunch* and *luncheon* may be an alteration of *lump,* the same relationship that exists between *hump* and *hunch* (hump, protuberance) and *bump* and *bunch* (protuberance). The primary source of *luncheon,* however, is probably Middle English *nuncheon* (a light snack taken between main meals and consisting typically of bread, cheese, and beer). *Nuncheon* ("Some say there is . . . no Dinner like a Lawyer's, no Afternoon's *Nunchion* like a Vintner's," 1694, Sir Thomas Urquhart, trans. of *Rabelais*) and its earlier form *noneschench* meant literally "noon drink," from *none* (noon) and *schench* (drink, cup). *None,* hence *noon,* is from Latin *non hora* (ninth hour or 3 P.M.) which changed to 12 o'clock when church prayers were moved back from the ninth to the sixth hour. *Schench* is from Old English *scenc,* akin to *scencan* (to pour out liquor), ultimately from Proto-Germanic **skankon* (shinbone), because a hollow bone or pipe was used to draw off liquor.

RAMSHACKLE (1830). In Norse law a house could legally be *ransacked,* that is, searched for stolen goods. Borrowing from Old Norse *rannsaka,* a compound of *rann* (house) and *saka* (to seek), Old English extended the word to mean "to plunder." A seventeenth-century variant of *ransack* was *ransackle,* which gave the verbal adjective *ranshackled* (ransacked, plundered). This became *ramshackled* (rickety, rundown), as if something were ramshackled from being ranshackled or ruined from plundering. Alternatively *ramshackle* may derive from Scots *camshachle,* to "distort" or "twist awry" ("An ye think tae *camshachle* me wi' your bluidthirsty fingers," 1819, Rennie, *St. Patrick*), compounded from *cam* (crooked), of Celtic origin and *shachle* (to distort), perhaps from the root of *shock. Shack* (a crude hut or cabin) is probably a back formation from *ramshackle.*

HUMBLE PIE (1830). It may be humiliating to *eat humble pie,* but to the hunter of old it was his exclusive privilege. Overlooking the dining hall from his dais, the medieval lord dined on venison, while the official huntsman and his henchmen took lower seats and ate a pie made of the deer's *numbles* (the inner organs of an animal: heart, liver, intestines, etc.). In Old French *nombles* (loin or fillet of beef or venison) was a considerable cut above the humble innards of English *numbles*. The French loan word is ultimately from Latin *lumbus* (loin), also the origin of English *loin, lumbago, lumbar,* and *sirloin.* By the fifteenth century, *numbles* was usually pronounced *umbles* ("I'll give them leave to give mine *umbles* to the kites and ravens if they find me conferring my confidence where it is not safe," 1826, Sir Walter Scott, *Woodstock*), and two centuries later the pie was called *umble pie.* Because it was the food of inferiors, *umble pie* was folk etymologized to *humble pie, humble* (lowly, not proud), itself being a thirteenth-century borrowing from French *umble* that goes back to Latin *humilem* (low, slight, mean, insignificant), referring to the lowly ground or earth, in Latin *humus.* But it was not until the nineteenth century that the metaphorical phrase *to eat humble pie* (to be forced to do something very humiliating, to apologize abjectly) came into use ("Trying to think what was the very *humblest pie* I could eat," 1883, Howells, *Register*), perhaps modeled on the Lincolnshire dialect expression *to eat rue-pie* (to rue, repent).

MATCH (1831). During the eighteenth century, many inventors tried futilely to come up with a chemical means of igniting a fire. Not until 1827 was a friction match invented by John Walker, an English apothecary. Four years later a French student, Charles Sauria invented a phosphorus match, and in 1836 a practical phosphorus match was patented in the United States. The name *match* was a natural choice, a simple extension from the older senses of the word. Since the sixteenth century, a match was either a long fuse made of rope or cord used for firing cannon and firearms ("It was a Morian slave that strangled him with a *match*," 1657, Sir Thomas North trans. of Plutarch's *Lives*) or a cord, cloth, or paper dipped in melted sulfur and ignited with a tinder box, used domestically to light a candle or set fire to fuel. Early chemical-tipped matches were sometimes called *lucifer matches* or *lucifers,* a whimsical reference to the ruler of hellfire, probably used to distinguish them from the old tinder-box versions. The original sense of *match* was "the wick of a candle or lamp," a Middle English borrowing from Old French *mesche*, thought to be ultimately a blend of Latin *muccus* (mucus of the nose) and Latin and Greek *myxa* (lamp wick, nozzle of a lamp, nostril), the spout of a lamp resembling a nostril, the wick corresponding to mucus.

HOBNOB (1831). To *hab or nab* meant in the 1500s "hit or miss" ("The citizens . . . shot *hab or nab* at randon [sic] up to the roodloft and to the chancell," 1586, John Hooker, trans. of Giraldus Cambrensis' *Irish Historie*). It derives from Middle English *habbe* (have) and its negative counterpart *nabbe* (have not) as in *habbe he, nabbe he* (have he or have he not, cf. WILLY-NILLY). By Shakespeare's time, *hab or nab* or *hab nab* had been altered to *hob or nob* or *hob nob* (have or have not, give or take). It often appeared in the expression *to drink hob or nob,* which referred to two persons toasting or drinking to each other alternately, one imbiber "giving" the toast and the other "taking" it. This was shortened to *hob or nob* ("Having drank *hob-or-nob* with a young lady in whose eyes he wished to appear a man of consequence," 1772, Richard Graves, *The Spiritual Quixote*) and often used as a verb meaning "to drink together" ("We *hobbed and nobbed* with . . . the celebrated bailiff of Chancery Lane," 1840, William Makepeace Thackeray, *The Paris Sketch-Book*). From the association with "drinking companion" came the latest senses of *hobnob,* "to be on familiar terms with" ("An honest groom jokes and *hobs-and-nobs* . . . with the Kitchen maids," 1844, William M. Thackeray, *Little Travels*) and "to be in close companionship with" ("I might be *hob-and-nob* with you now in your dungeon," 1859, Thackeray, *The Virginians*).

EVOLUTION (1832). Most of us think of Charles Darwin as the originator of the theory of evolution, which brought into question the whole Victorian world view of a divinely created and directed universe. But it was Charles Lyell who first used *evolution* in its modern sense, "the origin of species as a process of development from earlier forms" ("The testacea of the ocean existed first, until some of them by gradual *evolution,* were improved into those inhabiting the land," 1832, Lyell, *Principles of Geology*). *Evolution,* however, had been in the English lexicon since at least the mid-seventeenth century, when it was adopted from Latin, in which it meant the unrolling of a book, from *e-* (out) and *volvere* (to roll). Since in ancient Rome books were scrolls, to open one was to unroll it. The scroll or rolled manuscript itself was sometimes called a *volumen,* hence English *volume* (a book that is part of a set) as well as *vault, volt, voluble, involve,* and *revolve.* English books, of course, had long since evolved from rolled scripts to bound pages, so *evolution* was used metaphorically for any process of unfolding or opening out ("The whole *evolution* of . . . ages, from everlasting to everlasting, is . . . represented to God at once," 1667, Henry More, *Divine Dialogues*), a sense that was easily transferred in the theory of evolution to the unfolding of new natural forms from earlier ones.

VAUDEVILLE (1833). In Normandy there is a small river called the *Vire,* whose valley was home to a certain Olivier Basselin, the composer of many light, sometimes satiric, songs in the fifteenth century. So popular did his songs become they were given the name *chanson du Vau de Vire,* "song of the valley of Vire," which was shortened to *vau de vire* and *vaudevire.* The obscurity of the name *Vire* led to the folk-etymologized version with *ville* (town), *vau de ville* or *vaude-ville,* and sometimes further altered using *voix* (voice), *voix de ville,* though this latter did not survive. The English borrowed the word in the early eighteenth century to refer to any light, popular song topical or satiric in nature and performed on the stage ("Whenever Carbonel sings his delicious *vaudevilles* we think of you," 1818, Lady Morgan, *Autobiography*). About a century after the word first appeared in English, it was broadened to its current meaning, "an amusing or comic stage performance interspersed with light songs" ("Is this world and all the life upon it only like a farce or *vaudeville,* where you find no great meanings?," 1876, George Eliot, *Daniel Deronda*). But the British favored the French synonym *variété* (a variety or vaudeville show), and left *vaudeville* to the Americans ("There are *vaudeville* theatres in America and *variety* theatres in England," 1911, George Bernard Shaw, in London *Daily Graphic*).

TEETOTALER (1834). In early nineteenth-century America one of the many highfalutin creations of the exuberant, exaggerated backwoods lingo known as "tall talk" was *teetotally* (wholly, completely), an emphatic form of *totally* ("[A Kentucky backwoodsman said] These Mingoes . . . ought to be essentially, and particularly, and *tee-totally* obflisticated off of the face of the whole yearth," 1832, James Hall, *Legends of the West*). Tall-talk *teetotally* may be the origin of *teetotal* (complete, total), which the fledgling temperance movements in England and the United States adopted to refer to "total" or absolute abstinence from alcoholic drink. Another derivation claims that the temperance *teetotal* was first used by an artisan, one Richard Turner of Preston, England, in 1833 in a speech that took the advocacy of earlier reformers, who practiced abstinence from hard liquor only, one step further, maintaining that "nothing but *te-te-total* will do." One account of this event claims that Turner was a stutterer, but more likely he was merely being emphatic. Or he may have been using a colloquialism current in Lancashire meaning "absolute," "complete." Another account places the origin of *teetotal* in the American temperance movement. The principal in this story is one Reverend Joel Jewell, who founded a temperance society in 1817 that, like the early English reformers, bound the members to abstinence from ardent spirits only. But ten years later Jewell advocated total abstinence and in Lansing, New York, introduced written pledges binding the signers either to the "old pledge," hard-liquor abstinence only, placing "O.P." before their names, or to the "new" or "total pledge" indicated by a "T." on their pledge cards. The frequent need to explain the "T." eventually made the collocation "T.—total" familiar, hence, *teetotal*. Given the zealous and nearly simultaneous birth of the temperance movement in the two countries, it is possible that both stories are correct and that the word originated independently on both sides of the Atlantic.

LEFT, CENTER, RIGHT (1837, political spectrum). In 1789, the fateful year when the French Revolution exploded, the so-called Third Estate or representatives of the common people of France created the governing body known as the National Assembly. First meeting in the Church of St. Louis, the Third Estate was joined by the other two estates, the clergy and the nobility. The body of nobles took the seats of honor on the President's right, and the Third Estate sat on his left. This purely ceremonial arrangement quickly took on political significance. The commoners and the forces of change, and therefore democratic and liberal views, were associated with the *left,* a loan translation of French *la gauche;* while the politically and socially conservative stance of the nobility was represented by the *right,* from French *droite.* Both terms first appear in English in Carlyle's *The French Revolution.* Logically enough, the *center* became synonymous with politically moderate opinion located between the extremes of right and left parties.

PIGGYBACK (1838). The origin of *piggyback* (up on the shoulder or back) and of the earlier English dialect form *pig back* has nothing to do with pigs mounted on one another, except in the popular imagination. The original expression was *pick-a-back,* first appearing in the sixteenth century with variants *a pick back* ("To [too] easy . . . is that way to heaven, whereto we may be caried a *pickback* on a Roode [Cross]," a. 1565, James Calfhill, *An Answere to Martiall's Treatise of the Crosse*) and *a pick pack* ("[In China] we overtook a beggar and his wife traveling *pick-a-pack* along the stone road," 1894, *Outing*). These early versions refer to a *picked pack,* that is, a pack or parcel slung or pitched—in English dialect *picked* (pitched or thrown)—onto the back or shoulders. The variant *pick back* refers to the *back* on which the pack is pitched. The obscurity of all this gave the folk-etymologized forms *pig back* and *piggyback.* It is also possible that *pick pack* and its variants are instead a reduplicated form, like *tiptop,* of French *à pic* (vertically, perpendicularly).

THUG (1839). The first *Thugs* appeared almost a millennia ago in India and were a kind of organized religious mafia, a confederacy of professional assassins. Traveling in various guises and in discrete gangs of ten to two hundred, a Thug would follow a wealthy wayfarer and, after gaining the confidence of the hapless victim, at an opportune moment strangle him with a noose or handkerchief. The victim's body was then robbed and, after prescribed rituals in which the pickax used to dig a grave was consecrated and sugar was sacrificed, the corpse was wrapped and buried. The Thugs were worshipers of Kali, the Hindu goddess of destruction. They considered assassination a holy and honorable act, a religious duty performed for the deity, for whom a good portion of the plunder was set aside. Because they always used strangulation, they were sometimes called *Phansigars* or "noose operators." But at the height of the British Empire, when India was the crown jewel, they were generally known as *thugs* and their grim practices were *thuggee*. Derived from Hindi *thag* (a cheat, swindler), *thug* goes back to Sanskrit *sthaga* (a cheat), and *sthagayati* (he cheats), from *sthag* (to cover, conceal) and the Indo-European root *(s)teg* (to cover), which makes *thug* kin to many English words, including *thatch, deck, tile,* and *protect.* It took the British the decades of the 1830s and '40s to unmask the Thug system and stamp it out, though remnants remained as late as the end of the century ("When the Prince of Wales was in India, a *Thug* criminal showed him how victims were strangled," 1897, London *Daily News*). Once the word began to appear in writing about India around 1810, it caught the public's fancy and was quickly extended to refer to "a cutthroat," "killer," or "gangster."

HYPOCHONDRIA (1839). In medieval medicine *hypochondria* was not a psychological disorder but an anatomical structure, namely, the organs of the upper abdomen: liver, gall bladder, spleen, etc. Borrowed from the Latin singular *hypochondrium,* the original Greek was a compound of *hypo* (under) and *chondros* (gristle, cartilage of the breastbone). The hypochondria were believed to be the seat of MELANCHOLY and a source of the melancholic "vapours." Exhalations from these organs allegedly caused depression and other nervous disorders ("If our spleen or *hypochondria* . . . send up such melancholic fumes into our heads as move us to sadness and timorousness, we cannot justly call that vice," a. 1652, J. Smith, *Selected Discourses*). By the seventeenth century, *hypochondria* was transferred to the effect of these vapors: depression and melancholy that had no apparent real cause ("Will Hazard was cured of his *hypochondria* by three glasses," 1710, *Tatler*). It was not until the nineteenth century, however, that, under the influence of the related medical term *hypochondriasis* (a morbid concern about one's health), *hypochondria* was broadened to mean "mental depression centered on imaginary illnesses."

TAKEN ABACK (1840). Old English *on baec* (in the rear, at the back) was written as two words as late as the thirteenth century, but was eventually treated as a single word, with the preposition *on* (at, toward) being shortened to *a-,* giving *aback* (in a backward direction, in a position to the rear). During that same century, the *a-* prefix began to be dropped altogether, leaving *back* in its ordinary modern sense, essentially replacing *aback.* By the nineteenth century, *aback* was confined primarily to literary works of self-conscious archaic tone ("A temple fair / We came to, set *aback* midst towering trees," 1870, William Morris, *The Earthly Paradise*) and to nautical use. Sailors have used it since the seventeenth century to refer to the often dangerous situation when the wind suddenly shifts around to the front of the ship, laying the sails "back" against the masts. Sometimes a ship's captain would deliberately steer so that the sails were *taken aback* in order to slow or halt the ship's headway ("We instantly hove all *aback* to diminish the violence of the shock," 1847, Sir James Ross, *Voyage of Discovery and Research . . .*). But more often than not, it was a fickle and unexpected wind that took the sails aback ("This proves to my mind that the Captain was *taken* as flat *aback* as could be by a squall striking her from starboard," 1870, London *Daily News*). It is this surprise element in the nautical phrase that gave it its figurative sense "caught by surprise or unawares" ("I don't think I was ever so *taken aback* in all my life," 1842, Dickens, *American Notes*).

QUIZ (1847). One version of the history of *quiz* (to question, a student examination) begins with "an odd or eccentric person," known in the eighteenth century as a *quiz* ("She really means to marry that *quiz* for the sake of his thousands," 1852, Mrs. Smythies, *The Bride Elect*). Later, a *quiz* was "a person who banters or jokes," and then merely "banter," "witticism," or "jest," becoming the verb to "banter," "jest," or "make sport of" ("What a charming tongue Latin is for *quizzing* in," 1874, John Richard Green, *A Short History of the English People*). Probably influenced by *question* or *inquisitive*, bantering *quiz* took on its latest sense, to "question" or "examine." The history of the original *quiz* (an eccentric person), however, is a mystery. One story claims that a certain manager of a Dublin theater, one Mr. Daly, made a wager that he could introduce a new word having no specific meaning into the English language within twenty-four hours. He then proceeded to plaster every Dublin wall with the letters Q, U, I, and Z, which of course aroused the curiosity of the citizens, who soon attached the word to the eccentric perpetrator, Mr. Daly himself. The story, however, has never been verified. A much simpler history places the origin of *quiz* (an exam) in the Latin *qui es?* (who are you?), the opening question of oral exams in Latin when such things were taught in grammar school.

GUY (1847). "Nazis! I hate these guys." This is Indiana Jones *(The Last Crusade)* at his quipping best—intensity couched in snide, colloquial understatement. Even President

Bush uses the common *guy* (fellow), though his just-folks style creates a slightly different effect. Here is the president in his own words inviting the former prime minister of Jordan onto the Truman Balcony of the White House: "You guys have to come out here and see something before you leave." If a president early in the last century, say Andrew Jackson, had said this to a foreign dignitary, it would have been a diplomatic faux pas. At that time a *guy* was a person of grotesque appearance, like the *guys* or effigies of Guy Fawkes that were paraded and burned in English streets every November 5, the anniversary of the Gunpowder Plot. Guy Fawkes was a co-conspirator in the plot to blow up the king and parliament in 1605 in revenge for penal laws against Catholics. The pejorative connotations of *guy* quickly faded, especially in America, where the word is more common and where Guy Fawkes has little life in the popular imagination. By the 1890s, *guy* was a neutral if slangy way of referring to a male person. The name Guy itself is an old one and may go back to the Slavic god *Svanto-Vid,* who was worshiped with frenzied dancing. When Christianity arrived on the Baltic scene, it converted the pagan god into *Sanctus Vitus* or Saint Vitus, the name given to the Sicilian martyr (c. 300) and to a nervous disorder (St. Vitus' Dance, known in France as "la danse de Saint Guy"). *Vitus* then became in Italian *Guido* and in French and English *Guy.*

BUREAUCRACY (1848). *Bureau* is a French borrowing originally meaning "writing desk," and *-cracy* is a modern use of Greek *kratya* (rule). *Bureaucracy,* then, is literally "rule by writing desk," that is, by professional paper shuffling ("The work of government has been in the hands of governors by profession; which is the essence and meaning of *bureaucracy,*" 1860, John Stuart Mill, *Considerations on Representative Government*). The Old French source word, *burel,* the diminutive of *bure,* referred to a coarse woolen material used to cover writing desks. It is either from Latin *burra* (coarse wool) or from Old French *buire* (dark brown), the color of the cloth, from Latin *burrus* (red).

BERSERK (1851). In Scandinavian mythology, *Berserkr* was the name of the twelve sons of the hero Berserk, who was famed for his reckless fury on the battlefield and for fighting without armor. Since he went into battle essentially wearing only his shirt, his Old Norse name meant literally "bear-sark" or "bear-shirt" ("The *berserkars* were so called from fighting without armour," 1822, Sir Walter Scott, *The Pirate*). *Berserker* (a frenzied, savage person), adopted into English in the early nineteenth century ("Mere brotherhood in arms . . . did not distinguish the civilized man from the *berserkar*," 1861, Charles H. Pearson, *Early and Middle Ages of England*), was mistakenly interpreted as having the agent noun suffix *-er*, as though it meant "one who goes berserk." This misinterpretation gave the adjective *berserk* (frenzied, furious, crazed) by back formation, that is, by dropping the supposed suffix ("With her kindly, uncontrollable vivacity, in the brisk winter air she became more *'berserk'* as she went on," 1867, Henry Kingsley, *Silicote*).

YOB (1859). *Yob* (lout, hooligan) is one of the few examples of Cockney slang that has become accepted in general British English. It is from "back slang," the secret jargon favored by costers or costermongers (from *costard*, "apple," and *monger*, "dealer," "seller"), the vendors or hawkers of produce that worked the streets of nineteenth-century London. In back slang, a word is spelled backward (*rum* becomes *mur*, *pot of beer* becomes *top o' reeb*) and the closest pronunciation to the new form is used, for example, *yennep* for *penny* ("I've been doing awful dab with my tol . . . haven't made a *yennep*," 1877, Diprose, *London Life*). Because most words when spelled backward have impossible combinations of letters, vowels were often inserted, as in *tenip* for *pint*, *delo* for *old* (*cool ta the delo nemo* "look at the old woman"), and *kabac genals* for *back slang*, this last used to signal to another speaker that this mode of conversation is agreeable. Sometimes the word is rearranged, as in *nosper* for *person*, a common word for "stranger," not to be confused with *nosrap*, who was a *parson* or "devil-dodger." *Police* in back slang is *slop*, a variant of the earlier *esclop*. *Yob* is unusually straightforward, deriving from *boy*. In the 1850s, it meant simply "boy," "youth," before being extended to "lout," "hooligan" (" 'Let's go to the pictures.' . . . 'And have my enjoyment ruined by the Sunday night *yobs* in the front row?' " 1956, John Osborne, *Look Back in Anger*). Its offspring, *yobbery, yobbish, yobby,* and *yobbo,* are also in general British use ("A few *yobos* who had got nothing to do . . . hung around in irritated idleness, spitting manfully in the gutter and telling dirty stories," 1940, Raymond Postgate, *Verdict of Twelve*).

SCHEDULE (1863, timetable). French, as well as most of the other Romance and Germanic languages, borrowed Late Latin *schedula* (strip of paper) to refer to a document. It was originally the diminutive of *schida* (one of the strips that forms a papyrus sheet). In English from the fourteenth to the seventeenth century, *schedule* was written and pronounced like the French it was borrowed from, *sedule* or *cedule* (sed'yool), and meant "a written document or note" ("He had in hys honde [hand] a *cedule* wherein was wreton the oryson of our lord [the Lord's Prayer]," 1483, William Caxton, *The Golden Legend*) or "a list or table" ("I will give out divers *scedules* of my beautie. It shalbe inventoried and every particle and utensile labell'd to my will," 1601, Shakespeare, *Twelfth Night*). The British income-tax system, and later the American, adopted *schedule,* which, when combined with a designating letter (A, B, C, etc.), referred to specific tax forms ("The Chancellor of the Exchequer . . . jumped at the notion; for he saw in it the one and only plan for abolishing *Schedule D,* " 1863, Charles Kingsley, *Water-Babies*). In an effort to get back to the original or "pure" Latin form of the word, *sedule* began to be spelled *schedule* as early as the fifteenth century, but continued to be pronounced "sed'yool" into the nineteenth. But in the nineteenth in one of those odd twists of linguistic history, influenced by the French pronunciation of words spelled *sch-,* British English adopted "shed'yool" as the standard pronunciation. In America at about the same time a new sense, "timetable," and new pronunciation were born ("We tried our durndest to comply with your *schedule,* " 1866, Charles Henry Smith, *Bill Arp*). Under the prescriptive rules of Webster's best-selling "blue-backed speller," used in all nineteenth-century American schools, *sch-* at the beginning of words, like *school* and *scheme,* was supposed to be pronounced as "sk," and "sked'yool" became the standard pronunciation of *schedule* in America.

HALLMARK (1864). To ensure a standard of purity in gold and silver, a statute was written in 1300 granting the Goldsmiths' Hall of London the power to assay articles made of precious metals and to stamp an official symbol or mark on them as having met a certain standard. For gold the mark was a crown and for silver a lion rampant. The Goldsmiths' *Hall mark* had become such a fixed institution that by the eighteenth century *hallmark* was a standard term for an assay mark, sometimes called a *plate mark,* which, besides the standard symbol, included the place of assay; the date; the maker's touch—usually initials or a name; a duty mark; and an artisan's mark. From a mark of quality on gold, it was a simple matter to use *hallmark* figuratively of any distinctive trait or feature ("The *hallmark* of the adult human being is responsibility," Weston La Barre).

POPPYCOCK (1865). The next time you use the innocent-sounding *poppycock* (nonsense, foolish talk, bunk) in polite company, just hope that no one is aware of its history. The original Dutch word, *pappekak,* literally "soft dung," is essentially synonymous with *bullshit.* It is a compound of *pappe* (soft food, pap), borrowed from Latin *pappa,* a child's word for food, probably associated with *pap* (nipple of a woman's breast), from Latin *papilla,* and *kakken* (to defecate), also from Latin *(cacare)* and ultimately the imitative Indo-European root **kakka* (to defecate). *Poppycock* originally appeared in American English ("You won't be able to find such another pack of *poppycock* gabblers as the present Congress of the United States," 1865, Charles F. Browne, *Artemus Ward, His Travels*), perhaps via the Dutch settlements of New York.

PORTMANTEAU (1872). Borrowed from French, a *portemanteau* was originally an officer who carried (*porte,* "to bear," "to carry") the king's mantle or *manteau,* literally "mantle bearer" ("Here is arrived from the King of France a *porte-manteau,* who brought the ratification under the great seal of the agreements and treaty," 1597, George Gilpin, *Letters*). But by the time it became English in the 1500s, it referred to another kind of carrier of clothing, a valise or traveling bag. It was not until about 1870 that Lewis Carroll had Humpty Dumpty explain the latest meaning of *portmanteau:* "Well, 'slithy' means 'lithe and slimy.' . . . You see it's like a *portmanteau*—there are two meanings packed up into one word. . . . 'Mimsy' is 'flimsy and miserable' (there's another *portmanteau* for you)" (*Through the Looking-Glass*). Like two things packed together into a valise, a *portmanteau* is a word blended from the sounds and meanings of two distinct words, such as *motel (motor* and *hotel), brunch (breakfast* and *lunch),* and *guesstimate (guess* plus *estimate).*

MARGARINE (1873). In the late 1860s, Napoleon III sponsored a contest in France for a butter substitute. The chemist, Hippolyte Mège-Mouriès, won by using "oleo oil" from beef fat. The name given to it, *margarine,* was actually a misapplication of the chemical term *margarin,* which originally applied to a fatty substance supposed to be the glyceride of "margaric acid." In fact there is no such thing as margarin. Earlier in the century, the French chemist Michel Chevreul isolated what he thought were the three fatty acids that are the chief constituents of animal fat: *oleic, margaric,* and *stearic.* He took the name *margarique,* in English *margaric,* from Greek *margarites* (pearl) because the crystals of this fatty acid had a pearly sheen. But in 1852, Heintz showed that the three were instead *oleic, palmitic,* and *stearic,* and that Chevreul's margaric was really a mixture of palmitic and stearic. Hence, *margarine* from a scientific point of view is a misnomer. Because margarine could easily be passed off as real butter, the British parliament made it the legal name for anything used in imitation of butter, winning out over the alternatives, *butterine* and *oleomargarine* ("After adopting successively the names 'oleomargarine,' 'butterine,' and 'margarine,' Parliament finally, after several struggles, resolved on the last," 1888, London *Times*).

CHUMP (1883). *Chump* (a fool or dupe) evolved from a block of wood. Beginning in the late seventeenth century, a short, thick piece of wood was a *chump,* a blend of *chunk* and *lump* ("She fetched a hatchet . . . and showing him a *chump* . . . asked him if he would chop that up for her," 1863, George Eliot, *Romola*). By the mid-nineteenth century, like *block* ("knock one's block off"), it referred to one's head ("Think how unpleasant it is to have your *chump* lopped off," 1959, Vladimir Nabokov, *Invitation to a Beheading*). Further metaphorical stretching gave British English the phrase *off one's chump* (to be crazy or out of one's mind). From *chump* the block or head came *chump* the blockhead (a stupid person or dolt), which soon developed the nuance "dupe." Very recently in Black English, the noun has become the verb *chump off,* meaning to fool or get the better of someone, that is, make a chump out of a person, especially in a battle of words, as in *the dozens,* a black verbal "game" of ritualized or competitive insult. *Chump change* is an insignificant amount of money, the amount a chump would settle for.

RED HERRING (1884). When herring is smoked it takes on a red color and as early as the fifteenth century was called, not surprisingly, *red herring.* According to Nicholas Cox's *The Gentleman's Recreation* (1686), hunting dogs can be trained to follow a scent by "The trailing or dragging of a dead Cat, or Fox, (and in case of necessity a *Red-Herring*) three or four miles . . . and then laying the Dogs on the scent." Similarly a fugitive can put hounds off by dragging a smoked herring across the trail, which gave the figurative phrase *to draw a red herring across the track* (to divert attention from the real question) and the more usual *red herring* (something that misleads or diverts attention).

PYRRHIC (1885). In the metrics of poetry, two short, un-stressed syllables are called a *pyrrhic*. The term derives from an ancient Greek war dance or *pyrriche,* named after *Pyrrichos,* the inventor of the dance, which was performed in full armor ("Do they not still Learn there . . . / The *Pyrrhic* gestures, both to dance and spring / In armour, to be active in the wars?," 1630, Ben Jonson, *The New Inn*). The song to which it was danced was characterized by a pyrrhic metrical foot or *pous pyrrichos* (pyrrhic foot). A *pyrrhic victory* (a victory won at excessive cost) is from the name of another Greek historical figure, *Pyrrhus,* king of Epirus in Greece. In the first battle ever fought between Greeks and Romans in 280 B.C., Pyrrhus's cavalry and elephants overwhelmed the Romans but at such a great cost in lives and equipment that Pyrrhus lamented, "One more such victory and we are lost" ("Although its acceptance might secure for the moment the triumph of a party division, it would be indeed a *Pyrrhic victory,"* 1885, London *Daily Telegraph*).

GEEZER (1885). Although in American usage *geezer* (an odd, usually old person) almost always refers to old men, in late nineteenth-century Britain it usually applied to old women. And it is almost always derisive. By contrast, underworld slang uses the word and its variant, *geezo,* without derision to refer to young men, as in Graham Greene's *Brighton Rock,* when the central character, Pinkie, complains, "A *geezer* [fellow, guy] can't have an alibi for every minute of the day." A *geezer* is also a shot of hard liquor or narcotics (though perhaps with a different derivation, from *geyser*) and to be *geezed* is to be drunk. In Rhode Island *geezer* is a derisive term for a person of Portuguese heritage. *Geezer* derives from the fifteenth-century Scottish dialect *guiser* or *guisard* (a masquerader or mummer) from Middle English *gise* (manner, costume), hence *disguise. Gise* in turn comes, through Old French, from the Germanic root *wise* (manner, style), hence the suffix *-wise* as in *clockwise.* In the custom of shivareeing, Scottish *guisers* hazed newlywed couples: young men donned masks, tied shocks of straw to their bodies and danced drunkenly about, making a tumultuous noise. In a similar antic mode, children in Scotland to this day go door to door as *guisers* on Halloween, Christmas Eve, and Hogmanay (New Year's Eve) to collect gifts of cakes and nuts ("There's bairns [children] wi' *guizards* at their tail/ Clourin' [battering] the doors wi' runts o' kail [hard stems of kale]," 1921, Violet Jacob, *Bonnie Joann*). By the 1880s *guiser* had moved beyond its dialect borders into general English, the pronunciation changed from (gĭzər) to (gēzər), and the reference to a zany youthful masker shifted ironically to an odd elderly person, perhaps with the implication that age was being worn as a kind of guise. A similar late shift in meaning occurred in Scottish itself, when *guiser* came to mean any odd-looking person, a "freak" ("I'm maybe no' just sic [such] a black-avized auld [black-faced old] *guizard* as Hairry Cockburn maks out," 1925, George Douglas, *Cadger's Creel*).

CLICHÉ (1888). In 1725 the Scottish inventor William Ged patented a process in which a duplicate metal plate was cast from a mold of composed movable type. Only partially successful, his method was almost forgotten until Firmin Didot and other French inventors perfected it, eventually using papier mâché to create the mold. Didot applied the name *stereotype* to this form of printing, from Greek *stereo* (solid) and *type*. The French die sinkers or "dabbers" called the metal plate itself *le cliché*, from the verb *clicher*, a variant of *cliquer* (to click, clap)—the sound made when the engraved dies or composed type struck against the near-molten lead to create a plate. For the same reason German printers called it *der Abklatsch* from *abklatschen*, literally "to clap off," from *ab* (off) and *klatschen* (clap, smack). Because the *cliché* was a duplicate of an original form, it became a natural metaphor for an idea or expression that was worn out and trite ("The farcical American woman who 'wakes everybody up' with her bounding vulgarities . . . is rapidly becoming a *cliché*, both on the stage and in fiction," 1895, Westminster *Gazette*). The word *stereotype* similarly went on to achieve metaphor status ("The growth of brighter ideals . . . will go on, leaving ever further and further behind them your dwarfed finality and leaden moveless *stereotype,* " 1877, John Morley, *Critical Miscellanies*).

SCHLEMIEL (1892). In English the combination of the "sh" and "l" sounds at the beginning of words is not a natural feature, making such Yiddish words as *schlep* (haul, drag), *schlock* (cheap, shoddy) and *schlemiel* (a clumsy, blundering person) sound peculiarly expressive to an English speaker's ear and therefore readily adoptable into colloquial speech ("Don't talk like a *schlemiel,* you schlemiel. Sounds like you're letting them push you around," 1941, Budd Schulberg, *What Makes Sammy Run*). Yiddish *schlemiel* is itself a borrowing from the Hebrew, *Shelumiel,* the name of the chief of the tribe of Simeon mentioned in the Bible (Numbers 1:6, 7:36). The Talmud identifies Shelumiel as the Simeonite prince Zimri, who, caught in the act of adultery with a Midianite woman, was ignobly run through with a javelin (Numbers 25:6-15). The name was probably given fresh currency by Adelbert von Chamisso's story of *Peter Schlemihls . . .* (1814), a bumbling wretch who sold his shadow to the devil.

KAPUT (1895). English adopted *kaput* (broken, ruined, de-stroyed) from the Germans in the 1890s, and the Germans took it from the French during the Thirty Years' War (1618–48). The French expression was *faire capot* (be defeated), which the Germans translated as *caput* (or *capot*) *machen.* Later, they abstracted *caput* or *kaputt* from the phrase and pronounced the final *t.* The French *faire capot* or *être capot* is a card-game word and means "to make no tricks or be without tricks in *piquet.* " *Piquet,* pronounced "picket" or "peeket," was imported to England in the seventeenth century, its name said variously to derive from *pique* (a pike, a spade in cards), *pique* (a quarrel), and *piquer* (to prick, pierce, sting). It is a two-handed game played with a pack of thirty-two cards, the low-est cards, 2 through 6, having been dropped, and is scored on tricks and various combinations of cards. It has its own mini-terminology, including *capot,* which English borrowed directly from French when the game came to England, and *carte blanche,* which was a hand with no face cards, from *avoir cartes blanches* (to have blank cards). *Capot* itself is from *capot* (cover, hood, cape, bonnet). By taking all of the tricks in the game, one defeats the opponent so thoroughly that he is figuratively confused and disconcerted, as though "covered over" (compare *bury one's opponent*) or as though a "hood" had been thrown over his head (compare *hoodwinked*).

RUBBERNECK (1896). After Joseph Priestley discovered around 1770 that a small chunk of hardened latex imported from Brazil could make pencil marks disappear by "rubbing," this odd new material, which as yet had few other known uses, was soon called *rubber,* or in full, *India rubber,* a misnomer, Brazil being confused with the West Indies, itself a misnomer. Rubber was also known in Priestley's time by the native Quechua word *cauchuc,* which the Spaniards brought back to Europe in the sixteenth century (*"Caoutchouc,* very useful for erasing the strokes of black lead pencils, and is popularly called *rubber,* and lead-eater," 1788, Howard, *New Royal Encyclopaedia*). After Charles Goodyear revolutionized the industry with his discovery of vulcanization in 1839, *rubber* became a household word. But leave it to American English to employ it (1896) in a graphic colloquialism, *rubberneck* (to crane the neck and look around inquisitively). A *rubberneck wagon* or *bus* is a vehicle for sightseeing and is usually loaded with *rubberneck tourists* on a *rubberneck tour.* The colorful word was quickly adopted into British English ("They are the nobility—the swells. They don't hang around the streets like tourists and *rubbernecks,"* 1909, George McCutcheon, *Truxton King*) and is sometimes abbreviated to *rubber* ("She almost cracked her throat trying to *rubber* at him and play cards at the same time," 1901, Hugh McHugh, *John Henry*).

UKULELE (1896). When Portuguese immigrants from Madeira settled in Hawaii in the 1870s, they brought with

them a four-stringed musical instrument called a "machete de braga" or simply a "machete." A decade or so later a British army officer named Edward Purvis, serving as the vice-chamberlain of King Kalakaua's court, heard someone playing the machete. He took it upon himself to learn to play the novel instrument and was soon performing at the king's court. Purvis was apparently a man of small build and great energy, whose antics and lively playing led the amused Hawaiians to give him the nickname *ukulele,* literally "leaping flea," from *'uku* (flea) and *lele* (leaping, jumping). The new instrument became a great success, even the king learning to play, and because it was so closely associated with Purvis, it soon acquired his nickname.

MUMBO JUMBO (1896). European adventurers of the eighteenth century were the first to speak of *mumbo jumbo,* which was a grotesque idol worshiped in darkest Africa. In 1738 Francis Moore reported, "At Night, I was visited by a *Mumbo Jumbo,* an Idol, which is among the Mundingoes a kind of cunning Mystery. . . . This is a Thing invented by the Men to keep their Wives in awe" (*Travels into the Inland Parts of Africa*). *Nzambi* or *zumbi* means "god" or "fetish" in Kongo, a West African language, and is the origin of *zombie* (a voodoo deity, a walking dead person) and in West Indies English *jumbie* (ghost, evil spirit). It may also be the origin of *jumbo* in *mumbo jumbo,* the full expression being a rhyming combination (like *razzle-dazzle, fuddy-duddy,* and *teeny-weeny*), in which one of the elements is a pseudo-word. Moore's account, however, places *mumbo jumbo* among the Mandingo tribes of the Niger region, some distance from the Kongo source. According to an alternative explanation, it is a borrowing from the Mandingo *mama* (ancestor) and *dyumbo* (pompon wearer). But semantically this is less satisfying. Whatever the African source, a century after Francis Moore's expedition a *mumbo jumbo* was in English any object of foolish veneration, and by the 1890s the sense had been broadened to refer to obscure or meaningless talk or nonsense.

POLECATS
TO YUPPIES

American English

Shakespeare had only recently completed *Macbeth,* when the English brought their language to their first permanent colony in the New World, Jamestown, Virginia (1607). These first colonists had grown up in Elizabethan England and were speaking the language of Shakespeare, Bacon, Marlowe, and Donne. It was a time of great change and new worlds, the beginning of the British Empire and English as a world language.

Seventeenth-century American writing to us sounds quaint, with its Elizabethan features. But by the next century, American English, or as Samuel Johnson derisively called it, the "American dialect," was generally recognized as distinct from British English. Perhaps the earliest sign that British English was being Americanized was the adoption of Indian words into everyday speech.

The colonists encountered a strange landscape and unfamiliar forms of wild life for which they had no English names. When, for example, they came upon a furry, cat-sized creature with a masklike marking, they were at a loss as to what to call it. They naturally adopted the Indian name, which for

Europeans was difficult to pronounce. Captain John Smith spelled it *rahauqcum* and *raugroughcum* in his account (1608) of the Virginia colony. He was trying to write the Algonquian word *ärä`kun* from *ärä`kunem,* literally "he scratches with his hands," which probably alludes to the raccoon's habit of scrabbling for crabs and other tidbits on stream bottoms. The name was also used in the New England colonies and was spelled *rackoone* or *rockoon.* By 1672 the current spelling, *raccoon,* was established and the Indian word was fully assimilated into colonial English.

Some American Indian terms had already found their way into Elizabethan English, usually by way of Spanish and Portuguese borrowings from Nahuatl, the tongue of the Aztecs, and from various Indian dialects of the West Indies and Central and South America. Some of these words are *potato, tomato, chocolate, cocoa, canoe, cannibal, barbecue, maize,* and *savannah.*

Although there were numerous Indian languages spoken on the North American continent, only one language group, the Algonquian, is the nearly exclusive source of the Indian words borrowed by the colonists. This huge group encompassed many tribes including the Arapaho, Blackfoot, Cheyenne, Cree, Delaware, Fox, Micmac, Ojibwa or Chippewa, and Penobscot, each speaking a different Algonquian dialect.

About half of all the three hundred or so American Indian loan words current today entered the language in the seventeenth century, including *caribou, hickory, hominy, moccasin, moose, possum, papoose, persimmon, pone, powwow, skunk, squash, squaw, terrapin, tomahawk, totem, wigwam,* and *woodchuck.* Others like *pecan, caucus, chipmunk, toboggan, succotash, mackinaw,* and *mugwump* were borrowed later.

A colonial Indian would probably not recognize any of these words because they were radically changed in the course of being adopted into American speech. Algonquian has many sounds and sound combinations that were completely foreign to English speakers, making them difficult to pronounce. Often the words were abbreviated or clipped (*hominy* from *rockahominy, squash* from *asquutasquash, hickory* from *pawcohiccora*). Sometimes the Indian word was changed by folk etymology, an attempt to make sense of a new and unusual-sounding word by analyzing it (incorrectly) in terms of known words. For example, the Indian word *muskwessu* or *muscassus* became *muskrat,* a musky-smelling rodent; *otchek* or *odjik* became *woodchuck;* and *achitam* became *chipmunk.*

The influence of the Indian culture was not negligible when we take into account the numerous combinations that these loan words occur in (e.g., *skunk* cabbage, *skunk* bear, *skunk* weed), not to mention the couple of hundred combinations with *Indian* (e. g., *Indian pony, Indian mallow*). In addition there are many expressions derived from features of Indian life: *on the warpath, peace pipe, to bury the hatchet, to hold a powwow, Indian summer, paleface, brave* (noun), *firewater, Indian file, Indian giver, happy hunting grounds, Great Spirit, medicine man, war paint, war dance, to scalp,* and *ticket scalper.*

American English also borrowed many words from the Europeans who sought a new life in the New World, as well as words from Africa brought in with the slave trade. These, however, tend to be regionalized to wherever a given immigrant group settled—African in the South, French in Louisiana, Spanish in the Southwest, German in Pennsylvania, Dutch in New York—and have greater importance in the development of American regional dialects.

With the arrival of West African slaves, primarily to the Southern United States, came new customs and languages that inevitably influenced the English spoken in the American South. Some of the words adopted by Southern speech are *cooter* (turtle), *goober* (peanut), *gumbo* (a stewlike dish made with okra), *juke* (immoral, disorderly), *juju* (a fetish, amulet), *okra* (the edible pods of a tall annual cultivated in the South and the West Indies), *pinder* (peanut), *poor joe* (a great blue heron), and *tote* (to carry). Many African borrowings spread outside the South, such as *banjo, bogus, boogie-woogie, chigger, hep* or *hip, jitter, jive, phony, voodoo, yam,* and *zombie.*

Afro-American speech remains a creative influence on American English, though not in terms of African borrowings, and instead of being confined to the South, it is national and primarily urban. Most of the words that get into general use from urban Afro-American speech are highly colloquial, such as *bad* (good), *cool* or *chill out* (to calm down), *dude* (male person), *get down* (to do something in a more intense way), *gig* (job), *main man* (favorite friend, one's hero, boyfriend), *make it* (to go away), *out of sight* (excellent), and *rap* (to talk, converse). They also tend to be ephemeral, coming into use for a few years and then dying out or being replaced by fresh expressions.

Except for place names, French borrowings in American English are heard almost exclusively in southern Louisiana, which was originally colonized by the French beginning in 1717, when Jean Baptiste constructed an outpost at the site that is today New Orleans. Many of these words have spread into other parts of the Southern gulf states, but most remain close to their Louisiana source, such as *armoire* (wardrobe), *banquette* (sidewalk), *bayou* (small stream), *boudin* (a kind of sausage), *cabine* (privy), *coulee* (pool), *fais-dodo* (family party), *flottant* (bog), *jambalaya* (a rice dish), *marais* (swamp), *pirogue* (small riverboat), and *pooldoo* (coot, mud hen).

Of all the European languages that American English borrowed from, Spanish is the most pervasive. Examples from the large Spanish vocabulary in American English are *abalone, adobe, alfalfa, alligator* (literally "the lizard"), *armadillo* ("little armored one"), *bravado, canyon, cockroach, garbanzo, hammock, mosquito, mulatto* (literally "young mule" because mules have mixed parentage), *mustang, patio, pinto, ranch, stampede, stevedore,* and *vigilante.*

Other important linguistic processes operated to distinguish American English from British. The English spoken by the colonists almost immediately began to drift away from the mother tongue. Many words and pronunciations died out in England over two or three centuries, but survived in America, such as *adze, andiron, bay window, cesspool, clodhopper, copious, cross-purposes, din, flap-jack, fox-fire, greenhorn, home-spun, jeans, loophole, molasses, offal, ragamuffin, stock* (for cattle), *trash, underpinning.* Sometimes it was not the word that died out in England but one of its senses, which survived in America, such as *fall* (autumn), *raise* (to breed, rear, grow), *clod, quit,* and *cabin.*

Often English dialect terms became standard American words. This is the case for *cater-cornered, cordwood, deck, drool, pond, shoat, squirt, wilt,* and many others.

A word used in England with a particular sense frequently

developed new meanings after being transplanted to America. This happened with *apartment, baggage, barn, bug, cracker, creek, dry goods, fraternity, lumber, pie, rock, shop, sick, squat* (to settle on land), *store, tariff, team, to notify,* and *to haul.* For example, *lumber* in eighteenth-century English meant "disused goods," the sense that survives in England today, as in *lumber room.* But the American colonists used it to designate cut timber. *To haul* in England meant and still means "to move by force or violence"; in America since colonial times it has meant "to transport in a vehicle."

The American vocabulary during the nineteenth century began to be exported abroad, but by the twentieth century, with its economic, political, and technological prominence in the world, America and its language became one of the greatest forces for change and the expansion of English. Many of the new American coinages added to the English vocabulary are based on old processes, such as extending the meaning of an established word, like *apartment* or *folder,* or componding existing words, as in *boyfriend, bookstore, brainstorm,* and the 150 or so compounds using *corn,* such as *corn basket, corn bread, cornhusker, corn liquor.* American English also tends to coin and use more freely nouns compounded from a verb and a preposition, such as *blowout, brushoff, buildup, checkup, fallout, feedback, knockout, payoff, run-around, showdown,* and *workout.*

New words are frequently created by shifting the function of an existing word. Nouns are used as verbs: to *audition,* to *author* a book, to *chair* a meeting, to *park,* to *package,* to *program,* to *radio* a message, to *service,* to *vacation.* Verbs are used as nouns: a big *push,* an *assist,* a *release.* And adjectives can become nouns: *briefs, comics, formals, hopefuls, reds.*

To sample American coinages is to get a taste of American history and character: *abolitionist, automobile, baby-sit, ball park, basketball, bebop, bifocals, blowhard, bootleg, bourbon, carpetbagger, cheerleader, chewing gum, cocktail, congressional, crazy bone, credit card, custom-made, department store, district attorney, drugstore, electric chair, equal rights, firecracker, flophouse, flunk, fundamentalist, gasoline, genocide, gold standard, ghostwrite, graduate school, halitosis, highbrow, hillbilly, homemade, homestretch, homogenized milk, honky-tonk, immigrant, inaugural, installment plan, jaywalk, knowhow, lame duck, landslide, lumberjack, mail order, miscegenation, mo-*

torcade, organized labor, peanut butter, physical education, and so on and on.

POLECAT (1688). Although a skunk has a stripe, it is not called a *polecat* because it resembles a striped pole. When the American colonists first encountered a skunk, a strange creature unknown to Europeans, they called it a *polecat* because it reminded them of the fitchet or ferret back home. By the mid-seventeenth century, they had borrowed the Algonquian Indian word for the critter, *segakw,* which they pronounced *skunk.* The Indian word became the standard term, and *polecat* survived primarily in the Southern United States ("You recommend the domestication of the *polecat* on account of its playfulness and its excellence as a ratter!," 1870, Mark Twain, *Sketches New and Old*). The skunk, of course, is not a cat at all; but its feline semblance has given it many cattish folk names, including *civet* or *civvy cat, perfume pussy, piss-cat, sachet kitten, stink-pussy,* and *woods pussy.* Middle English *polcat* is from French and is a compound of *pol,* whose origin is problematic, and *cat.* One theory derives *pol* from Old French *pulent* (stinking). But in the first century after the word entered English there is no spelling *pulcat* to indicate the French pronunciation of *pul*ent. A more widely accepted explanation derives it from Old French *pole* or *poule* (chicken, fowl), with reference to the polecat's habit of raiding chicken houses ("Ther was a *polcat* in his hawe, That, as he seyde, his capouns hadde yslawe" [There was a polecat in his yard, / That, as he said, had killed his capons or chickens], c. 1386, Chaucer, *Pardoner's Tale*). *Polecat,* literally "chicken cat," would be parallel with such compounds as *sparrow hawk* (a hawk that feeds on sparrows) and *goshawk* (a goose-stealing hawk). *Poule,* the diminutive *poulet* giving Middle English *pullet,* is from Latin *pullus*

(young animal, chicken), also the origin through French of *pony*. The Indo-European root *pu-lo* (young of an animal), from *pou-* (few, little), is also the source of Old English *fola* (young horse, colt) and Modern English *foal*.

SKINFLINT (a. 1700). In sixteenth-century English, the verb *to skin* meant the opposite of its most common use today (to remove skin). Back then it meant "to cover with skin," hence "to clothe or attire," or "to heal over with skin" ("He looks like a death's head *skinned* over for the occasion," 1871–72, George Eliot, *Middlemarch*). It soon recovered its Germanic root sense "to peel off," "to remove or strip off the skin" and was used in phrases denoting meanness *(to skin a cat)* and stinginess *(to skin a flint)*. This latter phrase came into use after the invention of the flintlock musket early in the seventeenth century. The new firearm used a piece of flint held in a hammerlike device or "cock." When the trigger was pulled the spring-loaded cock struck the flint against a steel plate or frizzen, creating a shower of sparks. If all went well, the flash of the priming powder in the pan just beneath the frizzen ignited the charge in the bore and fired the weapon. Sometimes, however, it failed and there was only a *flash in the pan*, an expression that is still used to refer to someone or something that promises success but fails. After repeated firings the flint wore down and made poor contact with the frizzen, causing inadequate sparking. Most riflemen merely replaced the flint, but since it was a relatively scarce commodity, many penny-pinching backwoodsmen "skinned" or sharpened their flints with a knife. In 1807 Washington Irving alluded to this practice with derision: "The fool . . . who, in *skinning a flint* worth a farthing, spoiled a knife worth fifty times the sum" *(Salmagundi)*. It was a short step from the miserly action of skinning a flint to the actor, the *skinflint* (a miser, cheapskate). It may be, however, that *skinflint* has a somewhat simpler origin. *Skin* is used in other expressions of parsimoniousness, such as *tight as the skin on an apple* (or *on one's back*) and *stingy enough to skin a flea* (or *louse*) *for its hide and tallow*. *To skin a flint*, hence *skinflint*, may simply be colorful hyperbole the way *to skin a flea* is. That is, a tightwad could be said to be so niggardly that he or she would even try skinning a flint to get money.

BLUFF (1735). This is the first Americanism to have the distinction of being sneered at by an Englishman, even though it is well established in British use today. The adventurer and writer Francis Moore, who lived for a time in the new colony of Georgia as a storekeeper, described the fledgling city of Savannah as "a mile and a quarter in circumference; it stands upon the flat of a hill, the bank of the river (which they in barbarous English call a *bluff*) is steep" (*A Voyage to Georgia, Begun in the Year 1735*). This "barbarism" is a metaphorical extension of the earlier nautical sense of *bluff* (of a ship: having bows that present a nearly vertical front). Captain John Smith wrote the earliest-known reference to a *bluff* ship in his *Seaman's Grammar* (1627): "If her stem be vpright as it were, she is called *Bluffe*, or Bluffeheaded. . . . If shee haue but a small Rake [inclination], she is so *bluffe* that the Seas meet her . . . suddenly." Smith's term is probably a borrowing of obsolete Dutch *blaf* (broad, flat). When the colonists of South Carolina sometime in the mid-1600s encountered the high bluffs of the riverbanks, they naturally likened them to the steep and nearly vertical bows of a ship. Similarly, but in a more abstract vein, beginning around 1700, a frank, blustering person, one given to good-natured bluntness, was likened to the abrupt bluntness of a bluff ship. Henry VIII, for example, was known as "Bluff King Hal," though not in his own lifetime. Poker at times can be blunt and bluff, and indeed, in nineteenth-century America, *bluff* was a name for *poker*. To blindfold a person or an animal in seventeenth-century England was to *bluff* him or her, and a *bluff* was the blinkers for a horse. This sense, to "blindfold" or "hoodwink," combined with the bluffness of a bold front (of a ship or person) may be the origin of the poker sense of *bluffing* (deceiving an opponent as to the strength of one's hand by betting heavily upon it). Another possibility is that it is a borrowing from Dutch *bluffen* (to make a trick at cards, to boast), which in turn is from Middle Dutch *bluffen* (to strike).

DOLLAR (1785). The dollar was the currency of Germany and Spain over two centuries before it became American ("Resolved, That the money unit of the United States of America be one *dollar* . . . [and] That the smallest coin be of copper, of which 200 [sic] shall pass for one dollar," July 6, 1785, *Resolutions of the Continental Congress of the United States*). In 1516 a mine near Joachimstal (St. Joachim's valley, from German *Tal*, "valley," close kin to English *dale*), a town in northwestern Bohemia, now Jachymov, Czechoslovakia, began producing silver for a coin also minted there. The coin was called a *Joachimstaler* after the town's name, or *Taler* for short. The English borrowed the Dutch and Low German form *daler*, and by the eighteenth century began regularly spelling it *dollar*. This name was then transferred to the Spanish peso or "piece of eight" (eight reales), which was in extensive circulation in the British colonies of North America around the time of the Revolutionary War. To become independent of the British pound sterling after the war, Thomas Jefferson proposed that the Spanish dollar be the unit of currency. "It is," he wrote in 1782, "a known coin and the most familiar of all to the mind of all of the people. It is already adopted from south to north" *(Notes on a Money Unit for the United States)*. The dollar almost immediately was elevated to near divine status as the *almighty dollar*, "that great object of universal devotion throughout our land" (1855, Washington Irving, *Wolfert's Roost*), along with the *dollar sign* ("The *dollar-sign* has chased the crucifix clean off the map," 1920, Sinclair Lewis, *Main Street*), known earlier as the *dollar mark*. The *dollar sign* itself has many contested origins. One says that it was Jefferson's personal abbreviation. Another that it is a modification of the figure 8 as it appeared on the old Spanish pieces of eight. The earliest and best-known theory is described in a Boston newspaper in 1847:

> The dollar mark in question is only applied, properly, to the United States coin, or currency, of that name; and originally in order to distinguish it as such, it was written with the "U.S." affixed; as "US 100 dollars"; and in process of time the whole became abbreviated to "US 100,"—and then, by abbreviation, to the two letters in one, the "S" crossing the "U"—out of which has grown the "$."

After the more practical dollar note, redeemable for silver on demand, took the place of the gold coin, it was possible to describe the health or integrity of something as being *sound as a dollar* (1852), though the expression is more likely to be used ironically these days. However, it is still possible to say without irony that one *feels (or looks) like a million dollars* (c. 1945). To assert something with certainty and confidence is to be willing to *bet one's dollars* against someone else's *doughnuts* (or *buttons* or *cobwebs;* 1904), or to be willing to *bet one's bottom dollar.* This last phrase comes from gambling and refers to the bottom chip in a stack of poker chips. If one bets the bottom chip, one bets the whole stack. Similarly, *to pay top dollar* (to pay a full or excessive amount) for something probably alludes to the top chip on the stack of the highest bid in poker. Finally, *dollar diplomacy* (foreign policy used to secure opportunities for American business investment abroad) was first applied with reference to Secretary of State Philander Knox's administration (c. 1910) and is still alive and well today.

JUNKET (1814). According to the Wyclif translation of Exodus, the infant Moses did not go "on" a *junket* or "pleasure trip" when his mother sent him down the river, but "in" a *junket* or "basket made of rushes" ("Whanne he [she] mygte hide hym no lenger, he [she] tok a *ionket* of resshen [rushes] . . . and putte the litil faunt [infant] with ynne" [1382, Wyclif, trans. of Exodus 2:3]). Borrowed from Old North French *jonquette* (rush basket, especially one used for carrying fish), its ultimate source is Latin *juncus* (rush), also the source of *jonquil* (a plant with rushlike leaves). In the fifteenth century, a popular dish of sweetened and spiced curds and cream was typically served in a rush basket or on a mat made of rushes. So strong was the association between serving container and food that the cream dish itself became known as *junket* ("You know there wants no *junkets* at the feast," 1596, Shakespeare, *Taming of the Shrew*). Within another century the sweet delicacy of this dish gave its name to any dainty sweetmeat ("The people . . . do make of these Worms divers *juncats,* as we do Tarts, Marchpanes, Wafers, and Cheese-cakes," 1608, Edward Topsell, *The History of Serpents*). At about the same time (c. 1500), feasting and banqueting were called *junkets* ("Spendynge his patrimonie uppon *ionkettes,* mynstreles and scoffers [poets]," 1540, Sir Richard Morisin, trans. of Vives' *Introduction to Wysedom*), probably from the liberal use of rush baskets and mats for serving food, as well as the delicacies or junkets served. In America, this feasting sense was tempered to "a pleasure outing or picnic involving eating and drinking" ("I come . . . to ask the favor of your company . . . to a little *junket* at our farm," 1814, Fanny Burney, *The Wanderer*). The American political use of *junket* (a trip taken by an official at the expense of the government) is first recorded in 1886.

STOOL PIGEON (1830). If you picture a pigeon sitting on a stool when you hear the expression *stool pigeon* (a person acting as a decoy, an informer), you are not far from guessing the most popular version of its history. Professor Maximilian Schele de Vere originally proposed this derivation in 1871, and it has been repeated ever since, perhaps because it makes such a surreal, Magritte-like image:

> The *Stool-Pigeon* . . . [literally] means the pigeon, with its eyes stitched up, fastened on a stool, which can be moved up and down by the hidden fowler, an action which causes the bird to flutter anxiously. This attracts the passing flocks of wild pigeons, which alight and are caught by a net, which may be sprung over them.

Stool, however, does not mean the piece of furniture you sit down on, but refers to a bird, real or artificial, used as a decoy ("Two or three live Crows being previously procured as decoys, or as they are called, *Stool-crows . . . ,*" 1811, Alexander Wilson, *American Ornithology*). This is the American variant of the much older *stale* or *stall* (a decoy bird), borrowed from French *estale* or *estal,* which in the thirteenth century referred to a pigeon used to entice a hawk into a net ("As a faucon [falcon] free . . . / Which . . . for no *stale* doth care," a. 1542, Earl of Surrey, "Song"). The French word is itself of Germanic origin, probably from the root of *stall* (place, standing position). Like *stool pigeon, stale* was soon extended to any means of deceptively entrapping someone ("The trumpery in my house goe bring it hither / For *stale* to catch these theeves," 1611, Shakespeare, *The Tempest*). A *stale* or *stall* was also a prostitute who served as a pickpocket's decoy by distracting the victim's attention. A *stool pigeon,* then, is a pigeon used as a "stool" or decoy, not one sitting on a stool. This was readily transferred to a person used as a decoy ("A wag who keeps an oyster cellar in Newark, advertises, among other things, 'wildbirds domesticated and *stool pigeons* trained to catch voters for the next Presidency—warranted to suit either party,' " 1830, *Working Man's Gazette*). *Stoolie* (1924) is a shortening of *stool pigeon.*

POKER (1834). When the American ambassador to Great Britain, Colonel Jakob Schenck, taught Queen Victoria the rules of poker in 1871, he called it "the national card game of the U.S." The forerunner of the game of poker was a card game played around 1700 in Germany called *pochen* and in England called *brag,* both named from the brag or challenge that a player makes when he raises the bet. The name *poker* may derive from the German word *pochen,* or *pochspiel,* from *pochen* (to boast or brag), literally "to knock," because players who passed in bidding would declare "Ich poche" (I knock) or else would rap on the table. Though plausible, evidence for this derivation is slim. An alternative version, just as poorly documented, however, says that *poker* derives from French

poque, a similar game played in New Orleans at about the time of the Louisiana Purchase (1803). Ultimately, the game, though not the name, may have come from an old Persian card game called *As nas,* played with five cards per player from a twenty-card deck. Poker has given English, through American English, many terms, including FOUR-FLUSHER and PASS THE BUCK.

SUCKER (1836). In Middle English (c. 1380) a *sucker,* spelled *souker,* was an infant still at the mother's breast. It was used, for example, in *even-sucker* (a foster sibling), *even-* meaning "fellow" or "co-." More commonly, the term referred to an unweaned animal, especially a suckling pig. Sometime early in the nineteenth century *sucker* was used figuratively for a gullible person or simpleton—one who, like a child, is naïve. A quote attributed to P. T. Barnum embodies both the childish and foolish senses of the word: "There's a *sucker* born every minute." (*Sucker* at the time was a common circus term for a patron.) Then there is W. C. Fields's infamous motto "Never give a *sucker* an even break," which may punningly refer to children, Fields not being terribly fond of the little suckers. By the 1930s a "sucker" (a person easily hoodwinked) became the verb *to sucker* (to hoodwink). A sucker is also a person who lives at the expense of another, either by extortion or parasitism. Edward Hall, a sixteenth-century chronicler, wrote of the "flatterers to the kyng [Henry VI]. . . . *suckers* of his purse and robbers of his subjectes." The Scottish poet Allan Ramsay produced the following in 1728: "This *sucker* thinks nane wise, / But him that can to immense riches rise."

PUMPERNICKEL (1839). This delicious dark bread, originally a German recipe, made from coarsely ground, unbolted rye flour, has not always had a good reputation. One Britisher on his tour in Germany wrote in 1756: "Their bread is of the very coarsest kind, ill-baked, and as black as coal, for they never sift their flour. The people of the country call it *Pumpernickel.*" Though it did not catch on in England, the more ethnically eclectic Americans readily adopted it and its German dialect name ("The devil take you and your Westphalian ham, and *pumpernickel!,*" 1839, Henry W. Longfellow, *Hyperion*). In the German dialect of Westphalia, *pumpernickel* was an abusive term meaning "lout" or "boor," and is a compound of *pumpern* (to break wind, flatulence) and *nickel* (a goblin, devil, rascal; cf. NICKEL). The bread may have been coarse enough to make even the devil fart, but it was probably called *pumpernickel* by association with its rude or "boorish" country origin.

PANTS (1840). *Pantaloon* was an acceptable synonym for "trousers" in the nineteenth and early part of this century, but fickle linguistic taste considered *pants* to be vulgar ("It irks us, however, to encounter in a description of Mr. Legare's dress the term *'pants'* instead of pantaloon," 1843, *The Knickerbocker*). The increasingly common use of *pants,* however, eventually made it respectable. So common had it become by this century it spawned a bevy of colorful expressions, including *to be caught with one's pants down* (to be caught in an embarrassing situation); *to bore (scare, talk, beat) the pants off of someone; to wear the pants* (to be the dominant member of a household); *to keep one's pants on* (to stay calm); *to fly by the seat of one's pants* (to fly by instinct rather than by instruments); *have ants in one's pants* (to be restless); *to get into her pants* (to have intercourse with); *to have hot pants* (to be sexually eager); *pants rabbit* (body louse); *fancy pants; smarty pants;* and so on. *Pants* is shortened from *pantaloons,* which were a distinctive part of the costume worn by the character *Pantaloon* in the Italian theatrical productions known as *commedia dell'arte*. These improvised medieval plays always had a handful of stock characters who wore masks, including the *zanni*, the impudent servants with their jokes and irrelevant trickery (hence, English *zany*, "crazy," "wild"), and *Pantalone* (Pantaloon), a lecherous old Venetian *magnifico*, who wore a half mask with a long, hooked nose, a flat cap, and the blousy trousers tight at the calves that became his namesake. Pantalone's name was taken from *San Pantaleone*, a fourth-century physician and favorite saint of the Venetians. His name is from Greek *panata* (all) and *leone* (lion), that is, "completely lion" or "exceptionally courageous." One of the tricks a *zanni* could play on an American would be to send him to a British department store to buy *pants*. The American would be surprised to find that he could only purchase underwear.

GOUGE (1842, to cheat or defraud). "[The Georgians] can keep Negro slaves, race horses, *gouge* out eyes . . . and be honored in the land," or so *The Massachusetts Spy* in a pique of regional chauvinism contended in 1797. But twelve years earlier an English lexicographer had observed that *gouging* was "a cruel practice used by the Bostonians in America" (Francis Grose, *Classical Dictionary of the Vulgar Tongue*). Another horrified Englishman called it "A diabolical practice which has never disgraced Europe, and for which no other people have even a name." Along with butting, biting, and scratching, *gouging* reached its highest refinement among the scruffy boatmen of the Ohio and Mississippi, who developed with some pride a precise technique that consisted of twisting the forefinger in a lock of hair near the temple, and scooping the eye out of the socket with the thumbnail, which was grown long for that purpose. There was even a town called "Gouge Eye" (now Pleasant Grove, California). Today *gouging* is slightly less overt, and is usually confined to cheating, defrauding, or taking unfair advantage. This figurative sense has been current since at least James K. Polk's tenure, when the New York *Tribune* reported that his administration was paying some shady printers "$100,000 more than respectable printers would have done the work for. This is a clean plain *gouge* of this sum out of the people's strong box." Before coming to these shores, a gouge was a chisel with a concave blade (1495), and to gouge something was to pierce or cut holes in it (1570). It is one of the numerous borrowings from French, deriving from Late Latin *gulbia* (a hollow beveled chisel), ultimately from Celtic, the same source as Old Irish *gulban* (prickle, sting), Welsh *gylf* (sharp point, beak), and Cornish *gilb* (boring tool).

SHYSTER (1843). In New York around 1840 a lawyer named Scheuster was busy making a name for himself as a PETTIFOGGER, for which he was often rebuked from the bench. In time, his name became synonymous with professional unscrupulousness, and when it became generic it was respelled *shyster*. Not much else is known about Scheuster, and most scholars doubt that he even existed, though the word almost certainly originated in New York ("He must . . . wait next day for the visits of the *'shyster'* lawyers—a set of turkey-buzzards whose touch is pollution and whose breath is pestilence," 1849, George G. Foster, *New York in Slices*). Another version of its history suggests that *shyster* is a compound of *shy* meaning "disreputable," "shady" ("Rather a *shy* place for a sucking county member," 1849, William Makepeace Thackeray, *Pendennis*), extended from *shy* (bashful, retiring), and the suffix *-ster* (one who is), from Old English *-istre* or *-estre*. It is very likely that the suffix *-ster* is involved, but this use of *shy* has never been current in the United States. Another explanation claims that it is a blend of *-ster* and the name of Shakespeare's notorious lawyer, *Shylock* in *The Merchant of Venice*. The generally accepted history, however, is that *shyster* is a borrowing from German *Scheisser* (an incompetent, worthless person, a "son-of-a-bitch"), which also independently entered British and Australian English in the mid-nineteenth century as *shicer* (a worthless person, a swindler, defaulter). *Scheisser* was then altered under the influence of the disparaging suffix *-ster,* as in *gangster* and *trickster*. As for the German *Scheisser*, it means literally "defecator," "shitter" and is from *Scheisse* (excrement).

BONANZA (1844). The long-running TV series *Bonanza,* which portrayed a family of men working to maintain their enormous Nevada ranch, harked back to the *bonanza farms* and ranches of the late nineteenth century. Typically bonanza farming and ranching were done on a very large scale, as on the large irrigated fields of southern California or the vast acreage of the upper Midwest, where the latest harvesting technology was used. These operations were truly "mines of wealth," a figurative extension of the original mining sense of *bonanza* (a very productive mine, a rich vein of ore), which is itself a direct borrowing from American Spanish. The original Spanish word meant "prosperity" or "success," and comes from Vulgar Latin *bonacia* meaning "fair weather at sea." It is based on a misinterpretation of Latin *malacia* (calm at sea), the bane of sailing ships. *Mal-* in *malacia* was taken to be a prefix meaning "bad," from *malus,* hence the "bad" weather of a becalmed sea. Thus *bonacia*—so the reasoning went—must mean "good" weather from *bon-* or *bonus* (good). But in reality *malacia* is a borrowing from Greek *malakia* (calm at sea), from *malakos* (soft).

PODUNK (1846). Americans have always delighted in names for insignificant, out-of-the-way places, especially when they derive from strange-sounding Indian place names, such as Hohokus, Hoboken, Kalamazoo, Keokuk, Oshkosh, Skaneateles, Punxsutawney, Kokomo, and Kankakee. Vaudeville comedians sometimes softened up their audiences by announcing themselves from Punxsutawney or Yonkers, the companion stooge asking, "What are Yonkers?" The *k* sound seems to be a prerequisite to the humor, as does the grotesque improbability of these names, as if they were of imaginary places. A series of humorous magazine articles in 1846, titled "Letters from Podunk," established *Podunk* as one of the most durable and common names for a hick town or backwater burg ("A diploma from Harvard is much more marketable than a diploma from *Podunk* College," 1960, *Times Literary Supplement*). Originally it was the name of an Indian tribe that lived on the Podunk River in Hartford County, Connecticut. Their principal village, also called Podunk or

Potunk, was on a neck of land near the mouth of the river. The village name derives from an Algonquian word, like Mohegan *ptukohke* (a neck or corner of land).

SCALAWAG (1848). In pre-industrial Scotland, farm laborers were called *scallags,* the Scottish version of a migrant worker and a sharecropper combined. An Englishman, one J. L. Buchanan, who visited the Hebrides in 1793, described the lot of the scallag.

> The *scallag,* whether male or female, is a poor being, who, for mere subsistence, becomes a predial slave to another. . . . The scallag builds his own hut with sods and boughs of trees; and if he is sent from one part of the country to another, he moves off his sticks, and, by means of these, forms a new hut in another place. . . . Five days in the week he works for his master; the sixth is allowed to himself, for the cultivation of some scrap of land.

Though a scallag had little or no education, his etymological forebears were highly educated. The original Irish term, *scolog,* is from the root *scol* (school), borrowed ultimately from Latin *schola* (school). A *scolog* was a scholar, usually one studying in a monastery. Over time the associations of learnedness faded, and a *scolog* was merely a tenant of church land. By the time it became the Old Scottish form *scoloc,* it meant "a bondservant." In America *scallag,* which doubtless found its way to the New World in the great Scotch-Irish migration, became *scalawag* (a rascal, loafer, reprobate), probably under the influence of *wag* (a witty person). A *scalawag* is also a poor, undersized animal considered to be worthless ("Like feeding his weight in corn to a *scalawag* steer that won't fat up," 1902, George Lorimer, *Letters of a Self-Made Merchant to His Son*). This has led some to theorize that *scalawag* and its reference to "undersized animals" is an alteration of *Scalloway,* one of the Shetland Islands, in allusion to the small size of Shetland ponies. Although *scalawag* can be used affectionately to refer to a child, much the way *scallag* is used in Scottish English as a familiar form of address to a boy, in the Southern United

States after the Civil War it took on more odious connotations during reconstruction. Scalawags were Southerners who worked hand in hand with Northern carbetbaggers, taking advantage of the loopholes in the Congressional plan to re-build the South ("This invaluable class is composed . . . of ten parts of unadulterated Andy Johnson Union men, ten of good lord and good devil-ites, five of spuss and seventy-five of *scallowags*," 1862, Charleston *Mercury*).

GRINGO (1949). As the troops of Generals Zachary Taylor and Winfield Scott tramped across Mexico during the Mexi-can War (1846–48), they often sang a popular song of the time. The lyrics were from a Robert Burns poem: "Green grow the rashes [rushes], O; / The sweetest hours that e're I spend, / Are spent amang the lasses, O!" The soldiers sang this with such monotony—so goes this popular history of *gringo* (a North American)—that the unintelligible words were drummed into the Mexican peasants, especially the first two words "green grow," which to them sounded like "gringo." So strong was the association that the Mexicans began refer-ring to the Yankees as *gringos*. The problem with this colorful story is that *gringo* is attested in a Castilian dictionary (1787) long before the gringo invasion. That dictionary defines it as the name given in Málaga to foreigners who have such a thick accent that their Spanish is difficult to understand. In Madrid it is especially reserved for the Irish. This Spanish *gringo*, which was inevitably exported to Mexico, comes from *Griego* (Greek), foreign speech sounding like so much Greek to the Spaniards. Greek has had this reputation since medieval times, when the proverb "Graecum est; non potest legi" (It is Greek; it cannot be read) was as common as our expression "It's Greek (gibberish) to me" ("He spoke Greek. . . . Those that understood him smiled at one another and shook their heads—but for mine own part, it was Greek to me," 1601, Shakespeare, *Julius Caesar*).

BUDDY (1850). In a 1929 issue of *American Speech*, an ama-teur etymologist who had spent his boyhood in the Pennsylvania coalfields proposed that *buddy* (friend, companion, fellow) had its origin in the miner's term *butty*. The men with pick and shovel worked in coordinated pairs, laboring buttock to buttock in the cramped tunnels, or in comradely abbreviated form, "butt to butt." They were literally *butties,* a term the miners used in a technical sense without any connotation of emotional nearness. This history of *buddy* is more imaginative than actual. The miners were probably using the English dialect word *butty* (companion, mate), which did play a role. (In England a butty is also a middleman between the mine owners and the workmen.) The evolution of *butty* into *buddy* was probably hastened by the existence of the baby-talk word *buddy* meaning "brother" (" 'Look, sister, see; the sky's got the measles!' 'No, *buddy,* ' said she, correcting him, 'it's only freckled,' " 1858, *Harper's Magazine*). *Butty,* which is first recorded in 1802, is an alteration of *booty* (plunder, profit) in the expression *booty fellow* (a confederate who shares plunder or profits from swindling), which was only current in the sixteenth century ("One man lost an hundred pound land at shooting, [because] some that shot with him on his side were *booty fellows* against him," 1532, Gilbert Walker, *A Manifest Detection of the Most Vyle and Detestable Use of Dice-Play*). *Booty* ("Fortune . . . drops *Booties* in my mouth," 1611, Shakespeare, *A Winter's Tale*) is a borrowing through French of Middle High German *bute* or *buite* (exchange, barter), but can't be traced back any further. A related term, *boot* (advantage, profit), survives today only in the phrase *to boot* (to the good, in addition), and perhaps in *bootless* (profitless, without advantage).

JACKLEG (1850). *Jackleg* (unprofessional, incompetent, disreputable) is a dialect expression used throughout the American South, primarily with reference to preachers, but also to lawyers, doctors, carpenters, and virtually any other profession that lends itself to incompetence or disrepute ("The *jackleg* clergy, they preach so good they turn themselves on. . . . The Reverend Gorman, apparently out for revenge and knowledgeable in the ways of the *jackleg* clergy, reportedly stationed a photographer outside a motel, waiting for Jimmy Swaggart to turn up," 1989, *The Nation*). It can also refer to an incompetent person ("He has been told many a time how the born-and-trained novelist works; won't he let me round and complete his knowledge by telling him how the *jack-leg* does it?," 1894, Mark Twain, *Pudd'nhead Wilson*) or to anything done in a shoddy, makeshift manner, as in "he did a *jackleg* job repairing the table." Because it is very common, *Jack,* the nickname for *John,* came to mean in Elizabethan English "a lower-class man," "a commoner," or "a knave" ("A mad-cap ruffian and a swearing *Iacke,*" 1596, Shakespeare, *Taming of the Shrew*). This basic meaning appears in numerous expressions, including *every man jack of them* (everyone), *jack-tar* (a common seaman), *jack-fool, jackanapes,* and the name for the knave in playing cards. The expression *jack-of-all-trades,* with the rest of the phrase, *and master of none,* usually left unsaid, is closest in meaning and perhaps derivation to *jackleg.* The *leg* that it stands on is related to the one in *blackleg* (a race track gambler, swindler), which was sometimes reduced to just *leg* ("He was a horse chaunter [a deceitful horse dealer]: he's a *leg* now," 1837, Dickens, *Pickwick Papers*).

SHENANIGAN (1855). At first glance *shenanigan* (mischief, trickery, nonsense, foolery) has, as H. L. Mencken put it, an "Irish smack" to it. The *-gan* ending, for example, looks like the Irish diminutive suffix. One proposed origin is the Irish *sionnachuighim* (I play tricks), from *sionnach* (fox). Though the semantics fit well enough, the Irish word is just too different in pronunciation (shän′əho͞ogəm) to be a plausible origin. The Irish theory also relies heavily on the spelling *shenanigan;* but the early variant *shinannikin,* for example, looks like a Choctaw word. *Shenanigan* entered the American vocabulary around 1855 in California, when it appeared in the small San Francisco newspaper *Town Talk* ("Are you quite sure? No *shenanigan?*"). Mark Twain wrote from California in 1862, "Consider them all . . . guilty of *'shenanigan'* until they are proved innocent." The California pedigree has led one etymologist to look for an origin in American Spanish. A poster advertising a land sale at Palomar, Los Angeles County, in 1887 suggests one possibility. "Grand Railroad Excursion and Genuine AUC-

TION SALE! NO CHENANEKIN!!!" In Mexican Spanish *chanada* is a shortened form of *charranada* (a trick played on someone for the sake of mere diversion). Another educated guess seeks the origin in the German slang term *schinägeln* (to work or toil, especially under strain). This term is from Rotwelsch, the underworld argot of peddlers and thieves, and would have entered American English by way of lower-class German immigrants. But the indolence implicit in *shenanigan* is at the opposite pole from the German verb meaning hard labor. To bridge the gap, this theory claims that hard labor is usually done without enthusiasm, the worker striving mainly to give the impression of activity. Thus, the sense of trickery develops from the tricks used by the laborer to spare himself exertion. These explanations, however, may only amount to etymological shenanigans.

PRETZEL (1856). This now well-known salty cracker shaped like a knot and best eaten with beer was probably first borrowed into American English from German *Pretzel* or *Bretzel*. It is not of German origin, however, since it is found in Italian as *bracciello* (a cracknel or brittle biscuit). Its ulterior source is either medieval Latin *bracellus* (a bracelet) or, more likely, *brachitellum*, from *bracchium* (arm), because the knotted biscuit looks like a pair of folded arms.

BLIZZARD (1859). Davy Crockett was partial to the word *blizzard:* "During dinner the parson . . . called on me for a toast. Not knowing whether he intended to . . . have some fun at my expense, I concluded to go ahead, and give him and his likes a *blizzard*" (1835, *An Account of Col. Crockett's Tour to the North and Down East*). Crockett then launched a volley of cutting words at the Tory parson and his like. Earlier he used *blizzard* in the sense of "a shot or volley of gun shots" ("I saw two more bucks, very large fellows, too. I took a *blizzard* at one of them and up he tumbled," 1834, *The Life and Adventures of Colonel David Crockett of West Tennessee*). Crockett's uses are obsolete extensions of the earliest sense of *blizzard,* "a sharp blow," which is also obsolete. *Blizzard* (a violent snowstorm) may be an extension of the earlier sense (a volley of shots) or may have originated in England. A blizzard of etymologies have been offered for this puzzling word. The earliest-known citation (1829) is also the earliest attempt to explain its origin by appealing to German *Blitz* (lightning). Another version suggests French *blesser* (to wound), but neither this nor the German can be substantiated. Yet another claims that *blizzard* derives from English dialect *blizzer,* meaning "a blaze" or "flash" ("Put towthry sticks on th' fire, an' let's have a blizzer," *English Dialect Dictionary*) or from *blazer* (something that blazes or blasts), which gave the early sense "a volley of firing guns," that is, a general "blazing away."

TYCOON (1861). When Commodore Perry negotiated a treaty with the Japanese in 1854, his hosts used the word *taikun* (great lord or prince) as the fitting title of the shogun, Iyesada. The Japanese borrowed the title from Chinese *ta* (great) and *kiun* (lord, prince) at least as early as the reign of the third Tokugawa shogun, Iyemitsu (1623–51), who was referred to as *taikun* in a letter sent to impress the "barbarian" Koreans with his greatness. After Perry and the American diplomats that followed brought the word back with them, it was used first as an affectionate nickname for Abraham Lincoln ("Gen. Butler has sent an imploring request to the President to be allowed to bag the whole nest of traitorous Maryland Legislators. This the *Tycoon* . . . forbade," 1861, John Hay, *Diary*) and then extended to refer to any important businessman or politician. By the way, *shogun* (general) is also a Chinese borrowing, from *chiang chün* (leader of an army).

TACKY (1862). In the good ole American entrepreneurial spirit, gift shops were cashing in on the flood of visitors to President Bush's hometown, Kennebunkport, Maine. "That's getting close to tacky," the president of the Kennebunkport

Chamber of Commerce observed. She was referring to $30 bedroom slippers with rubber figures of President George Bush on the left foot and Mrs. Bush entwined with pearls on the right, both bedded in American flags. This is the latest extended sense of *tacky* (gaudy, in poor taste). Originally, *tackies* were the scrubby little horses that roamed the marshy areas of the south Atlantic coast in the nineteenth century, descendants of the wild horses of the Carolina colonies. William Tatham, one of the numerous English observers of early America, was the first to note the local name for the wiry horse: "You are thus asked (in local phrase and expression) to *truck* or *trade* for a horse, a cow, or a little *tackie,* etc. (which last term signifies a poney or little horse of low price)," 1800, *Communications concerning the Agriculture and Commerce of the United States of America.* This Southern name for an inferior breed of horse was extended sometime in the 1830s to poor whites or "crackers," considered to be socially inferior ("That indescribable class of people known in that region [central Georgia] as the piney-woods *Tackies . . .* steeped in poverty of the most desolate description, and living the narrowest lives possible in this Great Republic," 1887, Joel Chandler Harris, *Free Joe*). A *tacky party* (c. 1900) was originally a costume party to which the guests came dressed as hayseeds and hillbillies, or in a later variation, dressed in clothes that were gaudy or lacking in taste, a prize going to the "tackiest" costume ("I have a 'previous engagement' to a *tacky party.* I am going as I usually go when at home and I bet I take the cake. My very best friends would refuse to recognize me if they ever saw me in my farm rags," 1911, Letter of Harry S. Truman to his wife, Bess Truman). Beginning in the South in the 1860s but soon spreading throughout the United States, *tacky* was used as an adjective meaning "having the shabby look of a tacky horse," that is "the look of a poverty-stricken person" ("What a weary, bedraggled *tacky*-looking set they were," 1862, K. Stone, *Journal*), then by extension "dowdy," "seedy," "down-at-heel" and eventually "cheap," "in poor taste" ("Two little cards with his name printed on them in gilt. *Tackey?* Ugh," 1883, Isabella Rittenhouse, *Maud*). *Tacky* (a small, inferior horse) may derive from *tack,* which originally meant "foodstuff, especially low-quality food," as in *hard tack* (ship's biscuit), but was extended primarily in English dialect to refer to "anything of little or no value or of inferior quality" (" 'Ow dun yore tatoes turn out this time, John?' 'Mighty middlin', theer inna [isn't] many, an' whad theer is bin poor *tack,*'" *English Dialect Dictionary*). To this dialect word-base was added the common *-ie* or *-y* suffix, which means "little" (as in *dearie*), in keeping with the littleness of the horses.

GRAPEVINE (1863). In the early 1960s when Marvin Gaye sang about hearing through the *grapevine* (an informal network for conveying information or rumor) that he was about to lose his lover, he was invoking a hundred-year-old metaphor. The telegraph line constructed in 1859 between Placerville, California, and Virginia City, Nevada, was supposedly called the *grapevine telegraph,* possibly owing to the similarity between its strung wires and the continuous, circuitous vines that connect bunches of grapes. A metaphorical sense of *grapevine telegraph* arose very quickly and was widely used during the Civil War. Before the 1860s were out, the phrase had been abbreviated to *grapevine,* though the original *grapevine telegraph* also survived ("Dispatches report that the *'grapevine telegraph'* told every American soldier the news within twenty-four hours," 1943, *The Christian Century*). In Australia *grapevine telegraph* finds an analogue in *bush telegraph* ("Soldiers have a *bush telegraph* system of their own. The wildest furphies [rumors] travel over it, but sometimes it carries the truth," 1944, J. Hetherington, *The Australian Soldier*).

BUM, BUMMER (1864, Vagrant; c. 1969, a disappointment). In the underworld argot of the drifter and vagrant, fine distinctions are made between *bum, hobo,* and *tramp.* A *hobo* is a free spirit, unattached to anything except his own wanderlust, working only when absolutely necessary. A *tramp* too is homeless, but refuses to work at all and will steal whenever possible. A *bum,* at least from the hobo's point of view, is one notch lower, because he has sunk into alcoholism. In fact, an early sense of *bum* (1871) is "a drunken spree" ("I intend to celebrate their return by going on a tremendous *'bum,'*"

1885, Elizabeth Custer, *Boots and Saddles*). These nuances were kept more or less distinct, especially during the jobless Depression, but even then they were essentially interchangeable to the man in the street. *Bum* is shortened from *bummer* (loafer, sponger), which entered American English by way of northern California and Oregon ("Come, clear out, you trunken loafer! Ve don't vant no *bummers* here!," 1855, *The Oregonian*). It is probably borrowed and altered German *bummler* (loafer) from *bummeln* (to loaf). The most notorious bummers were not loafers but deserters during the Civil War, who robbed and plundered the countryside. Of these, the most infamous in the South were *Sherman's bummers*, named in honor of the Union General William Sherman, who razed Atlanta and marched his army to the sea ("The inhabitants were in mortal terror of the lawless crew known as '*Sherman's bummers*,' who rode on the flanks of his army, accounts of whose fiendish outrages were on every tongue," 1917, James M. Morgan, *Recollections of a Rebel Reefer*). In the late 1960s, a *bummer* was not a person but "something that turns out to be a disappointment" ("All the films released this summer have been box-office *bummers*," 1969, Pauline Kael, in *The New Yorker*), or more characteristic of the decade, "a bad drug experience," "a bad trip" ("The worst *bummer* of all time was recorded by Robert Louis Stevenson. It seems that the good Dr. Jekyll tripped out on a mysterious powder and ended up as the nefarious Mr. Hyde," 1971, *Science News*). This use of *bummer* is not directly from the earlier *bummer* (loafer), but is the adjective *bum* (of poor or bad quality, as in a *bum experience*) plus the noun suffix *-er*. The adjective itself derives from the phrase *to be on the bum*, which meant "to tramp about as a vagrant" and was then extended to something that is in bad condition ("I sized it up that the house was *on the bum* and she didn't want me to see it," 1896, George Ade, *Artie*). Subsequently *bum* was used as an adjective by itself as in *bum steer* (false information or bad advice). The *steer* in this 1920s expression, by the way, probably originally referred to an ox or castrated bull that is sold to someone and turns out to be of inferior quality ("*Bum ox*—wrongly directed," 1903, Cincinnati *Enquirer*), though *steer* (to direct or guide) has reinforced the usage. An alternative derivation of *bum* (vagrant) says that it is from Scots dialect *bum* (1540, a lazy, dirty person), transferred from *bum* (1387, rump, buttocks). This earliest sense may be from Middle Dutch *bonne* (Modern Dutch *bom*) "bung," "anus," or it may be merely onomatopoeic, this sound being associated with the general sense of "protuberance," "swelling," as in *bump.* In British English this evolution of senses did not occur, and a *bum* is always "the rump" and not "a vagrant." Both bums (the vagrant and the buttocks) coalesce in the expression *bum's rush* (1925), which is often preceded by a chorus of "throw the bum out" and consists of grabbing the collar and the seat of the pants and hurling the "bum" onto the sidewalk. It is very possible that both origins are at work in the history of *bum:* the bummer and vagabond who has been figuratively knocked on his butt by life or fate or his own foibles.

BUSHWHACK (1866). "I mounted the stump that had been cut down for the occasion and began to *bushwhack* in the most approved style." Davy Crockett was not ambushing Indians from the stump, but just giving an old-fashioned stump speech complete with vigorous gestures as if he were chopping bushes. This sense of *bushwhack,* one of the earliest, has died out. The original *bushwhacker* (a backwoods dweller) is close to the Dutch root *bosch-wachter* (forest keeper or watchman). During the first half of the seventeenth century, the New Amsterdam Dutch, the first European settlers of New York City and the Hudson Valley, spiced American English with many new words, including *stoop, cruller, waffle, boss, dope,* and *bush* (back country, uncleared forest). The Australians borrowed *bush* from the Americans and, by count in the *Macquarie Dictionary,* proceeded to create sixty-seven different words with it. American English isn't quite as crazy about the word, but does use it in such combinations as *bush league, bush ranger,* and *bush fighting,* and a handful of regionalisms: *bush bacon* (rabbit), *bush buster* (hillbilly), *bush meeting* (a camp meeting or extended revival meeting), and *bush whiskey* (moonshine). In the South, a *bush baby* is an illegitimate child, because the baby is conceived in the "bush," and is sometimes also humorously called a *bushwhacker.* Early in the last century,

to live in the wilderness or to explore or search through it was
to bushwhack ("He knew something about . . . *bushwhacking*
around for ogres," 1889, Mark Twain, *Connecticut Yankee*), but
if one were too long in the bush, there was a danger of becoming *bushed* (overwhelmed by the isolation, or tired and exhausted). During early riverboating along the Ohio and Mississippi, *bushwhack* meant to pull the boat upstream by
grasping bushes along the bank. But it was during the Civil
War that the most common sense of *bushwhack* developed, "to
hide in the woods and attack or plunder," "to ambush" (*ambush* itself has the *bush* of *bushwhack,* though it comes through
Old French). One Yankee officer harangued against *bushwhacking* in the New York *Herald* (1862): "We would be glad
to meet any number of the Confederates in a fair fight; but
this infernal *bushwhacking* shall not be practised on the men of
my command, without [my] enforcing the severest penalties
of military retaliation." A hundred years earlier the British
had complained of the same guerrilla tactics used by the
Americans.

CZAR (1866, a person with dictatorial powers). The Russian
czars (emperors) have long been dead, but *czars* (persons with
dictatorial powers, tyrants, bosses) flourish in America. Captains of industry are sometimes called *czars;* the baseball com-
missioner is a "baseball czar"; and the head of the Drug
Enforcement Agency is the "drug czar." The word was first
used in this transferred sense in reference to President Andrew Johnson (1866), but did not gain wider popular use until
the 1890s, when it was the nickname of Thomas B. Reed,
speaker of the House of Representatives. Reed's tyrannical
application of the rules of parliamentary procedure in Congress earned him the sobriquet ("I remember asking the ex-
Speaker how he felt . . . when he was being held up as 'The
Czar'—a man whose iron heels were crushing out American
popular government," 1893, *McClure's Magazine*). English
borrowed *czar* in the mid-sixteenth century from Polish and
used it only with reference to the Russian emperors. The
Russian form, transliterated *tsar,* ultimately derives from
Latin *Caesar,* the surname of Julius Caesar, whose name was

used as the title of the emperors from Augustus to Hadrian (30 B.C. to A.D. 138). Latin *Caesar* became Greek *Kaisar,* which was adopted in the Germanic languages, for example, Gothic *kaisar,* giving modern German *Kaiser* (emperor). Old Slavic borrowed the Gothic form as *tsesari,* which is the immediate source of the Russian.

MAVERICK (1867). *Maverick* (an individualist, an unconventional person) is all-American—Texas to be exact. In 1845 Samuel A. Maverick, lawyer, land speculator, and one of the signers of the Texas Declaration of Independence against Mexico, reluctantly received four hundred head of cattle as payment on a $1,200 debt owed him by a neighbor unable to raise the cash. Contrary to later legend, Maverick was not much of a rancher and placed the cattle under the stewardship of a poor family near Matagorda Bay. The family performed their duties indifferently, letting the cattle wander and breed untended, and branding only about a third of the calves. The neighboring ranchers were well aware of the situation, and naturally called the loose unbranded calves "Maverick's," often putting their own brands on them, making them no longer Maverick's. The word stuck and became a generic term for any stray calf or cow, especially if it had no brand. *To maverick* was to steal unbranded or newborn animals ("Numerous cases are reported of cows having their throats cut so that the *mavericking* of the calf would be more easy," 1889, Glenrock [Wyoming] *Graphic*), and a person who "strayed" from conventional or accepted behavior or beliefs was a *maverick,* this sense being quickly exported to non-American English speech ("A very muzzy *Maverick* smote his sergeant on the nose," 1890, Rudyard Kipling, *Life's Handicap*).

PAN (1868). Gold fever is at the bottom of *pan* (to yield results, work out). The California gold rush of 1849 ("Scores of dispirited looking objects are wandering up and down the Arroyo to-day, with their *pans* and picks upon their shoulders," 1849, *Alta California*) popularized the expression to *pan for gold,* a technique for obtaining the precious metal by filling a pan with the ore and gently washing away the soil and gravel, leaving the heavy gold at the bottom of the pan. *To pan out,* then, is to produce the yellow stuff by means of this technique ("In the mining camps of California . . . it is etiquette to say, 'Here's hoping your dirt will *pan out* gay,'" 1866, Mark Twain, *Letters from the Sandwich Islands*). This was figuratively broadened to refer to any activity, "to yield an outcome, good or bad," a usage soon borrowed by the British ("He was hoping all along that this fight would *pan out* big and that he'd be able to pay you back what you had loaned him," 1923, P. G. Wodehouse, *The Adventures of Sally*). It is not clear whether the next sense of *pan* (to criticize severely) is also an extension of the gold-mining metaphor ("Will Shakespeare . . . was *panned* by the critics because he dared to delve into the argot of his day," 1927, *Vanity Fair*). Perhaps it comes from the notion of unsuccessful panning; when all the dirt is washed away and one is left holding only the pan, one might be said to be panned. Alternatively, it might come from the notion of cooking in a pan ("Shellfish are preferable either raw, roasted or *panned,*" 1871, George Napheys, *Prevention and Cure of Disease*), which is probably the source of the American phrase *on the pan,* meaning "to be criticized or reprimanded" ("Even when the newspapers puts [sic] him *on the pan* . . . the safe-playing, money-grabbing middleweight king just laughs at us," 1923, Harry C. Witwer, *Fighting Blood*). Hence, to *pan* someone is figuratively to "cook his or her goose," to criticize or put the person down ("MacCarthy *panned* me, said the toughness was largely bluff," 1947, Raymond Chandler, *Raymond Chandler Speaking*). The first *pan* (an open shallow container) is ultimately from Latin *patina* (a shallow dish or pan). *Pan* in film making means to "rotate the camera to get a panoramic effect" and is completely unrelated to pans, either mining or frying. It is an abbreviated form of *panoram* with the same meaning ("We are before the Erie cut, and as the camera *'panorams'* around, we get a glimpse of our splendid Eleventh Avenue Stable in Jersey City," 1915, *Wells Fargo Messenger*), which in turn is from *panorama* (a complete view of an area). The Scottish inventor Robert Barker patented the Panorama in 1787, a cylindrical device that unrolled a landscape or other scene before the viewer. He originally called it *La*

Nature à coup d'Oeil [Nature view or Nature at a glance], but a couple of years later coined the catchier *Panorama,* from Greek *pan* (all) and *horama* (a view), from *horan* (to look).

SHEBANG (1869). A *shebeen,* pronounced with the accent on the second syllable, [shə bēn'], is an Irish speakeasy or low-class pub that sells liquor without a license. It derives from Irish *seibin* (bad ale, small mug), the diminutive of *seibe* (mug, bottle). Irish immigrants to North America early in the nineteenth century brought the word with them. In Canada it stayed closer to the Irish form than in the United States. In the relative isolation of Newfoundland, where the Irish influence was especially strong, *shebeen* remained essentially unchanged in both form and meaning ("Peggy Rose kept a snug *sheebeen* at Twenty-mile Pond, on which was read the following: 'I've trusted many to my sorrow. / Pay to-day and trust tomorrow," 1886, *Colonist Christmas Number*) and is still current there though considered old-fashioned. In the rest of Canada and the United States, *shebeen* was altered to *shebang.* The Irish root meaning "a low-class tavern," however, only survives in Canada ("Less picturesque were the *shebangs* dotted along the rivers, where squaws and whiskey awaited the shanty boys and their winter pay," 1963, Edwin Guillet, *The Pioneer Farmer and Backwoodsman*). The Canadian *shebang* may have been influenced by the French Canadian word *cabane* (a cabin or hut). In the United States, stripped of its association with liquor, the shabby shacklike *shebang* was extended to mean simply "a crude shelter" or "ramshackle hut" ("[I am] among the groups around the fires, in their *shebang* enclosures of bushes," 1883, Walt Whitman, *Specimen Days*). At just about the same time that it became American English, *shebang* developed a new sense, "concern," "affair," "thing" ("I like the book, I like you and your style and your business vim, and believe the *chebang* will be a success," 1869, Mark Twain, *Letters*), which today usually occurs in the phrase *the whole shebang* ("Camels placidly nibble *the whole shebang,* not merely the smallish but the spike thorns," 1933, E. E. Cummings, *Letters*). It remains a puzzle, however, how the earlier sense (hut, shelter) relates to the whole shebang, so to speak.

MAFIA (1875). *Mafia* became American English when many members of this Italian secret society of criminals, sometimes called "the Black Hand," immigrated to the United States in the 1860s. In the 1890s the lynching of eleven Mafia members in New Orleans made national headlines as the *Mafia affair* and gave the word much wider currency. The organization itself originated when medieval Italian lords hired brigands to guard their feudal estates in exchange for protection from the royal and legal authorities. The name derives from a term in the Italian dialect of Sicily, *mafia* (boldness, bravado), which is probably from Arabic *mahjas* (aggressive boasting, bragging).

KNICKERS (1881). When Washington Irving wrote *History of New York,* he created an American-Dutch narrator named Diedrich Knickerbocker. Irving took Diedrich's sensibilities and patronymic from his friend Harmen Knickerbocker, a prominent New Yorker whose great-grandfather, for whom he was named, came from Holland to settle in Schaghticoke near Albany, and whose fame and courtly hospitality earned him the sobriquet "prince of Schaghticoke" ("Lastly came the Knickerbockers, of the great town of Scaghtikoke, where the folk lay stones upon the houses in windy weather, lest they should be blown away," 1809, Irving, *History of New York*). Like Smith or Carver or Baker, *Knickerbocker* itself is probably derived from the kind of employment the early ancestors engaged in, namely, a marble (Dutch *knicker*) glazer or baker *(bocker)*. So well known was Irving's *History* that *Knickerbocker* became a general term for New Yorkers of Dutch descent, and more broadly for any New Yorker. But it was George Cruikshank's memorable illustrations for Irving's book, portraying the old citizens in knee breeches, that gave *knickerbocker* its best-known meaning (loose-fitting trousers gathered in at the knee). So popular did these knee breeches become, especially among boys and sportsmen who needed clothing that allowed freedom of movement, that *knickerbocker* was soon shortened to *knickers.*

SWIPE (1889). The earliest-known citation of *swipe* (to steal) comes from a Seattle clothier who had an ingenious way of preventing the theft of the shirt on a mannequin during the Christmas shopping season: "He runs a steel chain through the sleeve, and fastens the chain to the dummy with a padlock. 'By adopting this method,' said the merchant, 'we can stand back and laugh at their vain attempts to *swipe* our goods' " (1889, Seattle *Post-Intelligencer*). An 1890 slang dictionary claims that *swipe* was theatrical jargon used with reference to entertainers who stole jokes and routines from others. In any case, *swipe* is a dialectal variant of *sweep.* Around 1800 it meant "a heavy blow" and was often used to refer to a sweeping, full-arm stroke or swing in golf or cricket. But the sense of stealing probably is extended from *sweep* (to clear away with a broom) in a manner analogous to the development of *swoop* (to pounce upon and seize like a bird of prey in a sweeping movement) from Old English *swapan* (to sweep with a broom, to brandish a sword). Before being extended to the sense "stealing," *swipe* in English dialect meant "swoop and hastily seize or remove something" ("When awd [old] man deed [died], Bob swipet [swiped] all bit o' brass he had," *English Dialect Dictionary*).

DOPE (1890s). Around 1800 Dutch *doop* (a dipping sauce) became American *doup* or *dope* (gravy) ("Philo Dripping-pan was remarkable for his predilection to eating, and his love of what the learned Dutch call *doup,*" 1807, Washington Irving, *Salmagundi*). *Doop* is from Dutch *dopen* (to dip), which ultimately derives, through Proto-Germanic *dub-* (to drop, dip), from Indo-European **dhoub-* or **dheub-* (deep, hollow). Because of its clash with the other meanings of *dope* (a narcotic drug, a stupid person), except in a few isolated linguistic pockets this sense (sauce, gravy) is rapidly dying out in favor of the universal *gravy*. In much of Ohio and surrounding areas, however, *dope* can still be heard when someone asks for a dessert topping for pudding or ice cream. The underlying concept of a thick, sticky consistency is the source of most of the extended meanings. Any viscous liquid preparation is *dope*, from skin cream ("Give me some perfumed *Dope* that will restore a Peaches and Cream Complexion," 1901, George Ade, *Forty Modern Fables*) to axle grease ("They looked at his ear. 'Happen to any man careless around a horse. Put a little *axle-dope* on it and you wont notice it tomorrow though,' " 1940, William Faulkner, *The Hamlet*). A *dope* (a simpleton) is a thick-headed person, as if having dope for brains (cf. KLUTZ). The viscous preparation of opium used for smoking was dubbed *dope* in the 1880s and was soon extended to any stupefying narcotic drug. A decade later *dope* was transferred to the opium or dope user himself, also known as a *dope fiend* (1896) or *dope addict* (1933). At about the same time (1890s), *dopey* was formed from the noun and meant "stupefied" or "sluggish," as if one were drugged, and by extension, meant "dull" or "stupid" ("A Young Man with Hair who played the 'Cello. He was so wrapped up in his Art that he acted *Dopey* most of the time," 1900, George Ade, *More Fables*). Dope was also a preparation of drugs injected into a race horse to affect its performance, a practice known as *doping*, transferred to *blood doping* in the 1970s, in which athletes increased their blood-cell count by reinjecting their blood with most of the plasma removed. Because a bettor who knew that a horse was doped would have an advantage, *dope* came to mean "inside knowledge," "a tip." In the Southern United States, especially the South Atlantic states, *dope* is a carbonated drink, usually a Coca-Cola, which was originally a Southern beverage invented in Atlanta, Georgia, in 1893 ("Everybody likes Coca-Cola. There is nothing better to drink on a hot day, if the *dopes* are nice and cool," 1931, Erskine Caldwell, *American Earth*). This probably originated in a confusion between *Coke* (1909), another name for Coca-Cola, and *coke* (1908), a shortened version of *cocaine*, which of course is dope.

FEISTY (1890). When a linguist tramping the Kentucky hills first recorded it in 1890, *feisty* (spirited, excitable, irritable, impertinent) was a dialect term found primarily in the Upper Southern region of the United States. Since about 1950 it has become widespread. Its extended sense (putting on airs), however, has remained regional (*"Feisty* means when a feller's stuck on hisself and wants to show off—always wigglin' about wanting everybody to see him," 1917, *Dialect Notes*). *Feisty* was a regional term because it derived from a regionalism, *feist* (a small mongrel dog), even today virtually unknown outside the Southern United States. A feist is a spunky and contentious little dog that many Southern folks believe to be a breed apart, as distinctive as a Catahoula hog dog. One Southerner gave this definition to a linguist collecting dialect in the Smoky Mountains of Tennessee, "A *feist* is a little dog that stays around the house and keeps the varmints run off. He barks more than anything else. Just a 'scare dog' you might call him." *Feist* is a shortened form of *fisting cur* or *fisting hound,* which was a small pet dog ("The Puppy, or *Fisting-Dog,* [is] such as Ladies delight in," 1688, Randle Holme, *The Academy of Armory*). *Fisting* is the participial adjective of *fist* (to fart), pronounced with a long *i* (rhyming with *iced*), and was used as an epithet of contempt ("Where as your *fisting* Nonnes [nuns] were of Antichrist and the deuill [devil]," 1546, John Bale, *The Actes of the Englysh Votaryes*). *Fist,* from Old English *fistan,* ultimately traces back through Germanic to Indo-European **peis-* (to blow).

PANHANDLER (1897). Ed Koch, the former mayor of New York, made this characteristically acerbic pronouncement on CBS television: "When you give to the average *panhandler* you're simply feeding their addiction, which is generally drugs or booze." This was an ineffectual attempt to discourage panhandlers by discouraging the panhandled. The poor have always been with us, but *panhandler* (beggar) has only been around since the 1890s. It comes from *panhandle* (the act of begging), which was current some fifty years earlier. And *panhandle* derives from the beggar's outstretched arm, palm up, which resembles the handle of a pan. It is a *pan* handle because *pan* alludes to the beggar's bowl or cup held out to receive the offering, so that the donor does not have to touch the beggar, who often uses his scruffy appearance or diseased or maimed body to evoke sympathy. Among beauticians, at least thirty years ago, a *panhandler* was a beauty-shop girl because she labored over her customer's "pans" (faces).

THIRD DEGREE (1900). American gangster and prison movies popularized the expression *the third degree* (intensive questioning or rough treatment of a prisoner, usually by the police, to obtain information) and gave it world-wide recognition (" 'You don't think they're giving him *third degree* or anything of that sort?' 'My dear fellow, *third degree?* You've been watching too many old movies on the TV. The police don't use strong-arm methods in this country,' " 1976, Thomas Sharpe, *Wilt*). The expression probably originated with criminals and prisoners ("From time to time a prisoner . . . claims to have had the *Third Degree* administered to him," 1900, *Everybody's Magazine*). It was filched from the rank or grade in Freemasonry, the *Third Degree* (1772), that of master mason. In the ceremony conferring the degree, the candidate is interrogated, though without any strong-arming. The slang use was probably additionally influenced by the notion of something done with a greater than usual degree of intensity, as in a *third-degree burn.*

PHONY (1900). *Phony* or *phoney* (fake, counterfeit, false), which entered American English around 1900, has several phony etymologies. Early editions of Merriam Webster's dictionary tried to relate it to *funny,* though all editions after 1934 eschew this etymology with either silence or "origin unknown." A more far-fetched explanation seeks the source in *telephone* ("A statement is *phoney* if it is like the practical jokes and false impersonations that are so frequently perpetrated over the telephone," 1922, Boston *Traveler*). H. L. Mencken suggested that it derives from *Forney,* the name of a manufacturer of cheap jewelry. Forney's specialty was brass rings, which he distributed in barrel lots primarily to street peddlers, who called them *Forney rings*. *Forney* was then extended to all cheap jewelry and then to anything not genuine, the word being modified in the process to *phoney*. Although no one puts any store in this version, eventually including Mencken himself, the role of brass rings and bogus jewelry aré central to the true history of the word. *Phony* probably originated in the earlier English slang term *fawney* (a gilt brass ring), from Irish *fàinne* (ring). In the 1890s a *fawney man* was a seller of bogus jewelry, and a *fawney* was the key ingredient in a simple confidence game known as a *fawney rig*, described in the 1796 edition of Francis Grose's *Classical Dictionary of the Vulgar Tongue:*

> A common fraud thus practised:—a fellow drops a brass ring, double gilt, which he picks up before the party meant to be cheated, and to whom he disposes of it for less than its supposed, and ten times more than its real, value.

These confidence men were called *fawney droppers*. Although *fawney* is an English term, it was in America that it was extended to have the general meaning of "counterfeit" or "fake," and became *phony*. It was then reimported to England in its new form in the 1930s. But it was not until 1939 when American journalists began writing about the "Phoney War," the period of comparative inactivity from the outbreak of World War II to the invasion of Norway and Denmark, that it became widely known in the English-speaking world at large.

PUSSYFOOT (1903). *Pussyfoot* (to move or act cautiously or stealthily), which was either coined or popularized by President Theodore Roosevelt, had originally a positive connotation in contrast to its later extended sense "to refrain from committing oneself, to behave evasively or timidly" ("Ingalls once said of Senator William B. Allison that he was so *pussyfooted* he could walk from New York to San Francisco on the keys of a piano and never strike a note," 1924, D. S. Barry, *Forty Years in Washington*). William "Pussyfoot" Johnson

(1862–1945), a respected chief law-enforcement officer for the U.S. Indian Service, earned the nickname *Pussyfoot* because he implemented effective "catlike policies in pursuing lawbreakers in the Indian Territory," as he himself explained in *Who's Who in America,* obtaining some 4,400 convictions during his tenure (1908–11). Johnson was also active in the Anti-Saloon League and frequently lectured on temperance. Not only was he instrumental in the passage of Prohibition in 1919, he took the "cause" to London, where it was not always met with enthusiasm. In fact at Essex Hall an angry lush in the crowd he was lecturing to threw a stone and blinded him in one eye. Despite such setbacks, so effective was Johnson's crusade that he gave the British a new term for TEETOTALER, *pussyfoot* (*"Gloomy policeman.* 'You've had enough. Better go home.' *Reveller.* 'Shurr-up—*Pussyfoot!,* '" 1922, *Punch*). *Pussy,* which is first recorded in 1726, is the diminutive of *puss* (cat) used before 1530. *Puss* is perhaps imitative of a cat hissing or spitting, or more likely is a sound used to attract a cat. It is common to several languages, including Dutch *(poes),* Gaelic *(puis),* Low German (*Pus* or *Pus-katte*), and Norwegian *(pus),* all meaning "cat."

BUFF (1903). A *buff* is an enthusiast or fan, originally an enthusiast about going to fires. Early in this century, *buffs* were lads or men fascinated with the glamour and excitement of firefighting and were often seen hanging around the firehouse running errands for the firemen. Indeed, the first buffs (about 1820) were unpaid volunteer firemen, whose fascination itself was payment enough. *Buff,* which originated in New York City, is a shortening of *buffalo* and, though buffaloes seem etymologically distant from the Big Apple and firefighting, they come into the picture in either of two ways. The early volunteer firemen sometimes slept at the firehouse on buffalo robes and wore waterproof buffalo skins when responding to an alarm. The more widely accepted version holds that the volunteers wore "buff-colored" uniforms or overcoats, "buff" being the yellowish color of tanned buffalo hide.

FINK (1903). There are three different kinds of *finks:* "an unpleasant, contemptible person" first recorded in 1903 ("Anyone who goes against the Faculty single-handed is a *Fink,*" George Ade, *People You Know*); "a strikebreaker" (c. 1925); and "an informer" ("Now he's looking for the *fink* that turned him up eight years ago," 1940, Raymond Chandler, *Farewell, My Lovely*), first cited in 1929, though the verb (to inform on someone) is recorded earlier, in 1925 ("Suppose you had to hire a Private eye. . . . Would you want one that *finked* on his friends?" 1953, Raymond Chandler, *The Long Good-bye*). Likewise there are three or four different proposed etymologies, each emphasizing one of the three senses. The first addresses the earliest sense (contemptible person), suggesting it is a borrowing from German *Fink* (a dissolute person), originally university slang for a student who is not officially enrolled. It is probably taken from *Shmierfink* (a low, dirty person or hack), literally "a greasy or dirty bird." The second version focuses on the "strikebreaker" sense. It claims that *fink* dates from the Homestead Strike of 1892, when operatives of the *Pinkerton* detective agency, contemptuously referred to as *Pinks* and then *finks,* were employed to break the strike. Finally, *fink* (an informer) is given attention in two different derivations. The first and least plausible suggests that *fink* is an abbreviation and alteration of *finger,* "to inform on or point out a criminal to the police" ("Frank Lee . . . had *'fingered'* many, many dealers to the Feds," 1930, *Flynn's Magazine*). This American slang term, however, does not appear until almost thirty years after the first known usage of *fink.* An alternative version argues that it is a borrowing of German *fink* (finch) and is parallel to STOOL PIGEON and the old slang term *sing* (to turn informer). Unless the record is faulty, it seems reasonable to assume that the etymology corresponding to the first sense is the correct one. However, there is no direct evidence for any one of these; accordingly, most dictionaries play it safe with "origin uncertain."

FOUR-FLUSHER (1904). As early as 1529 a *flush* was a hand of cards all of the same suit, probably deriving from Middle French *flus* (a flowing), that is, a "run" of cards. Of the five cards of a poker hand, if only four are the same suit it is a *four-flush,* a usually worthless hand. A more worthless hand, one that can barely call itself a *flush,* is the *bobtailed flush,* which is a three-card straight or flush ("Mr. Wallace Offdean hurried to the bank in order to replenish his portemonnaie, which had been materially lightened at the club through the medium of unpropitious jack-pots and *bobtail flushes,*" 1894, Kate Chopin, *Bayou Folk*). *To four-flush* is to bluff with an incomplete flush, such as a four-flush, that is, to make opponents think the hand is more valuable than it is, or figuratively applied, to deceive or mislead people by bragging or being pretentious (" 'I thought he was going to fight.' 'Not that boy. He was *four-flushin,*' " 1896, George Ade, *Artie*), A *four-flusher,* then, is a pretender or braggart.

HAYWIRE (1905). In an industrial country with huge farms, baling machines were inevitably invented to bind automatically straw or hay with soft wire. And just as inevitably the new word, *haywire* (c. 1900), was extended to new senses. In the rough world of loggers, railroad workers, and hobos, *haywire* ("You can't run a logging camp without snuff and *hay wire,*" 1921, *Outing Magazine*) meant "inefficient or poorly equipped." A *haywire outfit* was a logging operation that had brokendown equipment repaired with haywire ("A rawhide railroad was a road that depended on cheap substitutes or extreme economies, just as a *haywire outfit* was one that had inadequate equipment," 1953, Benjamin Botkin and Alvin Harlow, *Treasury of Railroad Folklore*), and a *haywire line* or *road* was a small, inefficient railroad. The notion of broken, haywired machinery gave the sense "out of order," *to go haywire* ("When some element in the recording system becomes defective it is said to have gone *haywire,*" 1929, *New York Times*). Compounding this extended sense is the metaphor that equates springy, tangled haywire with emotional or mental confusion or craziness ("A married man . . . and absolutely *haywire* on the subject of another woman," 1934, John O'-Hara, *Appointment in Samarra*).

PASS THE BUCK (1912). Though most Americans know that President Harry S Truman had a hand-lettered sign on his desk that said THE BUCK STOPS HERE alluding to the expression *pass the buck* (shift the responsibility to someone else), few know that this is an old poker expression ("You ruther hold over me, pard. I reckon I can't call that hand. Ante and *pass the buck,*" 1872, Mark Twain, *Roughing It*). Instead of all players putting up an ante every hand, the dealer would ante and then pass a *buck,* usually a small article like a knife or a key, to the player on his left. When the hand was over, the player with the buck would ante, then deal the cards, and pass the buck on. Originally the buck was a *buckhorn knife,* a knife that had a handle made from deer's horn. A *buck* meaning "a dollar" comes from *buckskin,* back when deerskins were used as a unit of exchange (1748), especially in the Old West among frontiersmen and Indians. In modern casinos the buck used in poker is called a *button* or *puck.*

JAZZ (1913). *Jazz* has a convoluted and disputed history, New Orleans, Chicago, and San Francisco all claiming to be the birthplace. In the first two decades of this century, the *jazz* was a three-step dance done to the four-beat rhythm of ragtime. Very shortly the word was transferred to the music to which the *jazz* was danced. The dance soon vanished, but the music and the word, of course, survived. Several proposed etymologies seek the source in a proper name. On a planta-

tion in antebellum New Orleans (c. 1825), there was supposedly a famous dancing slave named *Jasper,* who graciously
lent his name to the dance and subsequently the music. A
similar story appeals to the name of a ragtime drummer from
Vicksburg, Mississippi, *Charles* Washington, famous near the
end of the last century. A Southern nickname for *Charles* is
Chas or *Chaz,* which supposedly became associated with his
free-form style of drumming. Yet another version claims it is
from the name of a black Chicago musician named *Jasbo (Jas)*
Brown. Other word historians seek explanations in Louisiana
French, *jaser* (to speed up, to chatter, make fun), and in an
African word, such as Mandingo *jasi* (to act out of character,
be unlike oneself) or Temne *yas* (to be energetic or lively).
The African connection seems to be the most likely source,
some unrecorded West African word giving the intermediate
English word *jasm* "enthusiasm, energy" ("If you'll take thunder and lightning and a steamboat and a buzz-saw and mix
'em up and put 'em into a woman, that's *jasm,*" 1860, Josiah
Holland, *Miss Gilbert's Career*). *Jasm* and *jazz* were also used
with reference to sex and sexual intercourse, and may have
been influenced by *gism* ("*Jazz* 'em all you like . . . but get the
money," 1929, Thomas Wolfe, *Look Homeward, Angel*).

BIMBO (1919). *Bimbo* (a woman, especially of loose morals),
sometimes abbreviated *bim* ("Studs Lonigan copped off [stole
from] a *bim* whose old man is lousy with dough," 1935, James
Farrell, *Studs Lonigan*), is labeled in most dictionaries "slang,"
and as such is difficult to trace, since slang is usually "secret"
or "in-group" language. In the nineteenth century *bimbo* or
bumbo was a punch made with cognac or rum, probably from
Italian *bombo,* a child's word for "drink." Like *tart* (a small
fruit pie, a prostitute), this potent punch may have been transferred to refer to a saucy woman. A more plausible explanation places its origin in Italian *bimbo* (little child, baby) from
bambo (silly), the diminutive of which gives *bambino* (baby).
But early in this century, if English borrowed the Italian word,
it quickly extended the sense "child" to "fellow," "chap,"
often used with derision ("*Bimbos* who went about the place
making passes at innocent girls after discarding their wives,"

1947, P. G. Wodehouse, *Full Moon*). By the late 1920s it was transferred to its current sense, first appearing in a glossary of vagabond lingo. This transfer of meaning from "fellow" or "man," to "a woman of questionable morals" occurs in the histories of several other words and reflects a cultural bias against women, also seen in the plethora of words for "loose woman" (*chippie, trollop, slut, whore, concubine, slattern,* etc.), and the dirth of corresponding terms for men. BROTHEL, for example, originally referred to a "worthless fellow" or "scoundrel" before it was transferred to a "prostitute," both senses now being obsolete. A HARLOT was originally a scoundrel or knave, and a *bawd* was a male pimp. Like *bimbo, wench* and *wanton* both originally referred to a child before taking on the sense of "a woman of ill repute."

COLD TURKEY (1920s). *To quit or go cold turkey* (abruptly to stop taking drugs, of a drug addict) came into use in the 1920s and probably developed from the earlier *to talk cold turkey* (to speak bluntly about something unpleasant), unfeeling abruptness being the underlying concept. It was also probably influenced by the resemblance of the pimply skin of a plucked turkey to the clammy skin of a sick and feverish junkie in withdrawal. In this century the turkey has suffered bad PR and is widely regarded as a stupid, ugly bird. In the 1920s, an unsuccessful movie or play was a *turkey* ("The boys at the studio have lined up another turkey for us," Groucho Marx wrote in a 1939 letter), and a few decades later the sense had broadened to refer to a stupid, inept person. The turkey, however, has not always been in such ill repute. In the nineteenth century, *to talk turkey* meant to speak affably and say pleasant things, often with flowery words. And in the eighteenth century there was a serious movement, led by Benjamin Franklin, to make the turkey the national bird. The name itself is a misnomer. *Turkey* originally referred to the guinea fowl, native to Africa, which Turkish traders introduced to England in the sixteenth century, hence the name. At about the same time Spanish conquistadors introduced turkeys to Europe from southern Mexico, where the Aztec Indians had domesticated them. By about 1541 they had spread to England. To the English, the North American bird with its bald wattled head resembled a guinea fowl, so both birds for a time were called turkeys. When they became distinguished, *turkey* stuck with the American bird. Almost immediately after being introduced to Europe, the turkey was associated with holiday feasting, especially with Christmas, and in the U.S. with Thanksgiving.

RAZZ (1921). To deride or make fun of someone is *to razz* them ("When I came to work the other girls used to *razz* me, call me 'Duchess' and say, 'Look at her, she thinks she's a lady,'" 1956, Billy Holiday, *Lady Sings the Blues*). *To razz* is to give someone the *razz* ("She'll prob'ly give me the *razz* for being out late last night!," a. 1919, C. Briggs, *Oh Man!*), that is, to give someone the *razzberry*. *Razzberry* is a variant of *raspberry* (1890), also known as a *Bronx cheer,* which is a derisive sound made by blowing through the closed lips, usually with the tongue in between. By 1920 one could give someone the *raspberry* without actually making the sound of contempt, because the word had been figuratively extended to mean "disapproval," "dismissal," "refusal" ("He was given the respectful *raspberry* by Jeeves, and told to try again about three hours later," 1924, P. G. Wodehouse, *Inimitable Jeeves*). It is the vulgar sound, however, that is the source of the word. *Raspberry* is an ellipsis for *raspberry tart,* which is rhyming slang for *fart* ("Then I sallied forth with a careless air, / And contented *raspberry tart,"* 1892, *Sporting Times*). Rhyming slang was especially popular in the 1890s and early in this century. It employs the substitution of a word or phrase that rhymes with the word substituted for. For example, *turtledoves* means *gloves,* and *tit-for-tat* refers to a *hat.* As with *raspberry tart,* the phrases are often shortened: *turtledoves* becomes *turtles* ("A long sleeve cadi on his napper, and a pair of *turtles* on his martins finished him," 1893, P. H. Emerson, *Signor Lippo*) and *tit-for-tat* becomes *titfer* ("I'll see Billy Fitt, with me *titfer* in me 'and," 1939, J. B. Priestley, *Let the People Sing*).

HIJACK (1923). "If we show fear in response to this aggression, all our institutions are *hijacked."* This was Susan Sontag's response to Ayatollah Khomeini's death threat made against her fellow writer, Salman Rushdie, in March, 1989. Her choice of *hijack* invokes the late extended sense, "to seize an airplane in flight and force the pilot to fly to a new destination," a common pastime of terrorists since the 1960s, sometimes referred to as *skyjacking* (1961). The first hijackers were robbers of robbers, stealing contraband or illicit goods from thieves and bootleggers. An early attempt to explain *hijack* claims that it was used by the Wobblies or members of the I.W.W. (Industrial Workers of the World) and comes from the command to raise the arms above the head, "High, Jack!," that is, "Stick 'em up." A more likely explanation is that it is a combination of *high* abstracted from *highwayman* (a highway robber) and *jack*. Which *jack* is in dispute. It could be the *jack* that refers to a man (cf. JACKLEG). Or the one that refers to the mechanical device that hoists things. Or it could be a reference to hunting at night with the aid of a *jacklight,* hijacking often taking place under the cover of night.

GOLD BRICK (1926, to shirk). A *gold brick* is just that, a brick-shaped chunk of gold—that is, unless someone tries to sell you one ("Gilmore swindled Patrick Burke, a citizen of St. Louis, out of $3,700 by the *gold-brick* trick," 1887, Louisville *Courier-Journal*). In this simple scam the brick may look like gold but it is in fact worthless, which is why by 1900 *gold brick* meant "to swindle" ("They always have coin. . . . They get it *gold-bricking* New Yorkers," 1908, *Saturday Evening Post*). By the outbreak of the First World War, a *gold brick* or *gold bricker* was an army lieutenant appointed to his rank directly from civilian life without going through the usual officer's training. In other words, as in the swindle, he was not the genuine thing, but was soft and pretended to be what he wasn't ("I think you're a *gold brick.* . . . You don't look as if you were wounded the slightest bit," 1926, Leonard Nason, *Chevrons*). The *gold bricker* cheated his way through the army and the war to avoid doing his duty or work. By the 1930s the contemporary sense, "a shirker," was fully developed, and the earlier meaning of an officer appointed from civilian life had faded away, though through that decade and the next the new meaning was still used primarily in a military context ("The

wise guy always complains when there is work to do. Sometimes [in the army] he is called a *Gold Brick,*" 1943, *Reader's
Digest*). Not until the 1950s did it really break out into general
use ("Students with applied art or science majors tended to
gold-brick on their reading courses," 1952, Mary McCarthy,
Groves of Academe).

KIBITZ (1927). In Yiddish *kibitsen* is to look over the shoulder of the players of a card game and to offer them gratuitous
advice ("Drax . . . [sorted] his cards . . . only into reds and
blacks, ungraded, making his hand very difficult to *kibutz,*"
1955, Ian Fleming, *Moonraker*). It is from German *kiebitzen* (to
look on at cards), which is itself from *Kiebitz* (pewit), a shore
bird. The connection between the pewit and the *kibitzer* (med-
dling onlooker) is the crux of this derivation. One version
offered by H. L. Mencken recounts a story from the reminis-
cences of the Austrian count Karl Schoenfeld (1828–66). It
seems that in the Italian campaign of 1848–49, a certain General Haizinger, who commanded the noncombatant Adjutant
Corps, owned a little dog he called *Kiebitz,* because it reminded him of the jittery pewit or plover. The officers on the
front line were soon referring derisively to the officers of the
Adjutant Corps as *Kiebitze.* To the line officers, the staff officers were mere onlookers of the war. Before long *Kiebitz*
began to refer to anyone who looks on at a game but does not
participate, a usage that spread from the army to the cafés of
Vienna. A simpler explanation interprets the skittish behavior
of the plover or *Kiebitz,* a ground nester that runs about ner-
vously when approached, to a busybody or meddler. *Kiebitz*
was then transferred to a person who interferes or meddles,
specifically at card games. The German word itself is from
Middle High German *gibitz* (pewit), which is imitative of the
sound that the bird makes.

BUTCH (1930). In 1902 Pinkerton's private detective
agency published in its February circular a wanted notice for
"George Parker, alias 'Butch' Cassidy, alias George Cassidy."
This famous American outlaw of the early 1900s popularized

the nickname *Butch,* which Damon Runyon adopted as the name of a tough character in his 1931 collection of stories *Guys and Dolls,* one of which is titled "Butch Minds the Baby." From then on *butch* was a term referring to a tough boy or man. In the 1940s and 1950s it was a popular name for a dog, as well as for a short haircut or crew cut, perhaps because toughs favored this particular hairdo. Around 1950 *butch* was transferred to lesbians whose appearance and behavior was considered masculine. Butch Cassidy's nickname, which started the whole thing, is probably a shortened version of BUTCHER (a slaughterer of animals, a ruthless killer), or less likely it may be from *butch* ("Boon bought . . . a bottle of beer from the news *butch,"* 1942, William Faulkner, *Go Down, Moses*), itself an abbreviation of *butcher,* an Americanism for a vendor of candy, newspapers, and other items. The American term is an extension of *butcher* (a vendor or tradesman who cuts and sells meat).

REEFER (1931). A hand-rolled marijuana cigarette or *reefer* ("The air of the trailer was heavy with the stinks of food and *reefers,"* 1940, Carson McCullers, *The Heart Is a Lonely Hunter*) resembles a rolled-up sail on a sailing ship known since the fourteenth century as a *reef* or *riff.* The *reef* was the portion of a sail rolled up to decrease the amount of canvas exposed to the wind ("The wynd was good, the See was plein, Hem nedeth noght a *Riff* to slake," 1390, John Gower, *Confessio Amantis*). If one lets down the reefs, the ship will go faster; hence, *reef* is also used figuratively to mean "to get the lead out," "to speed up" ("I lit out, and shook the *reefs* out of my hind legs," 1884, Mark Twain, *Huckleberry Finn*). *Riff* is found earlier in the compound *rifrope* (the rope used to tie the reef) and derives from a Scandinavian source. Ultimately it is probably transferred from *rif* (ridge), which in turn is from *rib.* Given the sometime habit of sailors to smoke the hemp of ropes, the nautical connection between *reef* and *reefer* seems reasonable enough. A plausible alternative derivation appeals to the Mexican connection, a primary source of the weed itself and much of the terminology, such as POT and *marijuana.* *Reefer* is probably an alteration and folk etymology of underworld jargon *griffa* or *griefo* (marijuana). And *griffa* is from Mexican Spanish *grifa* (marijuana, drug addict), a word that also means "drunkard," "cheap tavern," "spigot."

BOONDOGGLE (1935). *Boondoggle* (a trivial or wasteful project or activity) has been a favorite term in American politics for almost sixty years and was ubiquitous in the 1930s, when Republicans used it to criticize the alphabet soup of agencies (WPA, FERA, NYA, CCC) created by the Roosevelt administration to cope with the Depression. Roosevelt for his part took up the term to criticize the foreign loans made earlier under the GOP as "foreign boondoggling." One explanation of its origin claims that it is jargon from the iron-smelting industry and designates unprofitable attempts to retrieve good iron from slag. Another says that it is from Scottish, meaning a playing marble received as a gift without having been earned. A *doggle* or *dogle* is indeed English dialect for a common marble, but there is no evidence that it was ever compounded with *boon* (favor, gift), and in any case it is very difficult to see any relationship between "an unearned marble" and "a wasteful or trivial activity." The earliest citation for *boondoggle* offers a limited and undocumented explanation (" '*Boon doggles*' is simply a term applied back in the pioneer days to what we call gadgets today," 1935, *New York Times*). The most commonly accepted etymology holds that *boondoggle* was the fanciful invention of Robert H. Link, a New York scoutmaster. He supposedly began using it around 1925 to refer to the ornamental plaited neck cords made by Boy Scouts under his direction, an activity he considered "make-work."

TIZZY (1935). The American coinage *tizzy* (an excited and distracted state, a dither) usually found in the phrase *in a tizzy* ("Maybe it's better for the future of the race to live from daze to daze in a perpetual *tizzy* like Alix," 1938, *Ladies' Home Journal*), was happily adopted in the 1950s by the Australians, who thoroughly made it their own. When they use it in its original sense, they often abbreviate it to *tizz* ("*Peter:* Nothing matters. *Angela:* Practically nothing. All the things people get in such a *tizz* about—," 1954, B. Boland, *Return*). They bent its meaning to include "showy" or "gaudy" ("I send you lots of presents. Nice things, too. Nothing *tizzy,*" 1969, G. Johnston, *Clean Straw for Nothing*), which they also converted into a verb meaning "to dress up," "spruce up" ("According to children mothers get all '*tizzied* up' before they go out," 1960, K. Smith, *A Word from Children*). *Tizzy* may be related to the English slang term for a sixpenny piece ("So I gets a *Tizzy* for to let them alone," 1804, J. Collins, *Scripscrap*). The name for the coin may have been used in a play on words meaning a "little" amount of money and time ("A man reads, at a '*tizzy,*' what he had not read when priced at twelve times the humble tanner," 1901, *Longman's Magazine*). Alternatively, it may come from English dialect *tizzle* (to stir up or turn over), modified by the example of *dizzy*. One who is in a tizzy is emotionally or mentally "stirred up" or *tizzled,* dizzy and dithery. *Tizzle* is a variant of *teazle* or *teasel* (to raise the nap on cloth with or as with teasels, to tease). And *teasel* is a plant whose flowerheads with hooked prickles were used like brushes to tease or dress cloth so as to raise the nap ("The best clothiers still prefer the *teazel* to finish their cloth," 1870, John Yeats, *The Natural History of Commerce*).

G-STRING (1936). "What I know about politics you could put in a chorus girl's *g-string* and it wouldn't raise a lump" (1951, Irwin Shaw, *The Troubled Air*). To be sure there is not much to a *G-string* or *gee-string,* the bit of cloth—sometimes a mere string—today worn only by showgirls and strippers. In the nineteenth century, however, only American Indians wore *gee-strings* ("Around each boy's waist is the tight *'geestring'* from which a single strip of cloth runs between the limbs from front to back," 1878, John H. Beadle, *Western Wilds*). The spelling with *G* is probably influenced by the string on a violin or other instrument tuned to G. Why the Indian loincloth was called a *gee-string* is not known. One can be sure that it has nothing to do with a *g-suit*, a high-tech garment designed to partially protect a person from high *g* (from *g*ravity) force due to extreme acceleration.

BLOOPER (1937). When Rip Sewell died in 1989, one of the things the former Pittsburgh Pirates pitcher was remembered for was the *blooper*. This was a high-arching pitch that often reached some twenty-five feet in the air before plummeting with backspin toward the plate. Sewell was successful with the unorthodox pitch, which he called an *eephus* (apparently a term he borrowed from crap shooting), until he lobbed one too many to Ted Williams in the 1946 All-Star Game. Williams was the only player to hit a home run off one of Sewell's bloopers. Ten years earlier when a sports writer mentioned a blooper he meant a lofting fly ball hit to the unoccupied space behind the infield and in front of the outfielders. (A base-hit pop fly, for some reason, has been dubbed with numerous names besides blooper, including *awful, banjo hit, bleeder, drooper, humpie, humpback, humpback liner, Japanese liner, Leaping Lena, looper, percentage sinker, plunker, pooper, punker, smell hit, squibber, stinker, sucker,* and *Texas Leaguer.*) The oldest blooper (c. 1925), however, is a radio whose frequency causes other radios to howl or *bloop, bloop* being an imitation of the blooping sound. A bloop is also the sound a splice in a film's sound track makes when it passes over the tape head. It was probably the blooping sound's short unexpectedness, like a short pop fly that drops just out of reach, reinforced by the similarity of *loop* (the blooper fly ball was also called a *looper*), that created the baseball usage. Similarly, the sudden inappropriateness of a radio blooping in the middle of a suspenseful program or a Toscanini concert gave *blooper* the figurative sense of a publicly embarrassing blunder or howler.

POT (1938, marijuana). One dictionary of slang lists over six hundred names for marijuana and its types and grades. *Pot,* however, remains the perennial favorite ("Louisiana state cop displays a pot of *pot* discovered among 30 tons of Columbian reefer," 1979, *High Times*). Like REEFER it is probably from Mexican Spanish, an abbreviation of *potiguaya* or *potaguay,* which was adopted by American narcotics addicts in the 1930s. *Potaguaya* is probably a contraction of *potación de guaya,* literally "drink of grief," in reference to the practice of steeping marijuana buds in wine or liquor. *Pot* may have been influenced by the "pot" or pipe that it is often smoked in, or by the old British sense of *pot* (liquor) with the root meaning "intoxication" as in *pot-shaken* (tipsy) and *pot-valiant* (having drunken courage). Since the early 1950s *pot* has been folk-etymologized to *pod* with reference to the potent flower pods of the marijuana plant. The magazine *High Times* (1979), which specializes in articles about "soft-core" drugs, advocates that *pod* replace *pot:* "*Pod* suggests seeds, buds, pollen, odors, all the multidimensional sensual life of the fine plant, while *pot* ought to remain a word for a thing you plant *pod* in."

JITTERBUG (1939). When Cab Calloway sang "Jitter Bug" in 1934, he was not singing about dancing to boogie-woogie. Calloway's *jitter bug* was a heavy drinker of *jitter sauce* (liquor), who accordingly suffered from "the jitters ev'ry morn." Having the *jitters* (extreme nervousness, agitation), especially when the word first came into use around 1929, was usually associated with a hangover or delirium tremens ("The game is played only after the mugs and wenches have taken on too much gin and they arrive at the state of *jitters,* a disease known among the common herd as the heebie-jeebies," 1930, New York *Press*). *Jitter* is probably a variant of *chitter,* which in Chaucer's time meant "to twitter" ("Of hir song, it was so lowd and yerne [yearning] / As eny swalwe [swallow] *chitering* on a berne," c. 1386, *Canterbury Tales*) and is a parallel form to *chatter* but expresses a more attenuated action. Both *chitter* and *chatter* are ultimately imitative or onomatopoeic in origin. By the sixteenth century, *chitter* had been extended in English dialect—primarily Scottish—to mean "to shiver with cold," "to tremble." It is this sense that gives rise to the meaning of nervous trembling in *jitter.* The *bug* (an enthusiast, a person obsessed with an idea) of *jitterbug* is an American colloquialism (see BUG) first cited in 1841 and most often used in combination with other words *(firebug, litterbug).* It is transferred from the sense "insect." Calloway's *jitterbug* quickly caught on and soon referred to any jittery or nervous person. With its origin in a musical context, specifically jazz, it also meant a jazz musician or jazz enthusiast. All of these senses sprang into use in the 1930s, including the *jitterbug,* which was a hepped-up kind of new dance performed to the fast rhythm of boogie-woogie and swing. Its fast steps and free-form improvisations, in sharp contrast with traditional ballroom dancing, resembled the moves of a wildly nervous person, a jitterbug.

HASSLE (1945). In addition to the standard colloquial sense of *to hassle,* to "quarrel," "worry," or "harass" ("[They] are too blasé to *hassle* him," 1976, *People Magazine*), in the southeastern United States it also has the older sense, "to pant or breathe noisily" ("Lil dog run and set down in front of 'im and went to *hasslin'* and says, 'Me too,'" 1935, Zora Neale Hurston, *Mules and Men*). This regional word may have developed in imitation of the sound of loud breathing. It is also possibly related to English dialect *hassle* (to hack at or cut with a blunt knife in a sweeping motion). If two people are quarreling or are emotionally distressed, there is usually a lot of heavy breathing going on. To *hassle* (pant) is often a sign of a *hassle* (a quarrel, fuss, or difficulty). This latter sense appears in the 1940s in a jazz context and may have originally been the lingo of Afro-American jazz players, who introduced it from their Southern roots.

ZILCH (1966). This item in the "personals column" of a magazine called *Ballyhoo* appeared in 1932: "Zilch—A convention of Zilches will be held in Chicago during the Democratic Convention. Every loyal Zilch is asked to attend to give Elmer a good send-off." *Ballyhoo* was a burlesque humor magazine of the 1930s, whose first issue (August 1931) listed on its masthead: "President Henry P. Zilch . . . Executive Editor, Oscar Zilch . . . Editor Bolton Zilch, Associate Editors—Gus Zilch, Peter Zilch, Z. Z. Zilch, W. W. Zilch, Oswald Zilch." The name *Zilch* became a standing joke in the magazine, appearing repeatedly in its spoofs of advertising and in its cartoons. The name is doubtless a fanciful invention in part picked because of its ridiculous sound. Once it escaped into colloquial speech, it appeared in the succeeding decades with an assortment of odd meanings. In the early 1940s, a zilch was an imaginary wind instrument. In 1950s Air Force slang, a zilch was a snafu. In the 1960s, meaningless talk was zilch, and an unsuccessful party was sometimes called a zilch in college slang. The latest *zilch* (c. 1966) is by far the most widely known and most enduring: the adjective meaning "nil," "zero," "nothing" ("Our sex life is practically *zilch,* and he almost never pays any attention to me," 1977, *Playgirl*). These senses are so disparate that they may all be more or less independent, not continuous stages in the evolution of meaning that nearly all words pass through. It may have been the odd, unlikely sound of *zilch* that kept it in mind, a kind of blank word that slang of one sort or another could adopt and give short-lived, more or less arbitrary meanings to. That is until the adjective appeared on the scene. Its meaning is not as arbitrary because it sounds like the earlier *zip* (zero, nothing) and *nil,* as if it were a blend of these two. *Zip,* today heard usually with reference to a game or sports score, was student slang (c. 1900) for a mark or grade of zero and may itself be a colorful alteration of *zero. Nil* is a late (1833) borrowing of Latin *nil,* which is a contraction of *nihil* (nothing).

HYPE (1967). Given the mind-bending prevalence of advertising in the American free-enterprise system, it is no surprise that *hype* (misleading publicity, excessive advertising or promotion) originated in the United States, this latest sense first appearing (1967) in the pop music and record industry. In 1920s underworld slang, a *hype* was a short-change artist and *to hype* was to cheat. By the 1940s the meaning was extended to a "swindle" or "confidence trick" ("Life is a *bitch,* baby. It's the biggest *hype* going," 1962, James Baldwin, *Another Country*), and by the 1960s to "false or extravagant promotion." This development was influenced by *hyperbole* (extravagant exaggeration), ultimately from Greek *hyper-* (over, beyond) and *ballein* (to throw). In 1920s junkie slang a *hype* was an injection of a drug or the needle itself and is short for *hypodermic,* from Greek *hypo-* (under) and *derma* (skin). To *hype up,* then, means to "stir up," "stimulate," "excite" as if from the effects of a hypodermic injection. Ironically *hypo-* means just the opposite of *hyper-.* One could be so hyped up as to need a hypo ("As he works, Mitchell [George Mitchell, former U.S. Attorney General] has at times been so *hyped up* that Martha once asked his doctor to prescribe medication to slow him down," 1973, *Time*). *Hyper* (overly excited or stimulated) is also a recent Americanism (1971) and may be an adjective use of the ever-versatile *hyper-,* or more likely, an abbreviation of *hyperactive.*

KLUTZ (1967). "The sad, *klutzy* ballerinas of the Music Hall pollute children's first live experience of dance" (1970, *The New Yorker*). One need not be a ballet dancer, however, to be a *klutz* (an awkward, clumsy person), a term borrowed early in the 1960s from Yiddish *klots,* literally "a wood block," "a lump," from German *Klotz* (with the same meaning). Like

CHUMP and *blockhead* (a stupid or foolish person), *klutz* is based on the metaphor that a simpleton has a head that is little more than an inanimate lump of matter (cf. DOPE). Closely related to *klutz* and its Germanic parent, is Old English *clot* (lump), which evolved in a similar way. By the seventeenth century the same head metaphor extended the meaning of *clot* to "a dull fellow," "a clod" ("Feats of fine understanding / To abuse *clots* and clowns with," 1632, Ben Jonson, *The Magnetick Lady*). This sense died out and then reappeared over three centuries later in British English ("Jolly bad luck, what a *clot* she is," 1958, Penelope Mortimer, *Daddy's Gone A-Hunting*). In the fourteenth century *clod* (a lump of earth or other matter) appeared as a variant of Old English *clot* and soon was yet another term for a blockhead ("Not bred 'mongst *clods* and clodpoles," 1605, Ben Jonson, *Volpone*). Ultimately *klutz* and its relatives go back to Indo-European **gel-* (to form into a ball), also the root of *clump* (of trees), *club, cloud* (from Old English *clud,* "hill," "rock"), *globe,* and *conglomerate.*

YUPPIE (1984). Along with its awkward derivatives *yuppie-dom, yuppie-ism,* and *yupification, yuppie* (a young upper-middle-class professional living in a city) embodies a whole generation of Americans, the so-called Baby Boomers or 1960s generation ("The Yupification of a neighborhood is an awesome spectacle. . . . *Yuppies* descend in swarms and leave nothing behind but Dumpsters filled with discarded linoleum," 1984, *Time*). *Yuppie,* which appeared in 1984, is an acronym for *y*oung *u*rban *p*rofessional blended with self-conscious irony with *yippie* (a politically active hippie). It has a less well-known counterpart *yumpie* (*y*oung *u*pwardly *m*obile *p*eople), which, because it is essentially synonymous with *yuppie* ("The ultimate *Yumpie* status symbol is to have a child suffering flash-card burn-out," 1984, Chicago *Sun-Times*) and because it is more difficult to pronounce, will probably die out quickly, if it hasn't already. *Yippie* (1968) is also an acronym (*Y*outh *I*nternational *P*arty), with the *-ie* suffix taken from *hippie,* and influenced by *yippee,* an exclamation of delight or excitement ("Another [student] complains that the militants

❧ VI ❧

THE TECHNOLOGICAL CENTURY

Twentieth-Century English

BACKGROUND

To take a more or less random sample of terms that came into English use during the twentieth century is to sketch that turbulent century: *Bolshevik* (from Russian "large," "great," hence *Bolshoi Ballet*); *Gestapo* (an acronym for *Geheime Staatspolizei* "secret state police"); *latex* (from Early Modern English "body fluid," ultimately from Greek "drops of wine" or "dregs in a cup"); *propaganda* (from New Latin *Congregatio de propaganda fide,* "congregation for propagating the faith"); *psychedelic* (Greek "mind" plus "make visible"); *Rastafarian* (from *Ras Tafari,* the surname of Haile Selassie, worshiped as God by the Jamaican cult); *sabotage* (from French *sabot,* "wooden shoe"); *schmaltz* (from Yiddish "melted fat"); and *smog* (from "fog" plus "smoke," coined in 1905 by a representative of the Coal Smoke Abatement Society).

The more twentieth-century words we consider the fuller picture we get of this fast-paced century: *postimpressionist, Freudian, intelligentsia, profiteer, prohibition, fox trot, nylon, deepfreeze, existentialism, transistor, ecosystem, automation, bikini, disco, biodegradable, pulsar, op art, stagflation, biofeedback.* If the nineteenth century began to see the effects of science and technology on language, the twentieth saw a veritable explosion of new terms, and not just highly technical words or the jargon of scientists, but a vocabulary (*biochemical, atomic energy, fallout, ozone, DNA,* etc.) popularized through books, magazines, and newspapers. The highly publicized achievements in the exploration of space, for example, in the 1960s and 1970s made words like *astronaut,* GLITCH, *countdown, blast off, spacecraft, space walk, space shuttle, splashdown,* part of virtually everyone's vocabulary. But even in the so-called "soft sciences" such as psychology hundreds of new words have entered our common lexicon, including *apperception, egocentric, extravert, introvert, behaviorism, inhibition, inferiority complex,* and *psychoanalysis.*

The entertainment industry, which grew out of the inventions of radio, motion pictures, and television have brought many new words into general use, such as *cinema, motion picture, screen, reel, film, scenario, projector, close-up, fade-out, animated cartoon, radio, broadcast, aerial, loudspeaker, stand by, announcer, reception, microphone, transmitter, videotape, telethon, stereo, tweeter, woofer, tape deck,* and *reel-to-reel.* Another twentieth-century invention, the automobile, has had a profound influence on our language, with words like *carburetor, clutch, flat, garage, gas* (or in England *petrol*), *gearshift, hood* (or *bonnet*), *interstate highway, motel, shock absorber, spare, spark plug, station wagon, steering wheel, throttle, to backfire, to sideswipe, to skid, to stall, transmission, tune up, windshield* (or *windscreen*), and many more.

The world wars left their mark on the language. From World War I came *ace, air raid, antiaircraft gun, barrage,* BLIMP, *camouflage, cootie, dud, foxhole, gas mask, nose dive, sector, slacker, tank,* and *war bride,* to name just a few. World War II was perhaps more productive, at least vocabulary-wise, with the addition of *beachhead, blackout, blitz, blockbuster, bulldozer, crash-landing, decontamination, dive bombing, evacuate, Jeep, landing strip, paratroop, radar, resistance movement, roadblock, task force, to appease, to mop up, to spearhead,* and FLAK.

Despite the impact of new inventions and technology, nearly all of the new words are formed according to very old methods. There are "self-explaining compounds," such as *body language, hatchback, jet lag, know-how, lifestyle, lipstick, skydive, software, streamline,* and *think tank,* and compounds from Greek and Latin elements, such as *ad lib* (from Latin *ad libitum* "at one's pleasure"); *aerosol* (Greek "air" and *sol* from *solution*); *ambivalence* (Latin *ambi-*, "in two ways," and *valentia*, "strength," "vigor"), AMNIOCENTESIS, *isotope* (from Greek "same" plus "place," that is, occupying the same place on the periodic table), *psychedelic*, and *quasar* (quasi-stellar).

Another common method of expanding the vocabulary is to use familiar affixes appended to existing words, such as *trans-* (*transcontinental, transformer*); *pre-* (*prenatal, preheat*); *de-* (*defrost, debug, decaffeinate*); *-dom* (*stardom*), and *-ster* (*gangster, pollster*). Two productive affixes that were created whole cloth are *-aholic* (*bookaholic, workaholic*) abstracted from *alcoholic*, and *mini-* (*minibottle, miniskirt*) from *miniature* ultimately from Latin "to paint red."

Despite the dominant place of contemporary English in the world as a *lingua franca*, it continues to borrow words from many different languages. Its old standby, French, continues to contribute many terms, such as *the absurd* (taken from the philosophy of Albert Camus); *ivory tower* (*tour d'ivoire*); *marquee; velcro* (blended from French *velour crochet* "hooked velvet"); and *tutu* ("short, stiff ballet skirt," an alteration of *cucu* baby talk reduplication of *cul* "backside," "buttocks"). From German came *angst* and *strafe* (*Gott strafe England* "may God punish England"). From the Latin word for "desire," "lust" comes *libido* (via Freud) and from Arabic comes *ayatollah* (*aya* "sign," "paragon" plus *Allah* "God"). From Chinese we get *mahjongg* ("a dominolike game," from dialectal Chinese meaning "hemp birds," the design on the game pieces), and from Japanese *honcho* ("chief," "boss," from *hon* "squad," "corps" and *cho* "chief," "leader"). *Mandarin* (an important political person or intellectual) is ultimately from Malay and Hindi *mantri* (councilor). From a character in the Italian movie *La Dolce Vita*, English borrowed *paparazzo* (an aggressive photographer who hounds celebrities). From Russian we get *Sputnik* (literally "traveling companion"); from a Philippine language comes *yo-yo;* and from Jamaican English we received *reggae* (*rege-rege* "quarrel," "protest," literally "rags," "ragged clothes").

Many new words in twentieth-century English are deliberate coinages, such as *Frisbee* (from the toy's origin in the pie tins of Mrs. Frisbie's pies); *holistic* (coined by Jan Christiaan

Smuts, a South African soldier and politician, from Greek *holos*, "whole"); *scofflaw* (the winning entry in a national contest during Prohibition to coin a word referring to a person who drinks illegally); and *smog*.

Perhaps the greatest source of new "words" is the extension of the meanings of old words, as in *integration; gigolo*, in Middle English "a villainous man" (from French "dancing girl," "prostitute"); *nerd*, a variant of *nert*, itself a variant of *nut; in the offing*, originally a nautical expression referring to the more distant part of the sea; *queer*, ultimately from Old High German for "oblique"; *tout*, originally Old English for "to peep," "peer"; and *twit*, also Old English "to blame," "reproach."

More than in earlier periods in the history of English, slang has contributed a large body of words to the language. Some recent examples are *boob tube, vibes, rip-off, laid-back*, and *knee jerk*, as well as *gizmo, noodle* (head, simpleton), *sudser* (a soap opera), *stir-crazy* (*stir*, "prison," ultimately from Romany), and *umpteen* (military slang for "dash" in Morse code).

The truly modern process of word formation in this century is the use of *acronyms*, the word itself being coined around 1943 from Greek *akros* (tip, end) and English *-onym* (name). In fact, so common are acronyms in contemporary English that one dictionary lists over 100,000 examples. An acronym, of course, is formed by combining the initial or first few letters of two or more words, as in *radar* (*ra*dio *d*etecting *a*nd *r*anging), *scuba* (*s*elf-*c*ontained *u*nderwater *b*reathing *a*pparatus), *OPEC* (Organization of Petroleum Exporting Countries), and *NATO* (North Atlantic Treaty Organization).

If this century says anything about the future, it is that English will continue to expand its role as a world language, in the process enlarging its vocabulary to keep up with the accelerating pace of change.

FLAPPER (1888). Made popular in the 1920s, *flapper* refers to an unconventional young woman who is forward and flighty (" 'Oh, I *do* love you!' She embraced me in a *flapperish* manner, lifting one highheeled foot impetuously behind her," 1961, Iris Murdoch, *Severed Head*). The standard history

of the word supposes that it is a figurative use of *flapper* in its earlier sense, "a young wild duck or partridge" ("Lightbody happened to be gone out to shoot *flappers*," 1809, Maria Edgeworth, *Tales from Fashionable Life*). And there is precedent for referring to young women as birds, such as British slang *bird* itself and American slang *chick*. But *flapper* may instead derive from *flapper* (a young prostitute), which is from the old term *flap* (a girl or young woman of loose character), which survives in the modern dialects of northern England. It is a figurative use of the earlier sense of "something that hangs loose." Ultimately *flap* is imitative of the sound of something slapping or flapping. It is quite possible, however, that both *flappers*, "a young prostitute" and "a young duck," coalesced to give the 1920s *flapper*.

HOOLIGAN (1898). "The hoardings [billboards] were torn down and the terraces and railings broken up," said the report on *hooliganism* (violent, disorderly conduct) at a British football match. Another noted, "It is ludicrous to see how boys of a very tender age get possessed of a frenzy at some of these matches." These reports could have been written today, but they are from the 1890s, about the time that *hooligan* (a violent roughneck or street tough) was coined. Although hooligans and British soccer seem to go hand in hand—the worst incident being the catastrophe in April 1989 when ninety-five people died in a hooligan-inspired riot at a stadium in Sheffield, England—*hooligan* also appears regularly in stories about domestic violence in the two largest

Communist nations. After the Tiananmen Square massacre (1989), the Associated Press reported that the Chinese "radio and TV urged people to turn in fellow citizens who engaged in '*hooliganism* and destruction.' " Unlike the Chinese, the Russians borrowed the word itself as *khuligan* and widened its meaning to refer to criminals and political dissidents. Like *ballyhoo* (exaggerated publicity), *donnybrook* (a brawl), *blarney* (flattery), *murphy* (potato), *Mrs. Murphy* (toilet), and perhaps *malarkey* (nonsense, bunk), all of which derived from the Irish names of people or places, *Hooligan* probably originated in an Irish name. One derivation says that it is an alteration of *Hooley's gang,* supposedly "a name given by the police in Islington to a gang of young roughs led by one Hooley" (1909, James Redding Ware, *Passing English of the Victorian Era*); who Hooley was or even whether he existed has never been established. Another version is that the term originated with a rascal named Patrick Hooligan, who made the Lamb and Flag pub in the Southwark section of London his headquarters. Pat's unruly family may even have inspired an 1890s music-hall song that immortalized their hooligan shenanigans. Two well-known early twentieth-century comic strips gave *hooligan* a boost in popular usage: one called *Funny Folks,* which featured a comic Irish character named Hooligan, and the better-known American strip by Fred Opper, *Happy Hooligan.* The name itself probably comes from Irish *uallachán,* which, fittingly enough, means "braggart," "swaggerer."

ESCALATOR (1900). At the turn of the century, with the completion of the very modern Manhattan Elevated Railway, the Otis Elevator Company installed "movable stairways," which it called *escalators,* to carry passengers from street level to the trains. Soon this futuristic invention could be found in all the large buildings as well ("You will perceive that the Bee-Hive was not a fashionable department store, with *escalators* and pompadours," 1907, O. Henry, *Trimmed Lamp*). In coining the trade name, the Otis company adopted the rarely heard *escalade* (to scale something, especially the walls of a fortress, by means of a ladder) and altered it on the pattern of *elevator,* as if *-or* were the agent suffix *-er. Elevator,* however, is not from *elevate* (to raise) plus *-er* or *-or,* but merely Latin *elevator* (anything that lifts) from *elevare* (lift up, elevate), borrowed whole hog into English in the seventeenth century. *Escalade* is also borrowed from Latin, *scalare* (to scale), from *scala* (ladder). In one of those etymological goose chases that language sometimes plays, *escalade* has essentially been replaced by *escalate,* which is a back formation of *escalator.* In the 1920s, when *escalate* first came into use, it meant "to climb by escalator," and by the 1950s its figurative sense, "to increase by degrees," was well established, particularly with reference to the nuclear arms race.

LIMOUSINE (1902). In the pastoral hills of central France in the province formerly called *Limousin* (from the name of the capital *Limoges*), the shepherds customarily wore coarse woolen greatcoats. The long shepherd's cloak was so closely identified with the old province that it became known as a *limousine.* During the last century, wagon or cart drivers used these rough heavy cloaks, which were sometimes made of goat's hair. At the turn of the century a large automobile was introduced that had an enclosed compartment for passengers separate from the driver's seat which was outside and was eventually constructed with a cloth roof overhead. This luxury auto became known as a *limousine* from a comparison made between the earlier wagoner's protective *limousine* and either the passenger's compartment itself or else the roof over the driver's seat.

POSH (1903). When passengers of the P. & O. (Peninsular and Oriental) steamship line booked passage to India, if they were savvy, not to mention wealthy, they would request at considerably greater expense *"Port Outward, Starboard Homeward."* This meant that on the outgoing passage, their cabins were on the port side of the ship, and on the return homeward they were on the starboard side, thus ensuring that they had the shady or cooler cabins while crossing the broiling Indian Ocean. Such tickets were booked "P.O.S.H." and in time *posh* applied to first-class accommodations or anything that was luxurious. This clever derivation for *posh* (classy, stylish, first-rate) has been recently called into question, there being virtually no evidence for it. Instead, most dictionaries now refer to thieves' cant, which uses *posh* to refer to money ("That sort of patter . . . is the thing to get the *posh,"* 1892, M. Williams, *Round London*). Taken from Romany, the language of Gypsies, *posh* (half) originally referred to a halfpenny ("The paper makers get the tats and never tip the motts a *posh.* [*Translation:*] Thieves who pretend to belong to paper mills get the rags and never pay the women a farthing." 1839, H. Brandon, *Poverty, Mendacity and Crime*). In this derivation *posh* shifted from "money" to "expensive," "swank," "first-class." The Australians have put a slightly different spin on the word in their phrase *do the posh* (to spend lavishly).

CLONE (1903). Because the first *clone* was a plant propagated from a cutting, the name was borrowed from Greek *klon,* meaning "twig" or "slip." As biotechnology became more sophisticated, the word was extended to bacterial cells in the late 1920s. The verb meaning "to reproduce asexually" appeared in the late 1950s, and by the late 1970s, *clone* had escaped its scientific confines and meant "an exact duplicate or carbon copy" ("Both blond and blue-eyed . . . they are *clones* . . . squabbling over who is the original," 1979, *New York Times*). Because a clone is an unnatural product of science and technology, at least in the popular imagination, the word has also developed the recent figurative meaning "an automaton" or "a robot" ("Elsewhere, they suggest the possibility of using *clones* for work involving radiation or dangerous chemicals, or for fighting wars," 1978, *Manchester Guardian Weekly*).

DÉTENTE (1908). Although most Americans who lived through the cold war of the 1970s associate *détente* (a foreign policy that seeks amicable relations between countries of opposing political ideologies) with Henry Kissinger, Richard Nixon's Secretary of State and the implementer of the policy, *détente* first appeared in English in the seventeenth century. In Old French the *destente* was the mechanism of a crossbow that held the drawn or taut string, and that, when released, discharged the arrow. *Destente* became *détente* (trigger) in modern French. Extended from *détendre* (to slacken, unstretch, undo), which is from Latin *de* (from, away) and *tendre* (to stretch), the underlying meaning of the Old French word was to "slacken" or "loosen." But in English, influenced by *detention* and *detain*, it meant almost the opposite, "the part of a mechanism that checks a moving part, as in a clock," and more broadly "restraint" or "a holding back" ("A pinprick or a momentary whiff or hairbreadth motion freeth the *detent* of force," 1929, Robert Bridges, *The Testament of Beauty*). In the early twentieth century French *détente* (loosening, relaxation) was reborrowed and applied to the easing of strained relations between countries ("A change in the European situation . . . had . . . set in. . . . The characteristic feature of this transformation may be called a *détente,*" 1908, London *Times*).

S.O.S. (1910), **MAYDAY** (1927). Not only are S.O.S. the letters of the International Morse Code used by a ship in distress, they are the jocular abbreviation for other phrases, such as "*s*ame *o*ld *s*hit (or *s*tuff, *s*tory, etc.)" and "*s*hit *o*n a *s*hingle" (i.e., chipped beef on toast). Two phrases S.O.S. is *not* an abbreviation for are "*s*ave *o*ur *s*hip" and "*s*ave *o*ur *s*ouls," which are popularly believed to be the origin of the distress signal. In fact, the letters *s o s*—in Morse Code consisting of three dots, three dashes, and three dots—were arbitrarily chosen by the Radio Telegraph Conference of 1906 because they were easy to transmit and distinguish. Before that conference the Marconi Company used and advocated the letters *c q d* as a distress signal. With the perfection of voice transmission by radio and telephone, the cryptic dots and dashes were dispensed with. Instead, the expression *mayday* was chosen as the international radio-telephone distress call. It has nothing to do with the first day of May, but is the English spelling representing the pronunciation of French *m'aider* (help me!), shortened from *venez m'aider* (come help me!).

JINX (1911). Pindar, the ancient Greek poet in his fourth Pythian ode, invokes a love incantation that employs a turning magic wheel. This peculiar apparatus, also called the "moon wheel," had four spokes, and lashed to it was a bird, the spotted wryneck. The wryneck, or in Greek *inyx,* is related to the woodpecker and has the disconcerting habit of writhing its head and neck, especially when distressed. Its undulatory motions and its ability to hiss at intruders (it is also called the *snake-bird*), which Aristotle described in detail, probably led to its cruel use as a magic charm. Borrowed in the seventeenth century into English as *jynx* or *jyng* from Latin *inyx,* it referred both to the bird and to a charm or spell. From this latter sense comes American English *jinx,* meaning "a person or thing that brings bad luck" and "to cause or bring bad luck" ("What do you mean—humming love songs when their darn pitcher is forcing in runs? You *jinxed* my ball club," 1917, *American Magazine*).

SAMBA (1885), **TANGO** (1913), **RUMBA** (1922), **MAMBO** (1948). The tired ballroom dances of the nineteenth century, notably the stately but sedate waltz, led to the introduction of more flamboyant dances, whose immediate origins were in Latin America, but whose roots were ultimately in Africa. *Samba* came from Brazil and is shortened from Portuguese *zambacueca* (a type of dance), which is thought to be a borrowing from an African language. Alternatively it may be a blend of Portuguese *zamacueco* (stupid) and *zambapalo* (a grotesque dance) from *zamparse* (to bump, crash). *Tango* is from Argentine Spanish meaning "drum dance" and more broadly, "a Negro or gypsy dance festival." It is probably from a Niger-Congo language, such as Ibibio, which has the word *tamgu* (to dance). In English in the 1890s, the *tango* was the Spanish flamenco dance, which has nothing in common with the Argentine dance, but is instead of Arabic origin. *Rumba* or *rhumba* is originally Cuban Spanish, and though the dance itself is a Cuban modification of an African dance, the name is of Indo-European ancestry. Its circuitous history begins with the Spanish ship's compass marked with a rhombus or *rombo,* which the sailors believed was a magical symbol for guiding the ship. *Rombo* became *rumbo* (the ship's course) and then was extended first to "leadership," then to "ostentation" or "pomp," then, altered to *rumba,* it meant "party" or "spree," and finally meant the dance danced at rumbas. The *mambo* ("The difference between the *rumba* and the *mambo* is the difference between the regular foxtrot and the jitterbug," 1950, *Newsweek*) has darker roots in voodoo. It too is from Cuban Spanish, which took it from Haitian creole, *mambo* or *mambu,* whose ulterior meaning is "voodoo priestess." Ultimately from an African source, such as Yoruba *mambo* (to talk), the Haitian *mambo* was a ritual voodoo dance and initiation ceremony.

FLOOZY (1911). According to one derivation, *floozy* (a loose woman) has its roots in *Flora,* originally the name of the Roman goddess of flowers. *Flora* eventually became a popular woman's name among English speakers, with the pet forms *Florrie, Flo,* and *Flossie;* the last of these became a general term for a young woman, especially one who was attractive and had a hint of the lower class about her ("During the junior promenade there were many visiting *flossies* on the Hill," 1916, *Dia-*

lect Notes). Like the female pet names *Moll, Katy,* and *Kitty* (a wanton), *Flossie* soon connoted loose morals ("What was that high-farkin' [highfalutin] Annete going around thundered up like a saloon keeper's *flossie* for?," 1937, Mari Sandoz, *Slogum*). The word *loose* may have contributed to the evolution of *flossie* into *floosie* and *floozy.* There is, however, an alternative derivation. *Flossie* (fluffy, silky, soft) and its English dialect variant *floosy* are adjectival forms of *floss* (silk filaments, fluff), which is from either Old French *flosche* (velvet pile, down) or an unrecorded Scandinavian borrowing cognate with *fleece.* Silky or flossy women's clothing is fancy or showy ("I suppose I'll have to dress. She's sure to be all *flossied* up," 1957, Iris Murdoch, *The Sandcastle*). In its early use it was not necessarily unflattering to be called *floosie* or *floozy.* The meaning was extended to include "impertinent," "saucy," and "flirtatious" ("She had ol' Sagebrush locoed by the *flossy* talk she slung," 1914, Earl A. Brininstool, *Trail Dust*)—and thence to "a woman of disreputable character" ("I'm beginning to think that baby is half vamp and half *floosie,*" 1927, H. A. Vachell, *Dew of the Sea*).

INSULIN (1914). As often happens in science, as if there were one collective mind at work, different scientists working independently discover something almost simultaneously and propose the same name for the discovery. This was the case with *insulin,* a hormone that is vital in the metabolism of carbohydrates and the removal of sugar from the blood. A deficiency of insulin causes diabetes. The French scientist De Meyer suggested the name *insuline* in a 1909 publication, and though it was seven years later when E. A. Schafer suggested the same name, it was completely independent of De Meyer. Then in 1922 the Canadians Frederick G. Banting and Charles H. Best were the first to obtain the hormone using extracts of pancreas. Unaware of the earlier work, they too proposed the name *insulin,* from the Latin *insula* (island), the root also of *isle, insular, isolate,* and *insulate,* with reference to the *islets of Langerhans,* a specific group of cells in the pancreas that secrete this important hormone.

BLIMP (1916). The first lighter-than-air aircraft was called an *airship* (1819) because it floated on the air like a ship on water. An *airship* was distinguished from a *balloon* as being more navigable, though the first successful power-driven airship was not built until 1852 by the French inventor Henri Giffard. As the steering technology became more sophisticated, by 1885 the more descriptive term *dirigible balloon,* often shortened to *dirigible,* came into use. *Dirigible* had first been used in the sixteenth century to mean "capable of being directed or guided" ("It would avayle [avail] greatly to the furtherance of the Service, if . . . these Oaths were *dirigible* to the Justices," 1581, William Lambarde, *Eirenarcha*). It was adopted from Latin *dirigere* (to direct, make straight), which is a compound of *di-* or *dis-* (apart) and *regere* (to lead straight, guide, rule), the same source as for *direct* and *dress.* During the First World War the British classified dirigibles into two types: "A–rigid," those having a rigid hull of metal like the famous Zeppelin, and "B–limp," those that were nonrigid or "limp," having a balloon whose shape was maintained by the internal pressure of the gas. "B–limp" then became *blimp.*

TABLOID (1918). The term *tabloid television* is being heard and seen with increasing frequency these days, owing to the proliferation of network and syndicated "news" shows like *Geraldo, Inside Edition, Crimewatch Today,* and *The Reporters.* Although *tabloid television* may be hard to swallow, *tabloid* itself originally referred to a kind of pill whose contents were compressed and concentrated and relatively easy to digest. *Tabloids* were first manufactured by Burroughs, Wellcome & Co.; the company registered the term in 1884, apparently having coined it from *tabl-*, as in *tablet* (from French *tablette*, the diminutive of *table*) and *-oid* (ultimately from Greek *eidos* "form," "shape," "kind"), the common suffix meaning "having the shape or form of," as in *cylindroid, crystalloid, android.* Like the trade names *Xerox, Kleenex,* and *Cola, Tabloid* was almost immediately adopted into the spoken language despite legal efforts by the company to restrict its use. The 1894 edition of *Murray's Handbook for Travellers in India,* for example, recommends taking "plenty of quinine in 2 or 4 grain *'tabloids.'* " One of the first persons to use *tabloid* in a journalistic sense was Alfred Harmsworth, the first Viscount Northcliffe (1865–1922), who acquired and reorganized several well-known newspapers in England around the turn of the century. One of his innovations was to present the news in what he called *"tabloid* form"—that is, condensed for busy businessmen and in a small-sized format. Harmsworth's *tabloid* newspapers, the *Daily Mail* and the *Daily Mirror,* were half-penny illustrated morning papers.

BUG (1919). "Who ordered the *bugging* of the Democratic headquarters?" was the question in the minds of the millions of Watergate-bugs faithfully watching the latest episode of Senator Samuel Ervin's committee hearings in 1974. This most recent sense of *bug* (a concealed microphone, electronic eavesdropping) originated with the "bug-sized" microphone developed in the 1940s and may additionally allude to the expression about wishing to be a fly on the wall to overhear a private conversation. It may also be related to the earlier use in underworld slang of *bug* (burglar alarm), which, like the electronic version, is a concealed device that reveals hidden, often illegal activity. The secretive insect is also used metaphorically in the Southern United States expression *a bug under the chips,* meaning "an ulterior motive" ("To those uneasy over the alliance, he gave his word that there are 'no such *bugs under the chips*,' " 1946, *Newsweek*). An earlier sense uses the metaphor of a *bug* (defect) that had crawled into a machine causing problems—a fly in the mechanical ointment, as it were ("Mr. Edison . . . had been up the two previous nights discovering 'a *bug*' in his phonograph," 1889, *Pall Mall Gazette*). Later, this sense gave computer-speak *debug* (to remove "bugs" or flaws in a computer program). The imaginary creature can also metaphorically crawl into the brain, making a person *bugs* (crazy, insane). In prison argot a *bug doctor* is a psychiatrist. Similarly, to be afflicted or infected by a specific kind of *bug* is to be under the influence of a powerful desire or obsession ("Stanley Kramer . . . has succumbed to the Cecil B. De Mille *bug*," 1957, *The New Yorker*). In American English a *bug* is an insect, any insect. To an Englishman a *bug* is *Cimex lectularius*, the common bedbug, which, like *louse*, can be used with derogatory effect, as when Alexander Pope called Lord Hervey a *bug*: "Yet let me flap this *bug* with gilded wings,/ This painted child of dirt, that stinks and stings." Appearing in the mid-sixteenth century, "bedbug" was the original sense of *bug* in English. It may be an alteration of Old English *budde* (beetle), which is cognate with Middle Low German *budde* (thick, swollen). Or it may derive from Middle English *bugge* (hobgoblin, bugbear; cf. BOGEY). Or it may be a combination of the two. An enthusiast is also a *bug* but of a different species with a different origin. Appearing in American English in the mid-nineteenth century, it is almost always used in combination with a modifying term, such as *firebug* or JITTERBUG (*"Basketball bugs* believe Colorado never had a prep team like the Windsor Wizards," 1947, Denver *Post*). It is probably related to *bug* or *big bug* (an important person, a big shot) and English dialect *bug* (conceited, pompous), ultimately from a Scandinavian root that is also the origin of Norwegian *bugge* (an important man).

IRON CURTAIN (1920). Despite the recent melting of the *iron curtain*, most of us know this vivid metaphor from the Cold War decades as the barrier to information and free movement imposed by the Soviet Union at the outer edge of its political and economic influence. Originally, however, the *iron curtain* was literally a curtain of iron, first used in late-eighteenth-century theaters ("As a precaution against fire, an *iron curtain* was constructed, so as to let down in a moment of danger and separate the audience from the stage," 1829, Horace Foote, *A Companion to the Theatres*). It was almost immediately used figuratively for any impenetrable barrier ("On the 19th November we crossed the river Betwah, and as if an *iron curtain* had dropt between us and the avenging angel, the deaths diminished," 1819, Earl of Munster, *Journal of a Route across India*). The first use of *iron curtain* to refer to the Soviet barrier appeared in 1920, but it was not until Winston Churchill's 1946 address at Westminster College in Fulton, Missouri, that it became a household expression ("From Stettin, in the Baltic, to Trieste, in the Adriatic, an *iron curtain* has descended across the Continent," from Churchill's address). A few years after Churchill's speech, *bamboo curtain* was coined by analogy to refer to the political barrier erected by the Chinese Communist government ("The Communist bosses of Peiping dropped a *bamboo curtain,* cutting off Peiping from the world," 1949, *Time*). Just as there was a literal iron curtain, curtains made from split bamboo are common in Asia.

FASCISM (1922). When a prisoner in ancient Rome was to be executed, the officer or lictor walking before the chief magistrate carried the *fasces,* a "bundle" of elm or birch rods and an axe held together by a red strap, which were used to scourge and behead the criminal. Besides having a rather grisly practical function, the *fasces* was a symbol of official authority dating back to the Etruscans. The primary sense of *fascis* is "bundle," which is the source of such English words as *fascia, fascicle,* and *fascine.* When Benito Mussolini founded the *Fascismo* movement in March 1919, he was harking back to the Roman *fasces* as a symbol of absolute authority, underwritten by its violent power as an instrument of execution and its rigid unity as a bundle of separate elements.

ROBOT (1923). A *robot* (a machine often resembling a human designed to do the work of a human) may be a twentieth-century invention, but it has its linguistic roots in prehistory. In Indo-European, **orbh* meant "to separate" and **orbho* meant "to be separated or bereft of a father," hence "to be deprived of free status." In Greek it became *orphanos* (orphaned), the source of English *orphan,* and in Old Slavic it became *orbu* (slave), altered to *rabu,* giving *rabota* (servitude), which eventually became in Czech *robota* (forced labor, drudgery). The Czech playwright Karel Capek (1890–1938) modified it to *robot* in his 1920 play *R.U.R.,* the initials standing for "Rossum's Universal Robots," Rossum in the play being the manufacturer of the robots. After the play was translated into English in 1923, the word was immediately adopted into English ("If Almighty God had populated the world with *Robots,* legislation of this sort might have been reasonable," 1923, London *Times*). Because *robot* filled a strong need for a word expressing the profound impact that machines and technology were having on humankind, during the rest of the 1920s it spawned numerous derivatives, including *robotize, robotian, robotesque, roboteer, robotism, robotry,* and a little later *robotic* and *robotical.* If one did not know that a *robot* in South Africa is an automatic traffic signal, this passage from the Johannesburg *Star* could cause concern: "Johannesburg drivers . . . want to turn right or left while pedestrians, with the *robot* in their favour, are crossing."

GIMMICK (1926). One clever explanation of the history of *gimmick* (a gadget, an ingenious device or idea) claims that it should be spelled *gimac* and that this is an anagram of the word *magic.* Magicians were allegedly the first to use it as a synonym for "gadget" or "thing-a-ma-bob." Although *gimmick* sometimes refers to "a device for performing a conjuring trick or a deception," there is no evidence that it was ever spelled *gimac* or that it was first used by illusionists. Another derivation suggests that it is a blend of *trick* and *gimbal* (a contrivance for permitting a body to incline freely). A more plausible version holds that it is from *gimcrack* (a showy, insubstantial thing, knickknack). In use since the seventeenth century ("Ribbins, and Looking-glasses, and Nutcrackers, and Fiddles, and Hobby horses, and many other *gim-cracks* . . . and all the other finnimbruns that make a compleat Country Fair," 1676, Izaak Walton, *The Universal Angler*), *gimcrack* itself has a disputed origin. It is perhaps a dialectal compound of *gim* (spruce, neat) and Scots *crack* (a showy or boastful lad), giving its early sense, "a showy, affected person," from which evolved the more usual meaning, "a showy, trifling thing." Yet another history suggests that it is from the fourteenth-century *gibecrake* (an ornamental bit of inlaid wood), itself probably from Old French *giber* (to shake) and Middle English *crak* (a sharp noise). In this derivation, *gibecrake* is altered under the influence of the name *Jim*, *jimcrack* being an early attested spelling.

FIFTH COLUMN (1936). During the Spanish Civil War, General Emilio Mola on a rebel radio station declared that he would besiege Madrid, using four columns of soldiers from outside the city, and that a *fifth column* or *quinta columna* of supporters hiding within the city would join the invaders when they entered the capital. Troops marching shoulder to shoulder, row after row, creating a long line is an ancient military formation and has been called a *column* for centuries ("I would march my Army in two or three several Bodies divers wayes, which the French call *Columes*, but we, and I think more properly, Lines," 1677, Earl Orrery, *The Art of War*). Sympathy in the United States for the Loyalists, the extensive press coverage of the war—the *New York Times* picked up *fifth column* almost as soon as it was uttered—and Ernest Hemingway's 1938 play *The Fifth Column* quickly popularized the expression. Almost as quickly it became a term for internal subversives, persons living within the country that support the enemy ("If you call Stalin a bloodstained monster you must be shot as the most dangerous of *Fifth Columnists*," 1940, George Bernard Shaw, *Platform and Pulpit*).

FLAK (1938). The Second World War saw many innovations in the technology of death, including the greatly expanded role of aircraft and the inevitable countermeasures. For the Germans an antiaircraft gun was called *die Fliegerabwehrkanone,* literally flier or plane *(Flieger)* defense *(abwehr)* cannon or gun *(kanone),* "plane-defense-gun." This the Germans acronymically shortened to *Flak* (*Fl*iegera bwehr*k* anone), which British pilots picked up ("The word *'Flak'* is probably used in every Bomber Command pilot's report after a raid on Germany," 1940, London *Times*). Because planes were shot down by *Flak fire* ("One of the British bombers which raided Berlin . . . had been damaged when diving through heavy *Flak fire,"* 1940, *Flight*), *flak* soon referred to the shells and explosions themselves from the anti-aircraft guns ("The burst of orgasms coming as incessantly as a barrage of *flak* leave one a little sex-shocked," 1971, London *Daily Telegraph*). By the early 1960s in America, a barrage of criticism or a heated quarrel was metaphorically called *flak* ("We now have a tough anti-pollution law, and the city is taking a lot of *flak* because its own incinerators won't be upgraded in time for the deadline set by that law," 1969, *The New Yorker*).

GOOGOL (1940). As science in the twentieth century—notably math, astronomy, and physics—reached the limits of the ability of the rational mind to grasp the newest discoveries, a fabricated eccentric vocabulary reminiscent of the writings of Edward Lear, Lewis Carroll, and James Joyce began to appear (see also QUARK). Very large numbers, for which there are no names, for example, are frequently encountered in science. For the number "ten raised to the hundredth power" (10^{100}), that is, a one followed by 100 zeroes, the mathematician Edward Kasner asked his nine-year-old nephew to think up a name. The boy came up with the nonsensical *googol,* totally devoid of a history prior to its utterance ("George Brown . . . was the only one who came within a *googol* of light-years of guessing what they were," 1945, *Astounding Science Fiction*). And ten raised to the googol power, that is, a one followed by a googol of zeroes, he called a *googolplex.*

PASTRAMI (1940). The English word *pastrami* (beef smoked and highly seasoned) is, not surprisingly, a borrowing from Yiddish *pastrame,* it being a typically Jewish meat dish ("The catering was delegated to Levitoff, the demon *pastrami* prince," 1940, Groucho Marx, *Letters*). The Yiddish itself is a borrowing from Rumanian *pastrama,* in turn borrowed from modern Greek *pastono* (I salt), whose root, *pastos* (salted, also the root of English *paste*), is from *passein* (to sprinkle), that is, "sprinkled" with salt. Salt used as a spice and preservative is also the underlying meaning of *salami,* from Latin *sal* (salt), also the source of *sausage, sauce, salsa,* and *salad.* The -*mi* ending of *pastrami* was probably taken from *salami.*

GREMLIN (1941). Even in the age of technology unexplainable forces inhabit precision machines—mysterious GLITCHES appear in electronic devices, BUGS in computers, *gremlins* in high-tech jet engines. *Gremlin* was invented by Royal Air Force pilots to refer to mechanical behavior that cannot be explained by the laws of aerodynamics ("As he flew round, he wished that his instructor had never told him about the Little People—a mythological bunch of good and bad fairies. . . . Those awful little people, the *Gremlins,* who run up and down the wing with scissors going "snip, snap, snip" made him sweat," 1941, Graves, *The Thin Blue Line*). A 1942 newspaper account of *gremlins* quotes an R.A.F. pilot who claimed that gremlins have this name "on account of they were the goblins which came out of Fremlin beer bottles," Fremlin beer being a common brand in the R.A.F. messes in India and the Middle East. In this etymological scenario, the *goblins* in *Fremlin* bottles are *gremlins,* which when released attack the drinkers' planes. Most derivations of *gremlin* agree that GOBLIN played an important role. Another version suggests that *goblin* was blended with Old English *gremman* (to anger or vex), but since most pilots would not have been Old English scholars, it seems unlikely. Another explanation claims that the ending of *goblin* was appended to Irish *gruaimin* (an ill-tempered little fellow), but it seems unlikely that R.A.F. pilots would know Gaelic any better than Old English.

NIACIN (1942). Niacin, the pellagra-preventing vitamin, is derived in the laboratory from a highly toxic substance used in insecticides, nicotine. When nicotine, which is extracted from tobacco plants, is oxidized, it forms crystalline *nicotinic acid,* the English loan translation of German *Nicotinsäure* (1873). After pellagra was demonstrated in 1925 to be a deficiency disease, followed by the discovery twelve years later that nicotinic acid was the vitamin involved, American commercial food producers, notably bakeries, began adding it to their products. But no sooner was this done than anti-tobacco groups warned that eating "enriched" bread would foster the cigarette habit. Even though this was not true, the stigma of the name required a change. In 1942 the vitamin was rechristened *niacin* from the first two letters of its old name (*ni*cotinic *ac*id) plus the chemical suffix *-in,* a modification of the older *-ine* (a. 1860), used in such compound names as *globulin, gelatin,* and recently *dioxin.*

GUNG HO (1942). One can be *gung ho* (enthusiastic, zealous) about virtually anything ("In those days he was very *gung ho* for National Socialism and the pan-Germanic grandeur it was going to produce," 1967, R. M. Stern, *The Kessler Legacy*). But originally when U.S. Marine General Evans Carlson adopted the motto from Chinese cooperatives, it meant "work together" ("Borrowing an idea from China, Carlson frequently has what he calls *'kung-hou'* meetings. . . . Problems are threshed out and orders explained," 1942, *New York Times Magazine*), from Chinese *kung* (work) and *ho* (together). During the Second World War Carlson organized and commanded a guerrilla unit known as Carlson's Raiders, which achieved fame after its raids on Makin Island and Guadalcanal in 1942. The Raiders also called themselves the "Gung Ho Battalion" after Carlson introduced them to the Chinese motto. Their zeal and enthusiasm for combat soon gave the expression its current meaning.

BOGEY/JINK (1943). "O.K., *bogeys* have *jinked* back at me again for the fifth time." Those words were picked up in

January 1989 by the cockpit recorder of an American pilot just before he shot down a Libyan MiG fighter over international waters in the Mediterranean. As Air Force jargon both *bogey* (an enemy aircraft) and *jink* (to make a quick, elusive turn) go back to the Second World War, but both words also enjoy long Scottish pedigrees. *Bogeys* (ghosts, goblins, specters) have been jinking around in Scotland since at least the sixteenth century, when they were more commonly known as *bogles* ("Like an *bogill* all of ratland banis [rattling bones]," 1535, William Stewart, *The Buik of the Croniclis of Scotland*). Before that they were called *bugs* or *bugges*. When *bug* came to refer to an insect, its ghostly meaning was exorcised. *Bug* haunts contemporary English only in the word *bugbear*. The use of *bogeys* as a term for enemy aircraft—perhaps because of their spectral look when seen approaching from a distance—originated in the Royal Air Force and was adopted by American pilots. *Jink* has a less ethereal origin in Scottish English of the eighteenth century, when it was used pretty much the way the pilot used it, "to move or dart with sudden turns" ("He came *jinking* over Bowden moor with daughters and ponies and god knows what," 1819, Sir Walter Scott, *Letters*). It is probably onomatopoeic in its genesis, the sound of the word suggesting quick movement. In the twentieth century, it was used in rugby football before World War II pilots adopted it. Though in America the verb is primarily pilots' jargon, the noun is widely known in *high jinks* (pranks, frolic, merrymaking). In Scotland *high jinks* was the name of various drinking games ("The revel had lasted since four o'clock, and, at length . . . the frolicsome company had begun to practise the ancient and now forgotten pastime of *high jinks*," 1815, Sir Walter Scott, *Guy Mannering*).

KAMIKAZE (1945). American and British servicemen during the Second World War stationed in the Pacific primarily at Leyte Gulf and Okinawa were dismayed when Japanese planes loaded with bombs deliberately flew into their ships. The planes and pilots who made these suicidal crashes into enemy targets were called *kamikaze pilots,* or *kamikazes* for short ("As a British task force was hoisting victory pennants a *Kamikaze* darted out of the clouds toward the ship," 1945, *Newsweek*). The Japanese word means literally "divine wind," from *kami* (god) and *kaze* (wind). The kamikaze pilots were likened to the divinely sent storm that unexpectedly arose in August 1281 to destroy Kublai Khan's navy as it crossed from China to invade Japan. The incredible heedless bravery of the kamikazes made the word vivid in the minds of the soldiers, who brought it back to the United States, where it quickly became a part of the public imagination and vocabulary, eventually referring to anything that is reckless or potentially self-destructive ("He developed a contempt for the *kamikaze* liberals who prefer glorious defeat to sensible accommodation," 1968, *Evening Standard*).

CYBERNETICS (1948). "We have decided to call the entire field of control and communication theory, whether in the machine or in the animal, by the name *Cybernetics.*" With that calculated declaration in 1948, the American mathematician Norbert Wiener introduced a new word and new science. Because this field of theory explores the automatic controls that "govern" computers and brains, Wiener chose an Anglicized form of the French *cybernetique* (the art of governing), first used by the physicist André Marie Ampère (the *ampere* or *amp*, a unit of electric current, being named after him) in his *Essai sur la philosophie des sciences* (1834). The French word is from Greek *kybernetes* (steersman) from *kybernan* (to steer a ship), the same root as English *govern* through Latin *gubernare* (to direct, manage). The futuristic coinage *cyborg* (an organism whose functions are partly taken over by electro-mechanical devices)—the recent movies *Blade Runner* and *Robocop* have cyborg characters—is a contraction of *"cy*bernetic *org*anism." *Cybernetics* is also the root of the 1980s invention *cyberpunk*, a literary "movement" whose stories and novels are characterized by, among other things, cyborgs and a violent, dystopian world. *Punk* is a 1970s word referring to an aggressive, boisterous, and garish lifestyle copied from the bizarre appearance and outlandish behavior of *punk-rock* musicians and their fans.

NITWIT (1922), **NITPICKER** (1951). Though usually crude, military jargon is often very refined in the distinctions it makes, and bureaucratic Pentagon jargon is often at the apex of linguistic hair-splitting and nitpicking:

> Two long-time Pentagon stand-bys are *fly-speckers* and *nit-pickers*. The first . . . refers to people whose sole occupation seems to be studying papers in the hope of finding flaws in the writing, rather than making any effort to improve the thought or meaning; *nit-pickers* are those who quarrel with trivialities of expression *and* meaning, but who usually end up without making concrete or justified suggestions for improvement. (1951, *Collier's*)

A *nitpicker* (a pedantic critic, one who searches for trivial errors) is literally "one who picks out nits," nits being the very tiny eggs of lice. In fact, because lice have plagued us since prehistory, humans have always been nitpickers, as the Indo-European root **knid* (louse egg) testifies. A *nitwit,* however, is not a person having the wit of a nit, though *nit* during Shakespeare's time referred to a stupid person ("And his page . . . that handful of wit! Ah, Heavens, it is a most pathetical *nit!,* " 1588, *Love's Labour's Lost*), a sense that undoubtedly influenced *nitwit.* But the *nit* in *nitwit* is primarily from slang *nit* (nothing, nix) from Yiddish *nit,* a variant of German *nichts* (not, nothing). Hence, *nitwit* means literally "no wit" or "witless" ("The Vice-President announced loudly that he wanted a large cup of coffee with his dinner, and none of these '*nit-wit,* pee-wee, demi-tasses,' " 1928, *Daily Express*).

BEATNIK (1958). Almost every generation has its Bohemian movement. In the 1950s and early 1960s, it was the *beat generation* when "Suddenly everybody was slightly *beatniky*" (1964, *Listener*). As with the *hippies* a decade or so later, San Francisco was the mother city of the *beat generation,* an expression that first appeared in print in 1952. A *beat* or *beatnik* was typically a young person trying to be a writer or artist, whose unconventional dress, manners, and language expressed his or her often studied disdain for middle-class values. The *-nik* suffix is adopted from Yiddish (as in *nudnik* "an annoying person"), but is ultimately from Russian, popularized by the Soviets' famous satellite, *Sputnik*. The archetypal beat was Jack Kerouac, who claimed in a 1958 interview in *Esquire* magazine that "the *Beat Generation* is basically a religious generation" and that *"Beat* means beatitude, not beat up." But this may be a revisionist history of *beat*. It is also very possible that it derives from earlier American English *beat* (a worthless or shiftless fellow), as in *dead-beat* ("He would not loan money to policemen or firemen, stating that they were the biggest *beats* in the country," 1903, Boston *Herald*), which in turn is from the adjective *beat* (tired, exhausted), *dead-beat* being the emphatic form. At the same time, the new meaning was probably influenced by the *beat* of jazz, the music most often associated with the *beat generation*.

COCKAMAMIE (1960). During the 1840s in France and then in England in the 1860s, it was all the rage to pass one's time with *decalcomania,* an avocation that involved transferring pictures from treated paper to glassware and porcelain ("There are few employments for leisure hours which for the past eighteen months have proved either so fashionable or fascinating as *decalcomanie,"* 1864, *The Queen*). One authority claims that this fad may have started among fashionable ladies playing one-upmanship with fake beauty spots on their cheek, making them more and more elaborate, eventually using transfer designs. In any case, *décalcomanie* was literally "a craze" (*manie* or *mania*) for transferring tracings (*décalquer,* from *de-*, "off" and *calquer* "to press"), literally a "decalmania." Although the mania was short-lived, *decalcomanies* survived into the 1920s as *cockamanies* or *cockamamies,* which were painted strips of paper that children wetted with spit and applied to their wrists and rubbed until the image was transferred to their skin as a kind of temporary tattoo. Perhaps the silliness of this child's play, the odd sound of the word, and its association with *cock-and-bull* and POPPYCOCK, combined to give it its contemporary meaning "foolish," "absurd," which

did not appear until the 1960s ("You marched into the precinct with a tight dress and a *cockamamie* bunch of alibis,"
1962, Ed McBain, *Empty Hours*).

GLITCH (1962). In the jargon of electronics and aerospace
engineers a *glitch* is a sudden surge in an electric current or
signal. It is probably a borrowing of Yiddish *glitsh* (a slipping),
which in turn is from German *glitschen* (to slide or slip). Because a sudden change or "slipping" in an electric current in
a computer or electronic system can cause problems, *glitch*
quickly came to mean a "mishap" or "malfunction." This new
meaning may have been reinforced by earlier *hitch* (an unexpected obstacle or difficulty). Astronauts in the early 1960s
adopted the term—the earliest occurrence in print is a quote
from John Glenn—and popularized it in its extended sense.
Glitch, however, has stayed close to its technological origins.
Its newest sense is in astronomy (a sudden change in the
speed of rotation of a celestial body, especially a pulsar).

QUARK (1964). When the physicist Murray Gell-Mann
theorized that a group of subatomic particles, originally three
in number, composed heavier particles called *hadrons* (from
Greek meaning "thick," "bulky"), he needed a name for these
new particles. Like Edward Kasner's nephew's GOOGOL, he
resorted to a nonsensical and provisional "word," *quork.*
Then he noticed that his "word" appeared in the first line of
the twelfth chapter of James Joyce's *Finnegans Wake:* "Three
quarks for Muster Mark!" Gell-Mann interpreted Joyce's line
as a shout to the bartender in H. C. Earwicker's pub, "Three
quarts for Mister Mark," *quart* being closer in pronunciation
to his original *quork* than *quark* rhyming with Mark. Although
Gell-Mann's reading of the line from Joyce's deliberately am-
biguous and multidimensional book is "correct," *quark* is a
perfectly good English word for "croak," deriving either as an
imitation of the sound of croaking or as a borrowing from
Greek *quarken* "to croak" ("The gurgling and *quarking* of
spring frogs in a pond," 1860, John F. Campbell, *Popular Tales
of the West Highlands*). The three cheers for Mister Mark hailed

in the pub (with allusion to Aristophanes's play *The Frogs*) become three croaks.

BYTE (1964). A *bit,* which was introduced to computerese in the late 1940s, is a basic unit of information and is an abbreviation for *"b*inary dig*it,"* the binary numeric system based on 0 and 1 being the arithmetic of computers. A larger unit of information is the *byte,* made up of eight bits taken as a whole, like a spoonful of peas eaten in one "bite." Thus, *byte* is a coinage probably influenced by *bit* and *bite.* Another version of its origin suggests that it is an acronym for *"b*inary dig*it e*ight," a suggestion that is ingenious, even plausible, but unsubstantiated.

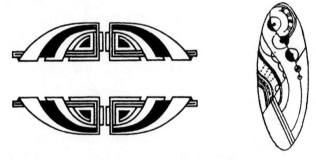

ART DECO (1967). This style of design popular in the 1920s and '30s is characterized by straight lines, bold colors, and geometrical forms, and was an attempt to capture the sleekness of modern technology. At the time, it was a revolutionary style that supplanted the Art Nouveau of the Edwardian years, but was called *art deco* only from the vantage of the late 1960s, when it was revived. The name is from the great Exposition Internationale des *Arts Déco*ratifs held in Paris in 1925, at which the art deco style was first presented to the public.

AMNIOCENTESIS (1970). Though *amniocentesis,* the technique of withdrawing amniotic fluid with a hypodermic needle and analysis of the embryo's cells, is a very recent development, the components of the name, *amnion* (membrane enveloping the fetus) and *centesis* (surgical puncture), are very old. *Amnion* was adopted in the seventeenth century from Greek *amnion* (caul, membrane), the diminutive of *amnos* (lamb), lambs being born still encased in the amnion. Another version claims that Greek *amnion* originally referred to the bowl that caught the blood of sacrificial victims. *Centesis* is from Greek *kentesis* (a pricking), *kentein* (to prick), also the root of *center* and *eccentric.*

ADIDAS (1975). This athletic equipment trade name has become synonymous with running shoes, nearly achieving the generic status that *Xerox* and *Kleenex* have ("We triple-tied our *Adidas* at the Staten Island staging area . . . and prepared to report on the marathon by joining it and going the classic distance," 1978, *The New Yorker*). In general use spelled with an initial capital, unlike the lowercase trademark, it derives from the name of the German manufacturer, *Adi Das*sler, who founded the company in 1948.

BOOT (c. 1980). Many who fear and loathe computers but must work with them anyway, when instructed to *boot* the infernal machine, might be inclined to kick it off its stand. But *boot* (to load the operating system of a computer) comes from *bootstrap,* not *boot* (to kick). A *bootstrap* is a short program or routine that loads the rest of the instructions into the computer or starts another program. To *bootstrap* or *boot up* is to initiate this short routine. Originally, of course, a *bootstrap* was simply a strap sewn on a boot to aid in pulling it on, and *to pull oneself up by one's bootstraps* (first recorded in James Joyce's *Ulysses*) is a vivid if impossible metaphor, meaning "to help or better oneself without the aid of others." The computer term is a play upon this latter expression: a *bootstrap* program by itself pulls up all the instructions necessary for the computer to operate. A *hot boot* is the automatic loading of a bootstrap program when the computer is turned on. It is *hot* because an electric current initiates the boot. This is the same *hot* as in the slang expression *hot seat* (electric chair) and *hot wire* (a "live" wire). A *warm boot* reloads the bootstrap but without turning off the computer, that is, while the machine is warm and running, and is synonymous with *reboot.* All of these uses of *boot* are quite recent, probably not occurring in print much before 1980.

GLASNOST (c. 1987). It is virtually impossible these days to read an article in the popular press dealing with the Soviet Union without running into the two buzz words *glasnost* and *perestroika.* Neither word has yet been fully adopted into English, which is why editors still usually italicize them. *Glasnost,* the more common of the two, is made up of the root *golos* (voice) and the suffix *-nost* (or *-ost*), which works much like our suffix *-ness* (as in *openness*). Thus *glasnost* means literally "giving voice to something," that is, "making something public." The English press takes minor liberty with the word by usually extending it to mean "openness," "frankness," or even "free speech" ("The Soviets put on an impressive show of *glasnost* for the world press. . . . All in all, it was an amazing lesson on the new scope of *glasnost* and also on its limits," 1988, *Time*), whereas a Russian speaker would probably not use *glasnost* in that way, but would use *otkrobennost* (openness, frankness) instead. *Glasnost* and its Russian root *golos* are distant relatives of the English words *call* and *clatter.* All have their common origin in the Indo-European root **gal* (to sound out, to call, shout), which also gave Latin *gallus* (cock, "the calling bird").

PERESTROIKA (c.1987). *Perestroika* is the name of General Secretary Gorbachev's program for "restructuring" the Soviet system and, of course, in the spirit of glasnost the name of his best-selling book. *Perestroika* is formed from the stem *stroika* (building, construction) and the common prefix *pere-,* which is exactly parallel to our prefix *re-* (again, anew). The stem stripped down to its immediate root *stroi* is related to the English stem in *structure, destroy, construct, instruct, obstruct,* and *construe,* all of which go back to the Latin *struere* (to pile up, construct). The Indo-European mother word to these Russian and English terms is **ster,* meaning "to spread." Thus, English *restructure* is an almost perfect, if somewhat literal, translation or counterpart to *perestroika.*